tappan library · · tappan library · tappan library · tappan library · tappan library · tappan library · tappan library · · tappan library

Tappan Library

FOUNDED 1956

Sudden Infant Death

Sudden Infant Death

Enduring the Loss

by

John DeFrain
Linda Ernst
Deanne Jakub
Jacque Taylor

Lexington Books

D.C. Heath and Company · Lexington, Massachusetts · Toronto

Library of Congress Cataloging-in-Publication Data

Sudden infant death : enduring the loss / John DeFrain . . . [et al.].
p.   cm.
Includes bibliographical references and index.
ISBN 0–669–24544–5 (alk. paper)
1. Sudden infant death syndrome—Psychological aspects.
2. Bereavement—Psychological aspects.   I. DeFrain, John D.
RJ320.S93S79   1991

618.92—dc20   90–21846
                                                                CIP

Published simultaneously in Canada
Printed in the United States of America
International Standard Book Number: 0–669–24544–5
Library of Congress Catalog Card Number: 90–21846

The paper used in this publication meets
the minimum requirements of American National Standard
for Information Sciences—Permanence of Paper
for Printed Library Materials, ANSI Z39.48–1984.

Year and number of this printing:

91 92 93 94 8 7 6 5 4 3 2 1

Life is precious.

Contents

Acknowledgments

For more than fifteen years we have been struggling to understand better the crisis families face in the aftermath of the sudden, unexpected, unexplainable death of a baby. Families have been losing babies for no apparent reason for as long as humans have walked this earth. And bereaved family members have, through the millennia, reached out in their pain and asked, Why?

"There is nothing new under the sun," it is written in Ecclesiastes (1:9). We believe this, sincerely. And the book you are about to read is not new or revolutionary. Rather, it is a small step forward in the human search for an understanding of the nature and meaning of death—one small step, based on the lives and experiences of literally hundreds of people who have contributed to the creation of this book.

The reader will not necessarily find answers to her or his questions in this book, for there are no answers to the profound questions posed here which humans will ever be able to agree upon. But the reader will perhaps find comfort and warmth meeting new, understanding friends in this book, friends who have been to the edge of the abyss, have looked down into it, and have chosen to stay here on earth, among the living.

If the reader then finds this book of any help, we are gratified in our work and thankful to the many people who have contributed immeasurably to it. We really do not feel, however, as though we as individuals wrote this book. We will take the responsibility for its shortcomings, but credit for its strengths must go to the family members whose testimony is its foundation.

Over the past fifteen years, 392 mothers, fathers, brothers, sisters, grandmothers, and grandfathers who have directly experienced the devastation of Sudden Infant Death Syndrome (SIDS) have contributed written testimony of their experiences. This testimony, written painstakingly and lovingly by hand as if to a sister or a dear friend, fills nearly seven thousand pages. We have read each of these pages, and cried—in a figurative if not literal sense—with each of these unhappy people. Without their kindness this book would not exist. This is, literally, their creation.

Hundreds of other people who have experienced SIDS have contacted us as a result of our research. They call on the telephone to talk about their questions, their fears, their sadness. They invite us to meet with their family or their support group. They come forward after a presentation to tell their unique stories. Some are parents, some are grandparents and surviving siblings. Others are nurses who haven't known what to say to grieving parents, or doctors, support group counselors, social workers, ministers, funeral directors, friends, child care providers. The death of a baby is like a stone cast into the stillness of a quiet pool: the concentric ripples of despair sweep out in all directions, affecting many, many people. These people, who have contacted us informally over the years, have each brought us insight into understanding the death of a baby and deserve our gratitude for sharing their experiences.

Besides those affected directly by SIDS, we are also indebted to the University of Nebraska. A university at its best is a community of seekers, and countless individuals have influenced our quest for understanding. John Woodward, professor of human development and the family at the University of Nebraska, Lincoln, decided fifteen years ago that research on families who experience sudden, unexplained infant death would be invaluable. Woodward wrote a successful grant proposal and hired John DeFrain into the Department of Human Development and the Family in the College of Home Economics to work on the project. The Agricultural Research Division of the Institute of Agriculture and Natural Resources (IANR) at the University of Nebraska funded Woodward's proposal for an initial five-year study of families in crisis; this blossomed into an ongoing project that has spanned fifteen years for DeFrain, Linda Ernst, Jacque Taylor, and Deanne Jakub. Administrators in the IANR at that time included Martin Massengale (now chancellor of the University of Nebraska, Lincoln), Howard Ottoson, Robert Kleis, and Roy Arnold. Others who have been at the University of Nebraska over the years were especially supportive of our efforts: Hazel Anthony, Lisa Morris Blankenau, Eileen

Curry, Ron Daly, Karen Eskey, Charlotte Jackson, Lee Kimmons, Kay King, Herb Lingren, Sue Losey, Betty Mendoza, Bill Meredith, Irv Omtvedt, Anne Parkhurst, Leon Rottmann, Gale Smith, Nick Stinnett, Helen Sulek, Sally Van Zandt, Dale Vanderholm, Ginger Woodward, and Xie Xiaolin.

Gratitude is also expressed to Alan Fisher, Charlene Gray, William H. Marshall, and an anonymous benefactor who read of our earliest work in *Psychology Today* and gave us a financial and psychological boost through his Omaha investment and banking advisers at Piper, Jaffray, and Hopwood.

We certainly cannot forget Margaret Zusky, our editor and friend at Lexington Books, and other fine staff there, including Sylvia Todd and Donna Vaillancourt. Margaret read our first book-length manuscript on SIDS ten years ago. She telephoned and said she could not read the manuscript without weeping. We knew instantly that we had found a sensitive and compassionate supporter for our efforts. Without her help this earlier book on SIDS, *Coping with Sudden Infant Death,* would not have been completed, for the task often seemed too long, too difficult, too emotionally draining. She encouraged, cajoled, and mothered us, and we eventually responded.

Finally, thanks to our own families who nurture us in the face of life's fascinating and terrifying ups and downs: Nikki, Amie, Alyssa, and Erica DeFrain; Orville and Harriet DeFrain; Margaret and John Schulling; Roger, Sara, Jennifer, and Aaron Ernst; Paul and Leona Skogrand; Rubin and Bernice Ernst; Leonard and Gladys Jakub; Parnell, Darren, Nathan, and Brennan Taylor; and Jeff and Sandi Keuss.

To all who contributed to the creation of this book, a warm and heartfelt thank you.

Sudden Infant Death

1

The Tragedy of SIDS

When a baby dies, suddenly, unexpectedly, and for no apparent reason, a unique crisis occurs in a family. No individual experiences the crisis in the same way another does, and each family is different. Though common themes of grief and bereavement occur time and time again, each family experiences the crisis in its own desperate way.

We do not use the word *desperate* lightly here. Every individual we have had contact with during the past fifteen years of our research has been plunged into dreadful unhappiness in the aftermath of the baby's death. More than four in ten parents in our most recent study considered suicide because of the death. Living becomes almost unbearable for most. Mothers and fathers tell us of slitting their wrists, trying to kill themselves in an automobile crash, trying to overdose on drugs, turning on the engine of the car in a closed garage. The vast majority of parents who have experienced sudden infant death see the loss as the most devastating crisis they have experienced in their lives. To repeat, we do not use apocalyptic terms lightly in this book. The baby's death is clearly a catastrophe for families—mothers, fathers, brothers, sisters, grandmothers, grandfathers, and other close relatives—and the responsibility falls to each of us in society to help these stricken people in any way. They are clearly crushed in a life-threatening and spiritually numbing situation.

"What Have You Gone through Since Your Baby Died?"

Families in more than 130 localities in thirty-four states have participated in our series of studies of the psychological and social effects of Sudden Infant Death Syndrome (SIDS) on surviving family members. We ask family members scores of questions, but the best question of all has proved to be "What have you gone through since your baby died?" That open-ended question gives people the freedom to respond in a very spontaneous fashion, and they have been wonderful in pouring their hearts out to us.

Written testimonies in response to our questions have come from every region of the United States; from cities, large and small; from rural communities, farms, and ranches. Parents, surviving siblings, and grandparents who responded to our calls for volunteers over the years were black and white, Hispanic, Native American, Asian American—a rainbow of color and ethnic variety. Some families were rich, some poor, and most were middle class. They represented many religious faiths and spiritual beliefs, and some had no faith anymore at all. Some had several graduate degrees, and some graduated from the eighth grade. They were homemakers, bankers, professors, ministers, truck drivers, farmers, clerks, teachers, electricians, computer programmers, carpenters.

They differed in these various ways, but one point became apparent: the one thing they had in common was their great need to share the experience of losing a baby to Sudden Infant Death Syndrome. In sharing their stories with us, they hoped to help others who would follow later on that terrible journey.

Here is one mother's story, just as she told it to us:

In the beginning I lost all sense of being. The second day after the funeral, I went out and tried to dig up her grave. I thought I could see her in her walker or hear her cry. I stayed up all day and night checking the other kids. I'd leave them several times a week and go to the cemetery and sit by her grave all afternoon. At the time I was four months pregnant. After my little boy was born, my husband and I took turns with four-hour shifts, watching the baby for several weeks. Then I would dress him in her clothes, until one day I put her shoes on him and I had to get my oldest child to take them off.

I wouldn't allow her to be put in a casket until the day of the funeral. We had taken pictures of her at the funeral home, but my husband wouldn't allow me to look at them. But they seemed to be some sort of a help. I can't really explain in words how they helped me. I never had but one other picture of her, and it was when she was a newborn. The best I can explain this was, just being able to look at her it seemed she wasn't so far away. The pictures from the funeral home were not taken of her in a casket and she looked as though she were asleep.

I still have periods of fear of losing the other children. Right after my baby died, my niece, four years old, drowned. Then my father was shot and killed. I lost all sense of reality. My husband started drinking, and I hated him. I couldn't sleep. If I did, I had dreams about bugs eating her, or I'd dream of the funeral. Somewhere in the back of my mind I decided if I could just stop loving the kids, my husband, and parents, I could never be hurt by anyone or anything.

I knew I needed counseling, but my mom and husband were totally against anything like that. It was only for crazy people. But I finally went to one doctor for almost a year, and I lived in my grief and could talk to him, and am thankful to God he told me what a selfish mother I was being. Oh, I hated him at the time, but he is the only one who really helped me out of the loneliness, because I'd shut myself off from any feeling relationships.

My stepfather made some harsh statements; some people thought we were really to blame. When it happened we were visiting my mother and the baby was in bed with us; my husband had been drinking and thought he had suffocated her. My husband wanted to send the pictures we had taken of her to his mother. I hated him and blamed him. She had awoken for a two o'clock feeding, and we played and she laughed and cooed, and at six o'clock she was dead. My husband never said so in so many words, nor did I, but we just became distrustful of each other.

This woman's marriage ended in divorce. Participants in our most recent study told us that only a small percentage of their marriages ended as a result of the SIDS death, but a great deal of strain was placed on everyone in the family and on their ability to relate to one another. Blame is sometimes placed on SIDS parents, just when they are at their weakest and most vulnerable. Some are investigated for child abuse. Public health nurse Janet Michel Nakushian found that often, because of the condition of the baby's body as a result of the parents' attempts at resuscitation, the parents may be suspected of child abuse and denied emotional support.[1] This can be devastating for the family, which is already weakened by the crisis of sudden infant death.

The resulting pain is not simply guilt over the death of the baby, however. The survivors spend many of their waking hours and many sleepless nights reliving every moment of their infant's short life:

> I felt an overwhelming feeling of guilt, coupled with remorse. Our baby had colic from about nine days old to four weeks old. That was very difficult for me to cope with. I resented her many times and sometimes wished I'd never had her. I even had fantasies I might harm her, and they surprised and upset me. She was getting to be a real pleasure to have shortly before her death at four and a half months, but I have reflected on my resentment and horrible fantasies.

For most parents there is time to outlive such negative feelings toward their children; none of us is a perfect parent and there are countless things we could have done better and do try to correct. But SIDS parents must learn to live with their feelings and failings.

Too often we found many of these parents still isolated in their guilt, being unable, or in some instances not allowed, to verbalize their feelings:

> Thirty-seven years have passed, and until four years ago I was not allowed to talk about it. Not to my husband and family or friends. I wasn't allowed to talk or cry myself out. No one wanted to know. I was blamed for letting the baby sleep on his stomach. I am seventy-two years old, and not until recently when a friend of my daughter's had a neighbor who went through the same thing was I finally able to talk and receive some comfort.

Defining Sudden Infant Death Syndrome

Sudden, unexpected, and unexplainable infant death is the leading cause of death in the United States for infants between the ages of one week and one year. It has been estimated that seven to ten thousand infants die of SIDS annually in the United States alone.[2] The deaths occur suddenly, with no warning. The medical term *Sudden Infant Death Syndrome* describes a specific condition and is useful in reinforcing the idea that no guilt should be attached to the caregivers of the infant.

Still, despite all the efforts at educating people, even physicians sometimes find that they are not immune to guilt feelings when an infant in their care suddenly dies. "What did I miss?" is a question they often ask themselves. One young resident in a family practice program talked to us about how he felt:

> It's very emotionally draining. We want to give support and encouragement. These parents have been doing everything right, doing a super job. Then they bring the baby in and there's no heartbeat. You feel terrible. You feel like you just want to leave. When the result turns out to be SIDS, you know there is nothing more that you could have done, but it is emotionally draining. I cried, and went home and talked about it with my wife. My wife is pregnant, and it really hit home in that regard too.
>
> You can return to work the next day because you know the statistics. You're playing the odds, and you know that ninety-nine times out of one hundred things are going to go well. To return to work and see other mothers with small children is kind of a lift to me. Much of medicine is saddening: seeing people with chronic disease, heart attack, something that can't be cured. In pediatric care things are usually happy. You realize that everything is not that way, and you've had excellent results in the past. You count on success in the future.
>
> There is an element of guilt in both the parents and the physician when something like this happens, because you think, Oh my God, did I miss something on the exam? The autopsy kind of helps absolve everybody. At times you're seeing so many people and going so fast you wonder if you've missed something and you feel terrible when the baby dies. You can use the autopsy to help reassure them that it wasn't something they could have prevented, and to reassure yourself that there was nothing you as a physician could have done.

The same kind of "what ifs" come back to haunt the parents who have lost a child to SIDS. This is common among people who are grieving over some kind of loss. But there is a difference: an infant is a small bundle of potential, with a future stretching out before her or him; an infant has not lived long and achieved but is still in the process of becoming.

When an elderly person dies, the grieving family can look back on his life and say, "Ah, but what a life he lived." With an infant, on the other hand, there is always the possibility of what might have been. Every time the parents encounter a child who is the age their child would have been, the parents are left wondering, What would my child have been like? What if he had not died?

A Prospectus

In this book we will explore some of the themes so common among SIDS families: the initial shock families suffer because of the sudden, unexplained death; the vivid, emotion-laden memories of that terrible day the baby died; the search for answers from doctors, from God, from deep within oneself; the symptoms of grief that lead many SIDS parents and grandparents to wonder whether they are going crazy; the thoughts of suicide that many SIDS parents (and some grandparents) have; the different ways mothers and fathers grieve; the good and bad things people in the community say and do; relationships with surviving children, and worries over having subsequent children; and the search for healing and rebirth. All these themes have been touched upon in this opening chapter and will be discussed at length in the chapters that follow.

The reader has realized by now how difficult this book is to read. No one we know has been able to get through the book without tears, for the families in the book are real and the events they describe are painfully true. But the families whose stories appear here also felt pain, tremendous pain, as they told us their stories. They risked that pain so that others who follow will better understand and, perhaps, better withstand the trauma SIDS brings.

Tears are cleansing mechanisms. They are an almost inevitable and useful part of the healing process. This mother described her experience reading the earliest draft of the book:

> I started reading your book at 10:00 P.M. I had lost a baby, and I cried and cried. I would read and cry and read some more. I finished at 1:00 A.M. I cried again for my lost baby . . . It felt good.

"It felt good." That struck us as a very curious statement at the time, but now we understand the profound truth in it. Our tears can help us heal; so can sharing our stories with others. Feeling the sorrow others have experienced can help us to feel not so alone in life's journey. Others too have been on this path, and other families, in so many ways just like yours, have been terribly wounded. But they live today and seem stronger.

When you feel up to it, then, try to continue on in your reading. And when you need to, please shed tears. Eventually it will get better. Not perfect, but better.

Tomorrow or the next day or the next month or soon enough thereafter there will be a time for dancing, a time for laughter. When you are ready, you will heal. Life is a delicate balance of sorrow and joy.

The People in This Book

A Short History of the Research

This book is the latest effort in a long series of investigations into the effects of infant death on families which began under Dr. John DeFrain's direction in the Department of Human Development and the Family at the University of Nebraska, Lincoln, in July 1975. The series of studies focused not only on Sudden Infant Death Syndrome, but also on stillbirth and miscarriage.

Nine separate studies have been conducted in these fifteen years; more than 1,050 bereaved mothers, fathers, grandmothers, grandfathers, and surviving sisters and brothers have formally participated in the research. Three hundred and ninety-two family members had experienced SIDS; 350 family members had experienced stillbirth; and 300 had experienced a miscarriage. Hundreds of other people have offered their thoughts on an informal basis over the years, and the insight gained through these discussions has been invaluable in the development of the formal research.

THE FIRST STUDY. Initially, a joint venture was begun in 1975 by John DeFrain and Linda Ernst in cooperation with the Nebraska State Department of Health, Division of Maternal and Child Health. Under the direction of Robert Grant, M.D., the division was working to identify SIDS cases more effectively in the state and to offer counseling for families. In that first study, the state Department of Health had identified ninety-one cases of SIDS that occurred between January 1, 1973, and June 30, 1975. Physicians and coroners involved in each incident were contacted, and after careful investigation it was determined that the baby had died for no explainable reason. It was found, however, that death certificates in some of the cases showed the death to be attributable to some other cause, and the parents had not been notified that their child actually died of SIDS. These particular parents were not asked to participate in the study. Parents in sixty-three out of ninety-one cases were sought for the research.

Two professional staff members of the state Department of Health tried to contact the parents by telephone in each of the sixty-three cases. If the parents could not be located, another telephone number for someone in the community with the same last name was tried with hopes of locating a relative. A grandparent was located in four cases, but in all four the grandparents would not allow the Department of Health to talk directly to the parents because they felt it would unnecessarily upset the parents. One grandparent stated that the couple had separated as a result of the death. Another stated that an arrest had been made after the death and the couple was still involved with legal problems. A third grandparent stated that the husband had left the wife because he blamed her for the death. This grandparent made it clear that she also blamed the mother. The fourth grandparent indicated that her daughter, a single mother, was in the hospital at the time of the study. Because of the difficulty we had in locating parents, we began to assume a high level of individual unhappiness and family disorganization as a result of the death.

All fifty parents who were contacted agreed to participate in the study and were sent thirteen-page questionnaires. (Our most recent SIDS questionnaire for parents is twenty-two pages long.) Of the fifty parents, thirty-two completed the questionnaire and returned it to us. Information collected from these thirty-two parents formed the basis for an initial journal article on SIDS published in 1978.[1]

We chose the mailed questionnaire technique for two important reasons: to preserve families' privacy and anonymity, and to ensure contact with a large and heterogeneous group of people. In subsequent years we have conducted many interviews with bereaved families and believe there is also a good deal to be said for that approach.

The questionnaire in our initial study began with four open-ended questions that allowed participants to express in narrative form their feelings about SIDS and the crisis in their families. The remainder of the instrument consisted of questions adapted from the literature of family crisis studies, death, and bereavement; from clinical impressions in the medical literature on the effects of SIDS on surviving family members; and from our own exploratory interviews with several SIDS parents. The questionnaire was greatly influenced by a number of perspectives, including family systems theories; family development theories; psychobiological stress theories; theories of bereavement and grief; and family strengths and family stress theories. More than a dozen professionals in pediatrics, social work, child development, and family studies critiqued the initial questionnaire. Its validity and reliability were further enhanced by piloting with a statewide (Nebraska) SIDS parents' group.

Over the past fifteen years, four distinct questionnaires have been developed for bereaved family members: (1) the SIDS questionnaire, which has evolved into an instrument not only for mothers and fathers but for surviving siblings as well; (2) the SIDS questionnaire for grandmothers and grandfathers; (3) a questionnaire for mothers and fathers who have experienced a stillbirth; and (4) a questionnaire for mothers, fathers, and surviving siblings who have experienced a miscarriage. These questionnaires range from fourteen to twenty-two pages in length.

From the very beginning we made a considerable effort to involve fathers. We felt that men had been generally neglected by researchers studying families. Fathers' experiences turned out to be a very important aspect of the research, as later chapters will show. After about seven years of work we also began to include grandparents and surviving siblings in the studies. After considerable effort we were finally beginning to develop a picture of the crisis with input from many members of the family system.

THE SECOND STUDY. Using a similar procedure, John DeFrain began a second study in conjunction with the state Department of Health Division of Maternal and Child Health in September 1977. All families experiencing SIDS in Nebraska between July 1, 1975, and January 1, 1977, were contacted by Lorene Wood, maternal and child health counselor and nurse. Thirty-seven of seventy-four parents filled out questionnaires in this sample.

A Nationwide SIDS Research Project

THE THIRD STUDY. Our 1978 article in the *Journal of Family Practice* was picked up by *Psychology Today,* and a small story featuring the research caught the attention of an anonymous benefactor, who, through his Omaha investment and banking advisers Piper, Jaffray and Hopwood, donated money to the University of Nebraska Foundation to continue the SIDS research. This modest financial boost proved critical from a psychological standpoint, and in the spring of 1979 John DeFrain and Jacque Taylor began a third study. We attempted to obtain a nationwide sample of families who had experienced SIDS. We also wanted to survey those families for whom a longer period of time had passed since the death in order to study the long-term effects of SIDS.

The nationwide study was done with the cooperation of newspapers and their family life editors. More than one hundred newspapers in all sections of the country were contacted, and fifty received follow-up telephone calls. Of the one hundred newspapers initially contacted, twenty ultimately ran news stories for us requesting volunteers for the study. Ninety-three families responded, and in most cases both the father and the mother indicated that they wanted to participate in the study.

They began telling us about their babies even before we had a chance to send them a questionnaire:

Dear Dr. DeFrain:

I saw your call for volunteers in my local newspaper and would like to participate in your study. Please send me a questionnaire. Our baby, Lynn, died on August 24, 1984. It was a very hot day here in Iowa, and I had just put her down for a nap not more than a half hour ago when . . .

Forty-three individual questionnaires were returned completed for analysis. A total of 112 parents had now participated in our first three studies. We felt we had a wealth of material to share with families and with professionals who serve families, and wrote

Coping with Sudden Infant Death, our first book on SIDS, which was published in 1982.

The Psychological and Social Effects of a Stillbirth on Surviving Family Members

THE FOURTH AND FIFTH STUDIES. After studying the effects of SIDS on families for seven years, it seemed in 1982 that it was time for a break. Leona Martens, a bereaved mother, was not about to let that happen, however. Leona and Al Martens's second child, Beth, died at birth on May 23, 1973. The death was a crushing experience for the Martens family, and it motivated Leona, a graduate student at the University of Nebraska at the time, to approach John about beginning a study of the effects of a stillbirth on surviving family members.

She began reading about stillbirths and found that an estimated thirty-three thousand babies were stillborn in the United States each year. She pointed out to John that these thirty-three thousand families were also grieving the death of their children and needed support also. Leona began her research by interviewing near her central Nebraska community forty-six family members in twenty-two separate families who had experienced a stillbirth.

After six months of interviews, Leona was exhausted and simply could not continue for a while:

> I set out to let the world know how much it hurts when your child is stillborn. I've visited with wonderful families who have shared their innermost feelings with me. I've spent hours upon hours crying and writing. After some time has passed, I realize that I've shared all that I can bear for the time being. I've turned a secret part of me inside out. My defenses are all down, and I'm weakened. I can go no further.

Teams of human beings are wonderful inventions, for when one member is down some other teammate will inevitably be up. Leona's interviews laid a foundation for the next phase of the research, and Jan and Warren Stork joined the project.

The Storks' twin baby boys, Nathan and Mathew, died at birth on September 30, 1976. A few years later they organized a support group for bereaved parents in Lincoln which was very successful in providing a haven for families to talk about their loss. John approached the Storks, and they were immediately delighted to begin working with us.

Leona's in-depth interviews served as the basis for the lengthy questionnaire used in the next study. Again, we solicited the aid of large and small newspapers across the country. Six hundred papers were contacted, and perhaps one hundred ran short news stories on the stillbirth project.

The three-paragraph news stories were usually buried deep inside the papers, but they bore fruit: within two months we had received letters from more than 550 parents in all fifty states. Each family was sent at least one twenty-page questionnaire, and over a period of several months 304 completed questionnaires were returned to us. Many people found the questionnaire too difficult to fill out. The memories were still too terribly painful. Others took several months or even years to complete the task but kept at it because they felt it was important:

> I hope your study is still going. It has been two years, and I finally can think about Cindy's death long enough without crying to write down my feelings. I hope this does some family some good. God bless you . . .

Simple multiplication does not do justice to the vast amount of material parents sent us: 304 parents times 20 pages or more each came to more than 6,000 pages of personal testimony. Each word the parents wrote was read and emotionally digested. The reading had to be done in small doses, because it touched too many exposed nerves in the researchers' lives. Leona and Jan and Warren synthesized and organized the material from the parents, and John did the final writing. This wealth of information and raw feeling with which the parents honored us took the team three years to analyze statistically, process emotionally, and weave into a book.

The Storks had come at the right time. Their energy and enthusiasm kept the project alive. The interviews with 46 family members and the questionnaire testimony from the 304 family members served as the bases for our book *Stillborn: The Invisible Death,* which was published in 1986.[2] Work on this project spanned a five-year period.

A Return to the Study of SIDS

THE SIXTH, SEVENTH, AND EIGHTH STUDIES. With the publication of *Stillborn: The Invisible Death,* it seemed time to go on to something else in life as researchers. Eleven years seemed long enough for studying infant death, a desperately grim subject. Even though much of the contact with parents was through the mail, there simply was no way to ignore or walk away from their tragedy. Reading the final proof sheets of *Stillborn* was a case in point: even though John had carefully gone over the manuscript four times earlier, the fifth reading was still an emotionally draining experience. Bereaved family members have no good way to escape their pain, but researchers, on the other hand, ought to be able to walk away from their studies, John reasoned.

Margaret Zusky, our editor at Lexington Books, made quitting impossible, however. Beginning in 1986 she would call and write regularly from Massachusetts to remind John that *Coping with Sudden Infant Death* was reaching as many new readers several years after publication as it had in its first few months. She gave copies of the book to bereaved friends, and they found some comfort in their grief. Margaret was intent on keeping the book alive, but it simply needed to be updated with the latest research. She did not twist our arms, but her efforts did work to twist our emotions.

Deanne Jakub joined the team, and the work began anew. We started slowly, planning carefully for our sixth, seventh, and eighth studies of the effects of infant death on families. This time we wanted to study Sudden Infant Death Syndrome from a much broader family perspective. In our earlier studies we had relied completely on bereaved parents for testimony. Though we had asked parents questions about surviving children and about grandparents' reactions to the death, we gathered little direct testimony. In the sixth study, we would focus on parents' responses to SIDS; the seventh study would look at children's responses to the death; and the eighth study would gather testimony from grandfathers and grandmothers.

The first task was to construct questionnaires for these projects. After going through perhaps a dozen drafts and field-testing with hundreds of people, we believed that our questionnaires were becoming quite sophisticated and all-inclusive. They were also becoming quite lengthy: the final draft of the SIDS parents' questionnaire came to twenty-two pages (two of these pages were questions for surviving children, with whom the parents could talk if they so desired).

The parents' questionnaire had eighty-three questions in it. Thirty of the questions were open-ended "story"-type questions, and the parent could write her or his response in any way desired. Parents were encouraged to add extra sheets of blank paper to the questionnaire to write more if they wished. Many parents added many extra pages of their own testimony. The other fifty-three questions in the questionnaire were closed, quantitative questions; parents responded to these simply by checking a blank, writing in a number, or circling the appropriate response. One hundred and twenty-seven parents completed questionnaires for this, the sixth study.

As noted earlier, two pages of the parents' questionnaire were questions the parent could ask surviving children, if the parents and the children agreed that this would be a good thing to do. There were eight of these questions. As always, we went to great lengths to assure people that as volunteers in this effort they were truly free to decide whether or not to participate, and we would be very understanding if they chose not to. After eleven years we were well aware of how sensitive the questions are. We believe that each question we asked people was an important one, but many were very difficult and we made it clear to participants that they could pick and choose which questions they wished to respond to. Seventy-three children participated in this, the seventh study; their feelings about the death are reported in chapter 11, "What Do I Tell the Other Children?"

The eighth study, that of grandparents' responses to SIDS, also gathered material via questionnaire. A fourteen-page instrument was developed. The questionnaire contains seventy-eight items (forty-eight fixed-response questions, and thirty open-ended "story"-type questions). We chose questionnaire techniques again because we believed a large sample of grandparents would be relatively difficult to contact, even if the study were advertised nationwide. This proved to be true, for it took twenty-two months to collect testimony from eighty grandparents. Also, we chose questionnaire techniques instead of interviews because we wanted to be less intrusive in people's lives, believing that those confronted by tragedy would appreciate working through the process of answering our questions at their own pace. Dealing with family members anonymously through the mail also made it easier for them to decline to participate, if they so desired.

Written testimony via questionnaire has disadvantages, when compared with oral interviews. We are well aware of this, but all things considered, written testimony seemed best for our particular work.

We found family members for these three studies through two basic sources:

1. *Newspapers.* A random selection of one thousand newspapers in the United States was made from the *Ayers Directory of Publications.* The family life editors of these newspapers were sent an introductory letter explaining the importance of the study and asking them to print a news release seeking SIDS parents and grandparents. It is impossible to say, precisely, how many newspapers volunteered to publish the news story. We estimate that fewer than one in ten did so.

2. *SIDS organizations.* Presidents of eighty-one local chapters of the National Sudden Infant Death Syndrome Foundation were contacted by letter and asked to talk with group members to stimulate interest in the study; some chapters advertised the study in their newsletters. Ninety directors and coordinators of SIDS information and counseling programs were also contacted, along with state offices of maternal and child health. Any assistance they could give in recruiting family members was requested.

Because it proved very difficult to find grandparents, we collected testimony from family members in this particular study over a much longer time period than we normally do. After two years we finally had enough data for our new, second book on SIDS, *Sudden Infant Death: Enduring the Loss.* Besides 80 grandmothers and grandfathers, 127 mothers and fathers completed questionnaires for the project. And many of the mothers and fathers with other children had interviewed the surviving siblings. We were delighted to have 73 children's responses to their parents' questions also carefully recorded for us to analyze.

Testimony from these 280 parents, surviving children, and grandparents would add immeasurably to our understanding of SIDS families. *Sudden Infant Death: Enduring the Loss* then, would be based on the experiences of 392 family members in thirty-four states. We began our work with confidence, knowing that the families had honored us with a priceless gift—the story of their baby's life.

Future Directions

THE NINTH STUDY. Over the years a steady stream of people kept telling us we must study the effects of a miscarriage on surviving family members. Friends would stop us in the parking lot to ask how our SIDS studies were going, or about the latest findings in our work on stillbirth, and then tell of the pain they experienced when they miscarried a baby. Or someone would phone from across the country or write to tell us that the book on stillbirth had done their sister so much good, and could we write something for them about miscarriage ". . . because that's the death of a baby too, you know."

To commit to such a project meant at least five more years of work. Our editor at Lexington Books, Margaret Zusky, as usual tipped the scales:

> I was exhibiting our books at a professional conference in Florida, John, and this lady came up and said, "Do you have anything written about miscarriage?" I told her we had books on SIDS and on stillbirth, and she said, "Yes, yes. Those are excellent. I've read them. But do you have anything on miscarriage?" I told her we didn't, and she said, "You know, a miscarriage is a death, also."

"John, that's got to be your next book," Margaret concluded.

A quick glance at the modest research literature on miscarriage and families confirmed Margaret's statement. We estimated that perhaps 875,000 or more women experience a miscarriage in the United States each year. Though our society views the loss of a so-called nonviable fetus as "just a miscarriage," the vast majority of the mothers who experience a miscarriage define the loss as a death. If we as researchers ever had any doubt about what the mothers were saying, these doubts were completely cast aside a few months later.

We had begun the study of miscarriage by again calling for volunteers through the newspapers. Once more, letters poured in from all across the United States. We began sending out questionnaires for family members to fill out. One morning a large, heavy-duty cardboard envelope arrived from Homeworth, Ohio. A copy of the questionnaire was in the envelope, carefully answered by Kathleen Gray Farthing. Also inside was a note, explaining the gift enclosed:

> This is a lithograph that I did in the weeks after my miscarriage. I needed to work through my feelings. And I wanted a permanent record of my baby's existence. After I finished the artwork, I put it away. Only about two people have seen it. It's hard for me to look at it. It's like a diary.
>
> Anyway, I thought I'd share it with your research group. I don't need it back because it is one print in an edition of eight.
>
> Thank you for doing the research project. I hope your work will help others. I'm glad I participated. I don't want to ever forget my second baby.

Carefully wrapped in thin paper was a beautiful picture. A young mother stared vacantly at the viewer with the saddest eyes imaginable. A tiny baby, like a photograph of an embryo in the womb, was in the background. And along the edges of the picture, the artist had written, "Little baby that didn't grow/I'll always keep you in my heart."

If we, the researchers, had ever doubted that a miscarriage was the death of a baby, we could doubt it no more. This stunning lithograph makes an indelible impression on the viewer.

Kathleen soon after agreed that her lithograph would grace the cover of our book on the effects of miscarriage on families. And in a second letter she remembered the rest of her story:

> Thank you so much for your phone call about my print. It really means a lot to me to share it with people that understand and appreciate the feelings behind it. I later remembered that the title of the print that I had been doing before the miscarriage was called, "Two Miracles in One Lifetime" . . . and then I lost one of them!

Kathleen's lithograph was another spark for the researchers. The work simply *had* to continue. Elaine Millspaugh and Xie Xiaolin began working on the project. Today, more than three hundred mothers, fathers, sisters, and brothers have now participated in the study of the psychological and social effects of a miscarriage on surviving family members. Soon we will begin writing a book, *Miscarriage: The Death of a Dream.*

After that, perhaps, it will be time to rest.

An Important Note

One decision we have made in reporting the results of our various studies over the years is to go to great lengths to preserve and protect the anonymity of the families who have offered their testimony. As the reader has already concluded, the pages of this book include very sensitive material and certain "family secrets" that, if divulged in the wrong place, could be of potential harm to families. For this reason we have carefully changed identifying details—names, dates, cities, towns, states, and many other clues to people's identities. The essence of each story, however, remains basically intact. The people in this book are real people, and the stories in this book are true. Painfully true.

Testimony: Ellen and Bill

Ellen and Bill live in a pleasant, middle-class neighborhood in a well-kept house in the heartland of America. This is the story of what happened to them after their baby Christopher died. They are among the majority of couples who have survived SIDS, in spite of all the pain.

Ellen's Story

"I was born in a very small town in the Midwest, a farming community of about fourteen hundred people. The thing I remember most is that my father was the town drunk. He was successful when he first got married. He owned a couple of farms and had a grocery store, and then he went through a variety of things: he was a mail carrier, a truck driver, and then he finally hit rock bottom and wasn't anything for about four years. Eventually he went through an alcohol treatment program at a hospital.

"I was a junior in high school when he finally quit. And he did extremely well. He came home and started a rock-hauling business. Within about four years, he had an empire. Making incredible money and doing extremely well, a regular riches to rags to riches story.

"I don't like to look back at it, really I don't. But if I had it to do over again, I would probably do it the same way because of what came out of it. The part of me that came out of it all has been helpful in later life. I think I have become a real survivor.

"He didn't drink around the house, but he was always drunk. I didn't watch him pour the alcohol in his body, but he was a sloppy, nasty drunk. We used to have to leave when he came home. My mom was smart enough to get us out of there. I can remember many nights that we drove around for hours, until she knew he had gone to sleep. Then we would go home and she would get up the next morning and go to work as a nurse. She did this throughout the entire thing. There was a period of time that I was very angry at her for allowing this to go on. I was angry at her for not getting out of the relationship. But she is an incredible lady, and I guess she knew—I don't know how. But she knew that it was all going to come out okay in the end. When I was growing up, it seemed like everybody else had a 'normal' family. And I know now that they didn't. They just were faking it like everybody else.

"It seemed like I was missing a real father figure. It was very humiliating to be down at the bowling alley with the crowd and watch your father go weaving back and forth down [the] main street. The kids were all cracking up.

"But instead of letting it get the best of me and crawling into a shell, I didn't do that at all. I did tons of things in high school, and really put forth a lot of effort toward succeeding.

"The most important thing about my experience is that it made me really understand that some people are very calloused toward alcoholics, calloused toward drug addicts, calloused toward all sorts of people with problems, basically because of ignorance.

"I think having an alcoholic father has enabled me to understand and accept life experiences I may not be able to control. That experience during my childhood also has made me accept the fact that people often can be insensitive to what you may be experiencing, often because they really don't understand.

"After a few years of college in California, I came back here and started working for a bank. The people who owned the bank thought that I was a promising person, so they sent me to St. Louis and put me through extensive training, and when I came back I went into management. I met Bill shortly after that. And my big career in banking went out the window. I worked while we were dating; we got married and I worked for about ten months after we got married.

"The demands of my job did not really go well with being a bride, and really caring more about my marriage than the position, I decided to quit and devote more time to our marriage.

"When Bill and I first got married we really didn't discuss having children. I really didn't feel I would ever be a mother, basically because I really had never been around children and I can honestly say they scared me to death. I had grown up an only child and had virtually no exposure to them. I like children and felt they could bring great joy to a relationship, but then again they were frightening, and moreover, I was afraid of the great responsibility of raising a child.

"There were many things that Bill and I did discuss when we first got married and one of those things was arguments. I have always felt strongly about never bringing up the past in an argument. It never seems to help to dredge up past wrongs; it only adds more hurt and anger to the problem you are dealing with at the time. This attitude I have can probably be attributed to my mother, for she never held my father's past behavior over him during or after his drinking problem. I always admired her for this, and I really felt that is one of the reasons their marriage survived what it did.

"Drinking was another thing Bill and I discussed. Bill likes to drink and let loose, but he doesn't make a habit of it. Bill knew from the beginning I wouldn't tolerate a drinking problem. I know I sound a little hypercritical, but I guess I felt if I laid down the law from the beginning maybe I would never have to deal with it later. Realistically, I'm really not sure how I would handle it. We are not the kind of people that have that ritual drink before dinner to relax, basically because I feel it can become a very dangerous habit. I feel very confident that neither one of us will ever have to deal with a drinking problem.

"Another major problem we had to deal with before we got married was religion. Fortunately it did not become a major problem with us as it does for many people. I had been raised Catholic and Bill had been raised Lutheran. We both felt that one should not change for the other; we felt we should both make a sacrifice, so we became Methodist. This compromise was good for us, for that way we were both adopting something new together. By doing this neither one of us could feel like we sacrificed something for the other one.

"We were married a little over a year when I got pregnant. We really hadn't discussed it much, but once I knew I was pregnant I felt very positive about it. I decided to do the best job I could at being a mother. I didn't read a lot of literature on parenting, and sometimes I'm not sure if that's a curse or a blessing. James, our first child, is not your ideal child, but I don't believe reading more would have helped. James is a really neat little kid, but he and I do have personality differences; we just don't mesh well. James and his father get along famously, and Bill read even less about child development than I did, so I'm not convinced some parents have more difficulty with a child than others do.

"James was born two weeks early, and I was prepared to go over my due date so it was quite a surprise. Bill had been at a business meeting that night at which they had cocktails, and Bill had certainly had his share. When he finally arrived home I was furious with him, first of all for drinking, and second because I was unable to find him all evening. Bill decided not to respond to my anger and went to bed. He had no more gotten to bed and my water broke and off to the hospital we went. Bill was really very little help during the labor, and I think he's still convinced he was in greater pain than I was. James was born after a long six-hour labor. The labor and delivery were difficult at the time, but now after having more children I feel the difficulty was merely not knowing what was going on or what was to be expected.

"James was a beautiful baby and a very good one. I was quite scared of him at first, but somehow Mother Nature took over and I managed quite well.

"Bill and I decided we wanted our children to be two years apart, so I became pregnant again, which ended in a miscarriage after about six weeks. Then I became pregnant again. I loved being pregnant, I always felt terrific, and it was always a wonderful experience.

"When James was born I had a fear of crib death. When the second baby, Christopher, was born, SIDS never entered my mind.

I had had one beautiful baby that lived, so there was no reason for me to worry about this baby.

"James was two and a half when Christopher was born. Chris was born the end of September. James never showed any jealousy toward Chris at all.

"The labor and delivery of Christopher was very long, although after Chris decided to be born the delivery went very smoothly. He was a small baby when he was born, but he grew and progressed very normally.

"He was an extremely good baby, an absolute angel. He never caused a problem at all, although he always got up for a four o'clock feeding at which he was quite delightful. There was something I noticed shortly before he died and that was that he seemed to have a lack of a startle reflex. I could slam a door right next to him, and he didn't seem to react at all.

"He died in December. December twentieth. A week before Christmas. Upstairs. Two and one half months old. Almost three months old. I wanted to move immediately.

"I loved this house. I had worked my fool head off here. With all that work I had really kind of neglected Chris, and now this damned house has killed my baby.

"The week that led up to Christopher's death has bothered me a little bit in that I was so busy getting ready for Christmas. I didn't spend as much time with him as I would have liked to. Fortunately, Bill's parents were here that week and Bill's mother just idealizes her grandchildren, and they really hadn't spent as much time with Chris as my parents had. Bill's mother took care of the boys most of that week as I was running errands, making drapes, and making Christmas cookies.

"The next week on Wednesday—Chris died on Thursday—Bill was home all day as we were getting ready for Christmas, and we had a Christmas party to go to that night. I was in and out of the house all day, and Bill was hanging the draperies I had made. Christopher wouldn't go to sleep; he was very content to sit in his infant seat and watch his father work and his big brother play. He never did take a nap that afternoon.

"I tried to rock him to sleep. At one point he lay there and smiled at me and was so happy, and I figured, 'Well, this is ridiculous.

Face it, the kid is not tired.' He got a little fussy when I was getting ready to go to the party that night, so I just took him from room to room where I was getting ready, and as long as he could see me he was all right. We left him with the baby-sitter and we went to the party.

"It was very strange that evening; much of the conversation revolved around our children, particularly Christopher and what a delightful and good baby he was. Most of our friends at the time didn't have any children, and so we rarely talked about our kids. But that night was different. When we came home that night I did something I had never done before and that was I took the baby-sitter into Christopher's room to check on him. He had the sniffles, nothing serious, but we went in and checked on him and he was just fine. This was about 1:00 A.M. I took the baby-sitter home, and she knew that he was fine when she left.

"We woke up at eight o'clock, and I couldn't believe that he hadn't gotten up for his two o'clock feeding. He was finally sleeping through the night, I thought. He hadn't napped that whole day before, so I figured he was just so tired.

"Then Bill went in to check on Christopher, and the first thing he hollered out was that 'My God, he is gone.' I thought somebody had taken him. That thought got planted in my mind, and I had nightmares for months afterward that somebody was going to kidnap James.

"But then Bill said Chris was dead. I dialed 911, and I said, 'Our baby is dead.'

"And the operator said, 'Do you know mouth-to-mouth resuscitation?'

"I thought to myself, You dumb idiot, I just told you my baby is dead. But I said, 'Yes, I know mouth-to-mouth resuscitation.'

"He said, 'Can you apply it?'

"I said, 'It isn't going to do any good. My baby is dead.'

" 'My baby is dead. My God, my baby is dead.' There are no words to really explain the horror I felt, the anger, the confusion. I gave the rest of the information to the operator and hung up the phone. The fireman arrived within minutes of our phone call.

"James had woken up and was sitting on the steps crying and didn't know what was going on. Bill would not let me go in the bedroom to see, and I didn't because of the fear of what I might see. I then came down the steps. I said to the fireman, 'You have got to do something with James.'

"He said, 'Can we take him next door?'

"And I told him to take him next door to the Svobodas' and he did. The fireman picked Jim up and carried him over there. I didn't know where Bill was, so I went back upstairs and I did see Christopher. I am very glad that I did see him for Bill's sake.

"It is not a pretty sight. But I was glad that I at least saw him because Bill would have alone had that vision forever and I would have never known that pain. Bill would have always known. He would have been the sole person who would have seen that horrible sight of our baby discolored and deformed.

"I don't know if I could have stood it alone. This way we can share that awful feeling, and I can say, 'I understand, I know what you saw and I know how awful it is.' Had he had to cope with that by himself, I think it would have been hard. It would not only have been hard on him, but it would have been hard on me because I would have never known what he saw. It was awful—it was awful.

"I went upstairs and the fireman had him. I never really held him, and I regret that terribly that I never really held him. The fireman had him, and I put my arms around the fireman and I just collapsed on the fireman holding Christopher. And when that happened there was a push of air out of Christopher. I looked at the fireman, and the fireman started to work on Christopher again. And then he explained to me that having both bodies push against Christopher worked some air out. That was the last time I ever saw him looking that way. And then they wrapped him in a white blanket. I then came downstairs, and there was a nurse from the mobile heart team.

"She knelt by me and cried with me. And told me over and over again how it wasn't my fault and how there wasn't anything we could have done. She was the one who really got me headed in the right direction. Just the fact that she sat there. How can you say thank you for crying? But I did.

"Our doctor arrived about an hour later to pronounce the body dead, and at this time he requested that we have an autopsy done. We had been told that it was SIDS, but he felt for our own well-being and for research it would be helpful. At first I was very resentful; I felt as if he were accusing me of something. We did decide to have the autopsy done, and I'm grateful that we did. The autopsy relieved any questions I had about the fact that it really was SIDS.

"That day was a busy blur. With friends and relatives arriving I remember very little of the details. The one thing I remember vividly was that I was never going to have another child. I was never going to be put through this again.

"Bill seemed to accept Chris's death so easily at the time, and this angered me. Bill has always had a stronger faith in God, and I believe this was the reason he took it better.

"The next day the mortuary called and told us Christopher's body was ready for viewing. Viewing dead bodies has always bothered me, but I so desperately needed to see Christopher. When I saw Chris lying there for the first time it really sunk in. He was dead. That horrible sight that we had found had been wiped away, and he lay there so angelic and peaceful. It was very comforting to see him that way.

"We got through the funeral and the next few days quite well as we were surrounded by friends and relatives. Christmas came and went and all I can really remember was such emptiness. Then they were all gone and we were alone.

"Bill and I had started a pattern of Bill always putting James to bed and I would put Christopher to bed. Bill took care of James at the table, and I took care of Christopher. All of a sudden I had nothing to do. I had been robbed of my baby. So many times I thought, Why me? Why my baby? I would look at James sometimes and actually hate him. He constantly rejected me and wouldn't allow me to do anything for him. I thought to myself, I hurt so badly; how can you do this to me?

"Bill and I had a number of arguments about James. He felt I was short-tempered with James and that I wasn't very understanding of his needs. Bill felt what had happened really had affected James much more than we understood. In a way I was resentful, because I kept thinking, This thing has affected me too!

"Bill and I never pulled away from each other emotionally or sexually. If we ever needed each other, it was at this time. Often when married couples experience a crisis they pull away from each other in every way, but for Bill and me it was different. We seemed to come closer together.

"I was convinced in the beginning that I could never have another baby, although the day of the funeral I remember standing in our bedroom getting ready and saying a silent prayer to myself. I was asking God to help me get through the day, and then I realized that our life as a family had to go on and having another baby was part of that going on. I strongly believed God wouldn't put me though this again, and if He did I would have to deal with it. I didn't make a decision then to have another baby immediately, but I really didn't fear getting pregnant.

"Two months after Chris died I found out I was pregnant. I'm not sure when I got pregnant but it had to be within days of Chris's death. I wasn't trying to replace Christopher, but I knew I wanted to have more children. I just wasn't sure if I was emotionally ready.

"I didn't realize what the birth of Benjamin really did for all of us until a few months after he was born. There was fear, incredible fear, but along with that fear came a great healing process. Much of my anger was leaving me and to be able to love and be loved by another human being was wonderful. I was once again feeling good about myself and my life.

"By the end of the pregnancy, I didn't think that this baby was going to solve any problems at all. I felt that maybe there were going to be a whole lot of problems. I thought I really was going to become a mental case, that it was going to be constant worry. I wasn't going to be able to sleep, I was going to make this baby crazy with overprotection.

"Benjamin is without a doubt a very special child. I don't love him any more than James, but when I look at Ben I remember all the pain he managed to wipe away.

"I worried more about Jim after the baby died. I still go in. I will go in often in the evening and just sit and look at him. Not so much just to check that he is still breathing, but just to sit and look and be thankful that we have gotten him to five years old. Maybe everybody sits and looks at their children and appreciates the fact that they are alive. But I don't think so. I think a parent that lost a child has a tendency to cherish those moments. My heart sinks a little bit every time James gets hurt.

"Bill and I have always had good communication between us,

and about a year ago I found we were being short-tempered with each other, so we decided to make a pact to be nicer and more considerate of each other's feelings. We both realized that we were wasting such precious time in nagging each other, and you never know how much of that time you have left. When a family experiences a loss you become very aware of how impermanent things are.

"After Benjamin was born, my cousin, who is a general practitioner, urged us to have Ben monitored. Our family doctor didn't encourage us either way. I strongly felt that if we were going to lose Ben there was nothing we could do about it. I still believe that way, although I understand monitoring much better now and I see how beneficial it can be in many cases.

"Bill and I have a strong belief in God and have accepted Chris's death and feel that that was the way it was to be. Many people don't feel that way, and I think it may change their way of handling it. I do believe that the faith we both share has helped us deal with the guilt that often accompanies parents after the loss of a child to SIDS.

"I always feel somewhat more fortunate that my child died of SIDS than the mother who lost her child to a disease. My baby was apparently healthy; the autopsy reported that there was no apparent cause of death. Knowing that helps to erase some of the guilt. I feel confident that I took the best care I could of Christopher. In a sense we parents who lose children to SIDS are taken off the hook. There is still guilt, but at least there aren't those what ifs that often go along with losing a child to some sort of disease.

"After Christopher died, someone said something to me about my smoking while I was pregnant. I felt so guilty and at the same time I wanted to wring her neck. I spoke to my doctor at length about my smoking and he was wonderful. He encouraged me to cut down my smoking, but he assured me that the smoking was not the reason Christopher died. He knew that I was not emotionally able right then to quit, so he didn't urge it.

"The pregnancy was hard emotionally. But there were some light moments. We were on our way out to Rockford and the sun was setting. It was a glorious sunset. As we were driving out, we were heading west. It was that time of the evening when you could literally see the sun going down. We are visiting and all of a sudden

Jim pops up in the back seat and he says, 'How does Christopher stay up there?'

"And I said, 'What do you mean?'

" 'Well,' he said, 'The sun is coming down; how does Christopher stay up in heaven with God?'

"And I looked at Bill and we both looked at each other and we thought, Gee, what do you say?

"Bill replied, 'Well, he has a chair up there to sit on.' [Laughs.] I was waiting for this profound statement to come out of Bill and that was it. Jim never asked another thing. The silliness—it's something you've just got to have to stay alive.

"We had a horrible time the Christmas after Ben was born. I thought I was going to lose my mind. James just began to behave horribly. In the back of my mind I thought maybe.

"Ben was the same age as Chris was, and it was the same time of the year. I was afraid that James was having fears of Ben possibly dying. Maybe this was the reason he was behaving so badly. I didn't want to bring up the subject. I feared if that wasn't the reason for his bad behavior, I didn't want to plant a fear there that wasn't there already.

"Down deep I was afraid of the same thing. It seemed like I was sitting on a time bomb. One morning about a week before Christmas, James crawled into bed with me and said, 'Mom, when is Ben going to die?'

"And I said, 'Well, Honey, we hope that he won't die.' I knew that I couldn't say he is not going to die because I thought, As soon as I say that, I'm going to get caught in one big mess. And I talked about it and said, 'We hope that babies don't die, but sometimes they do.'

"And he said, 'Well, it is Christmas, Mom, and Chris died at Christmas.' He said, 'Mom, all babies die,' because all his babies had died.

"The only baby that he had was Christopher, and he had died. We got another baby and he was going to die too. So then I talked about different babies that we knew that didn't die and grew up. We had a little girl next door that was a baby about the same age as Christopher and she was almost two.

"James seemed to accept the explanation, and we got through

Christmas pretty well. Bill and I both cried after Christmas was over. We cried because we had gotten over another mountain in our lives.

"Everyone told us that James would never remember the death of Christopher. He's only two and a half and he will forget. James didn't forget; he never will. Maybe if Christopher had died in the hospital it wouldn't have affected him so deeply, but going through the trauma that day with both of his parents half crazy with fear and bewilderment has really stuck with him. He has fond memories of Chris and often mentions him. Small children don't know how to release their grief, and so James never cried. But he just seemed to ask endless questions. James finally was able to mourn when he was five years old. He and I took a bouquet of flowers to Chris's grave on Chris's birthday. When we got there James started to ask me some questions about Chris, and then all of a sudden he began to cry. He sobbed hysterically, begging me to get Chris back and all the time asking why. I held him and loved him and allowed him to get it all out. Together we sat and talked for nearly an hour at Chris's grave, sharing our feelings. And ever since that day I believe James has a better understanding of what really happened.

"After Christopher died, in the first few days I started to withdraw badly. I was scared. I started to withdraw, and it started to scare me because I usually don't back away from situations, I usually go full speed into them. I didn't want to talk and I didn't want to be talked to. I was feeling very sorry for myself. I was the only person this could happen to. Bill seemed to bounce back so quickly, I was a little angry. I thought, What in the hell? I wasn't talking. People were asking me questions, and I wasn't answering them in the car on the way back from the funeral home. I could tell it was getting to Bill, but at this point I didn't care.

"We got home and we got the phone call shortly afterward. At that time, I still didn't know for sure if it was SIDS. We had been told it was, but I thought, God, I wonder if he got bumped. Maybe the baby-sitter dropped him and she didn't tell me, and he bled to death. A million things went through my head. Then when I got the autopsy report—Dr. Fritsch has a way of calming you—he said, 'There was nothing you could have done, Ellen.' He said, 'The autopsy shows he was in very good health; he was just a normal baby.' And it was like the whole world lifted off my shoulders. I hadn't done anything wrong. Thank God, I hadn't done anything wrong. And so then I got to feeling better.

"I have never backed away from anything, and I felt this crisis in my life wasn't any different. I had to go on. Not only for Bill, James, and the baby I was caring for, but mostly for myself. It wasn't easy, and I didn't do it alone. Bill was truly my strength, and all our wonderful friends and family were so good too. They all listened, and they never seemed to say the wrong thing. I have worked with SIDS families who have had someone say something hurtful and stupid to them. That makes it all the more difficult to heal. Maybe somebody did say something to me that could have been taken the wrong way. Maybe, but I just didn't hear them or I didn't want to hear it.

"Now when I think of Christopher, I think, I have lost him for now, but I know I will find him again. The word *dead* is very final.

"In my mind that means he is gone forever and that is not the way we look at it. He is still very much a part of our family, very much a part of our life. I feel we have three children, unfortunately one of them isn't with us.

"I don't ever want to forget him, and we never will. There are things that still hurt and times that are very hard. When I hear 'Away in a Manger' played it always tears me apart. But it's not bad to cry. It's not bad to be human.''

Bill's Story

"I was born in Chicago and I lived there until about third grade and then we moved to Springfield. I graduated from high school in Springfield and was in chemistry for three years at the University of Illinois before switching to business. After graduation I went to work for a small industry, and I'm a manager now.

"I met Ellen through her cousin. We weren't too crazy about each other at first, but I needed a date for a fraternity function and I couldn't find anyone so I called her. Nine months later we were married. It was a real whirlwind romance. We had good communication after we decided to like each other. I really don't know what happened. We could talk and we didn't have any problems.

"After about a year Ellen got pregnant and our first son James was born. Two years later Christopher was born.

"I don't really like little babies. They have got to grow a little bit. I don't feel right handling five-pound creatures. They just have got to grow a little bit before I feel comfortable. I feel like I'll break them. Christopher was about three months old when it happened. We had been to a Christmas party that night.

"The funny thing about this is that I hadn't had very much to drink that night at the Christmas party. I came home and I drank some coffee and I was not tired at 2:00 in the morning, so I stayed up until all the television shows were off at 3:30, drinking milk and eating cookies. Ellen was sound asleep. I was up until after 3:30, when I went to bed, and to the best of my knowledge, Chris was dead at that time. It was at or around the time he died that I went to bed. There was no sound and we had the doors wide open.

"The next morning he slept late, and I went in and checked on him and thought, Somebody has stolen him. He wasn't lying there in his crib. I saw his blankets over in the corner. He was under them. I picked him up. I knew he was dead. I didn't know what to do. I was panicked.

"I tried to keep Ellen out of the room. I didn't want her to see him, because he was pretty, well—he looked bad. I got very loud. I was angry. I was yelling at her to stay in our room and I was over in the baby's bedroom with Christopher. I just didn't want her to see him because when I took the blankets off him his mouth was distorted and his eyes were open. I didn't want Ellen to see him like that. I knew he was dead.

"I am talking slowly about it now, but as it was going through my head, it was unbearable. Do I call the morgue or do I—Who do I call? I put the baby on the bed, on the other bed. And then, by this time James was awake and crying on the steps.

"I yelled at Ellen, 'I don't want you to—don't come in here— stay out!' And she was handling the phone so she stayed out, and to be honest with you I don't know if she went in or not because she called 911, and I thought I had better get some clothes on: Someone will be here. I laid him down, then I had him covered up, and I went in and put on a pair of jeans. I came back out of the bedroom, and a fireman was standing at the front of the door. They were here immediately.

"I couldn't believe it. If there had been any chance, we would have saved him. That fireman took him and worked with him in the bathroom, and he tried everything. I can't blame anybody.

"The fire department came; they were the first. The heart team was here and then the sheriff. Then the coroner. The fireman closed his eyes. I didn't want Ellen to see the baby, and yet—I can understand the mother not really wanting to touch the child but wanting to touch to see if it is true. To realize the baby is dead.

"Seeing him in the casket helped. Ellen had always said that she had never wanted to ever have an open casket. She changed her mind after we lost our baby.

"I have my memories now of Christopher the way I want to remember him. I think that maybe in our case it was extremely relieving. It helped to soften that earlier ugly memory. He looked very angelic, and just to have his face back in an undistorted manner was so relieving.

"When I found him he appeared to be in such pain, even though everyone said it was a painless death. It's good to be able to remember him the way he was in the casket, at peace, his face natural and calm.

"The day that Christopher died, it fell to me to talk to Jim. That night when he asked Ellen about what happened to Christopher, she froze right there and she gave me a look that signaled help: I can't tell him, her eyes said. Nothing would come out of her mouth. So I took Jim upstairs and talked to him.

"I took him into Christopher's room. The big one. It had a bed in there and a crib. I took him into Christopher's room—what came about is that Jim had moseyed upstairs, and he went into Christopher's room and for the first time realized the firemen were not going to bring Christopher back and Christopher wasn't in the crib.

"He started asking the questions: 'When are they finally going to bring him back?' He just thought that the fireman had him for a little visit. So I just sat him down and tried to explain it to him. Christopher went to heaven and God had chosen him and wanted him to be with God. And it would be sad for us, but Chris was very fortunate. And Jim said, 'Well, when is God going to bring him back?' This is when I told him Christopher wouldn't be coming back. I thought he did an excellent job of comprehending.

"The next morning was worse. We went to Christmas Eve services, and I didn't want to take him in at first, but neither one of us really thought what was going to come would come. We were sitting in the pew and he said, 'Well, we gonna see Christopher tonight?'

"I said, 'He is with God.'

" 'We are here, where is he?' He knew the church was God, and you know, we are here. What was the deal?

"Telling anyone was a problem. The day Chris died, I called my best friend, Fred, and then I thought I would call my folks and let them know. That didn't work, because I called Fred to tell him, and that took me five minutes to get out of my mouth what I was trying to say. And I thought, If I can't call my best friend, there is no way I am going to call my parents.

"When I called Fred I just tried to say, 'He is dead.' The word *dead* is very hard to say. I started to say it. I just kind of choked up, and I couldn't get it out in one nice sentence, what had happened to Christopher.

"Fred finally asked, 'Has something happened to Christopher?'

"And I said, 'Yes. He is gone.' I could get *gone* out.

"Then he knew what I meant. He said, 'Do you want us to come over right now?'

"And I said, 'I would really appreciate it.'

"The hard part for the next few days was the planning. The fellow at the funeral home, he said to us many times, 'This is very difficult. It is very difficult for me, I had a grandson just exactly the age of the baby, your baby, that died. And I've got to be honest with you, this is hard for me.' He had seen death thousands and thousands of times, and it was hard on him.

"I talked to the people at the funeral home afterward and thanked them for the very professional job. They did an excellent job. They were fantastic. They were very professional. The bill was very inexpensive. I just couldn't believe it. When I asked them about it they said that is just their policy and the way I got it, it is kind of a common thing in the whole industry. They just figure the last thing you need is a financial burden. They feel that the death of a young child is a trauma for everybody involved. And they don't want to make it harder for you if they can. That is the way they do it. I questioned it because I thought they had forgotten something on the bill.

"One of the hard things besides finding him, I had a hard time at the mortuary that night. The next hardest thing was at the funeral. We were sitting in the limousine and people were filing out of the church and I saw six guys from my National Guard group in their uniforms. They had come, and they had come in a hell of a snowstorm, and it was kind of—there were lots of friends there, that we knew would be there, but these were people who I had commanded. They knew us, but they didn't know us real well. It wasn't a thing where they had to be there. It was a very genuine act for them to do this and to be there in full uniform. It meant a lot to me.

"I didn't feel like I was being strong for others. But in a sense I was strong. I think a lot all gets back to the achievement aspect of what you think of yourself and what you want to contend with. A lot of it came from my military background. I have had to tell men how to face death, what death is, and I can't tell them if they believe in God that is the answer. But I can't tell them that door isn't open either. I can't say, 'Okay, if you believe in God you can face death. If we go into battle and your buddy gets killed, if you believe in God, you will make it right on through on trust.' I can't say that because half of them don't believe in God. That is why it is hard for me to tell you my beliefs because going through the stages we do to try to prepare men for war—whether we ever see war or not—we still have to teach them. But after you get done talking about death, there is still the one thing that always comes up in the military and that is the mission. And to accomplish the mission. Whether it be at all cost. My belief was to do that at as small a cost as possible. But still the fact remains that in the indoctrination that I had to administer, the mission was always number one. And you know, after you preach that for so many years, and then it happens to you, you are faced with death—when I wanted to break down, I never could. I preached it for too damn long to turn around—I had to be strong.

"In the initial few days, I wanted to go out and knock down garages with a sledgehammer. I wanted to fly off in a rage. And I couldn't because of the state Ellen was in. That was true and was the only time that I ever felt that I just had to stay together, and that was all there was to it.

"I feel I have been allowed to mourn all I wanted. I don't feel that I have been restricted at all. We communicate, Ellen and I. I can let a lot of grief out just by talking. Maybe it is relaxing for me to talk with Ellen, I don't know. But that is one way I can express my grief.

"I have met people who can't talk at all. They just can't let anybody know anything. And how they would get across, then, that feeling I had inside the first day, or what they could do with their grief, I just don't know. They have got to do something. They have got to let it out somewhere, some way. Each marriage, you know each other, and you know when to let each other be strong or weak.

"I would say on this particular subject, the death of Christopher, I was stronger because I had less feelings toward the baby than she had. They were so much closer; in my mind I had to be strong, in this particular instance.

"It is a hell of a lot easier to be strong if there is someone who is strong with you. We share power. There is no struggle.

"You can never erase a mistake, but you can sure offset it with achievements. And so, consequently, it is the same way with death. You might have a wound over here, but all the good things that happen are building up together on the other side of the fence. It never goes away. No way does it go away, but these good things over here continue to grow and pretty soon your scale is going to weigh out. Still, thirty years down the road, Christmas is going to be hard.

"When we chose the music for the funeral, we had 'Away in a Manger' played. Thirty years from now that song is still going to affect me in the same way it does now. I think the only thing that is never going to change in thirty years is that I will never forget the way he looked when I found him. No way. What I did all day that Thursday and Friday in thirty years is probably going to be forgotten. But the way he looked will never pass.

"Little things bring back memories. Like I went to a funeral that was for an older person that had passed away; he was a vet. And there was a color guard right there. These guys never did any ceremony when Chris died, but they were in uniform. Anytime I go to a funeral and see a uniform, it is going to get me. Just little things. They are always going to be there, and they are always going to come back. When they reoccur, when you see them, you think about it all over again.

"It is hard to know what you will remember, but that night at the mortuary I remember feeling that I was looking at Christopher for the first time. I realized for the first time that Christopher would never get to what I call a father stage, like James had. 'I am never going to get a chance for that kid to get to me.' He had already got into the mother stage. Ellen could feel a loss I wasn't really part of. I didn't know that before I actually saw him there in the casket and realized that I am never going to get that experience.

"My son Jim has his own tools. They are not play tools, they are a real-life hammer and saw. And everytime I do projects, he is right there with me, he takes them along. It gives him something to do. He nails nails and saws boards. I enjoy having him there. The kid is good. I'd just as soon have him doing that as anyone. It is great.

"Christopher never got to that stage, of course, since at three months he died. That afternoon I was hanging curtains—the little guy wouldn't go to sleep, so I had him right there, and I would give him a toy hammer and he was chewing on it or something. But he was awake and with me. It was the only time that I had ever spent any real time with him because he had never got to that stage. When I saw him in the casket, that is when it hit me, what I really lost.

We had pictures taken at the funeral, which may seem morbid. But after we talked about it, in my mind I kind of wanted the photographers there so that I could get the picture of him when I found him out of my mind. It keeps recurring, and I have to have something to go back to and remember. Something that is tangible that I can look at. I am looking at two memories and one is horrible. One is more impressed on my mind—the one where I found him, not the one of seeing him in the casket. I got to thinking, I know which one is more likely going to stick in my mind the longer. I would like not to have it there. So we have the funeral pictures. If I didn't, then I lose that memory and that would be awful.

"We don't want to lose him. You don't ever want to lose him. They are just so much a part of you. To put that baby away forever would be awful. He wasn't here that long, but he was here. He existed. And it is just like trying to erase—you just can't erase part of your past. It happened. Just try to take something out of it and try to put it into your life and make something out of it. Mold it into a positive experience. There is something there you can get out of it.

"When I think of my family, we are still missing one. One is missing. And we feel that. There should be one in the middle. You know, a two-year old.

"It's funny. Ellen has a cousin who has three boys. The oldest is kind of artsy, a very sensitive person, very strong-willed. The middle one, he couldn't care less. He is a hard worker, quiet, but he couldn't care less about win or lose. Not competitive at all, a big mediator. The third one is rather ornery, and he keeps trucking right on down the line. The middle one keeps peace in the whole household. It is just kind of funny; Ben will be getting kind of ornery, and Jim and Ben go at it. I say to Ellen 'You know we are missing that middle one to keep the peace around here.' Christopher was very gentle and quiet. When you see that, you wonder. What could have been?"

A Year Later

Bill and Ellen are surviving quite well. Their relationship is strong and healthy, and their love for each other seems to be even greater than ever. They both have gotten involved with a SIDS support group in their area and find it to be very rewarding. They are doing well, but they still have some difficult times. It is a struggle, and they both have agreed that there will always be difficult days, difficult times. But these days are farther apart, and the time is not so long. The struggle to heal never ends, but without the struggle they would not have survived. Life will never be the same for Bill and Ellen; it has become infinitely more precious.

The Day the Baby Died

The stories of what happened the day the babies died were painful for parents to describe and will certainly be painful to read for those who have experienced a SIDS death in their family. These experiences, however, may help parents understand that their own experiences were not so unique and that they do not need to feel guilty about things they did or feelings they expressed the day the baby died. After leaving the hospital, one parent drank beer for the next several days. Another parent bent a metal chair in the hospital waiting room with his hands. Another parent put his fist through the wall after calling 911 from his home. Although these reactions may seem extreme, the stress of losing a child so suddenly does create all kinds of feelings and responses unique to that day and time.

Baby-sitters Who Cared for the Baby

Approximately one-third of the parents said their babies died while in the care of a baby-sitter. Our research does not explore what happens to these individuals, but they should be the focus of further research. Some parents provided clues as to the possible agony baby-sitters experienced:

> She called 911 and could not get herself to apply CPR because she had gone through the same thing three years earlier with another infant boy. She told me she knew there was no hope, but apologized that she hadn't tried CPR anyway. I had to console her when I arrived at her home. She was literally a madwoman, tearing her hair

out, walking from room to room amidst all the police and rescue people. I finally got her attention, and all she could do was apologize. . . . My sitter was taken to the hospital by her family and had to be under sedation for a couple of days. The next day we tried to see my sitter, but she was still at the hospital, so we didn't try again for several days.

She [the baby-sitter] took the death *very, very* hard. Much more, I believe, than we did. She felt a tremendous amount of guilt. We had the SIDS chapter, the public health nurse, and the pathologist who did the autopsy contact her, answer her questions, and reassure her that she was not at fault. To the best of our knowledge she is doing okay now.

Two of the parents who participated in our study had their child die while in the care of their sisters. One of the parents said, "She was the only person I truly trusted to watch my children. I still trust her." This same parent went on to describe the effect of the death on her brother-in-law:

The first person I saw when I got to the hospital was my brother-in-law. When I saw his face I fell to the ground, but somebody caught me. They had a wheelchair waiting for me. How did they know I would need it? I remember my husband made a comment later, referring to my brother-in-law when we first got to the hospital. He said he had never seen a face that was so expressionless before.

The other parent referred to the guilt her sister felt over the baby's dying. She said,

My sister kept telling us over and over what happened. I know she felt tremendous guilt. How could I comfort her? I knew she had nothing to do with this and she had done all she could.

We can only speculate about the grief and guilt these baby-sitters experienced as a result of a child in their care dying of SIDS. What effect does this experience have on their ability to care for other children? Because they do not receive the in-depth counseling SIDS parents typically receive, how do they deal with the self-blame or the real or perceived blame of the parents?

Premonitions about the Baby's Death

Some parents described a premonition they had about their baby's death. One mother said she knew her child would die very young but had been afraid to tell anyone but her husband because people would think she was crazy. Another described her experience:

> When I awoke again, I noticed the clock read 9:00 A.M. Since I had had a dream that someone was telling me, "The baby is dead," I was scared to go and look in on him. I noticed that my older son was up and watching cartoons in the living room, and he had to look at the baby before leaving the room, since he had slept in the same room with him that night. Then my husband got up and rushed to the bathroom to shower. He ordinarily looked in on the baby also, so I figured the dream was absurd. I went into the room to wake the baby for his feeding, since it was late. As soon as I entered the room I felt a presence, and when I looked at the baby's hand I realized, or knew, that he was dead and that the dream was true.

Parents often described an uneasiness or just a general feeling that things were not as they should be. One couple had a feeling something was wrong and came home early from going to a movie. Many parents had a feeling of something being wrong when they woke late in the morning and realized the baby had slept so long:

> It was Christmas morning, 1984. I woke up, looked at my watch. It was 7:15 A.M. I knew before I jumped out of bed that something was wrong, because he always awoke about 5:30 or 6:00 A.M. I was in the same room. When I got to the crib and realized he was dead, I screamed.

Some parents described a feeling of death when they entered the room where the baby slept. One typical response came from this parent: "I walked into the bedroom. Before I turned on the light I had a terrible feeling. Then I found him." Another parent said, "I went in to get her. I felt funny, but I didn't know why." Yet another said, "I woke up about 10:00 A.M. on Sunday morning and knew something was wrong, because the baby hadn't waked me up to feed him."

Some Unusual Examples

Several children lived for a period of time after being revived, and one of the children survived. Other children died while being held in their parents' arms, and one baby died in the car.

THE BABY WHO DIED IN THE CAR. One mother described how her baby died in the back seat while she was driving:

> My father and I were returning to my home on the central California coast after visiting my college friend and her new baby in Portland, Oregon. I put him down for a nap right behind me while I drove. We stopped at a gas station and parked for dinner. He had been asleep for almost three hours. I turned him over and he was dead, newly dead, because he was still quite warm, except for his hands.

The baby had died quietly since neither the mother nor the grandfather heard anything that would have made them concerned about the child's welfare.

THE BABIES WHO LIVED FOR A WHILE. For some parents the death was not so sudden. For some there was hope, for a little while, that the child might survive. The anxiety of not knowing whether their child might live and possibly have extensive brain damage, or might die at some later date, created additional stress for some parents.

One set of parents rushed the baby to the hospital while administering CPR. After approximately half an hour in the emergency room, the doctor announced there was a heartbeat:

> The pediatrician said my child was a sick boy with internal bleeding. . . . We waited through three hours of anxiety, with his blood pressure rising and falling. Around daylight the medical team from Boston arrived. Their prognosis was also grim. "If he lives he'll be a very sick child." Later, a doctor pulled us into a room and we heard the words "I'm sorry to say your baby could not be saved."

Another couple found their baby not breathing and also administered CPR until the paramedics came to their home:

> At the hospital his heart was started after a shot of adrenalin, and he was flown by life-flight helicopter to Toledo. . . . We couldn't know how much damage the baby had suffered from lack of air. Total recuperation, a coma for weeks, brain damage to some degree, death? I really wondered which would be harder to face, a brain-damaged child after having had a lively, happy, normally developing, bright child, or death? Both alternatives seemed so devastating.
>
> He was stabilized, still unconscious and unable to breathe by himself. . . . The doctor called to say that part of his intestines had been eliminated, indicating organ death from lack of oxygen and

that he would die within hours. We returned immediately to the hospital and sat by his bed just watching the heart monitor lose ground beat by beat. I was able to hold him once there was no hope, and, therefore, no concern over causing further brain damage by moving his head. He had so many tubes hooked up to him. I just rocked him and stroked his soft head until his heart stopped beating shortly after 6:00 A.M. on the sixteenth. . . . It was so hard to lay him on the bed and leave the hospital.

One child lived for four days after what medical personnel referred to as "interrupted SIDS." A sister who had been caring for the child started CPR after she found the baby was not breathing. The child was taken to the hospital with no pulse or heartbeat. The child was on a respirator, unconscious:

> He needed to be moved to another hospital, but we were told he might not survive the trip. He was still alive when we got to the hospital [where he had been transferred]. Hope was coming through. We didn't get to see him for two hours. . . . All the doctors kept telling us that he was dying and they couldn't help him. He had been too long without oxygen. Even if he did live he would be a vegetable. His brain and all other organs were devastated. He would never be our beautiful baby we knew and loved. When we were allowed to see him, my heart just shattered. He was connected to machines from everywhere on his body, and he was having terrible seizures. How could this have been true? He was fine at 6:30. Why would God let this happen? My whole life was dying in front of my eyes, and no one could stop it.
>
> The things my precious baby went through took a little piece of me away every minute. . . . Those days were full of hope, despair, tears, and asking why and how one hundred times a day.

Parents Who Saw Their Babies Stop Breathing

Three of the parents were watching as their babies stopped breathing, and they made efforts to revive their children but were unsuccessful. Parents who think they should have done something differently, or believe they somehow could have prevented the death from happening might find comfort in knowing that even parents who witnessed the event could not protect their child.

One woman was holding her child on her chest in bed when he

stopped breathing. The child had "just snuggled down and popped his thumb in his mouth."

> He then gave a little sigh, and I felt him go "dead weight." I screamed for my husband to call the paramedics. I turned him over and started mouth-to-mouth. One look at his little face told me that he was gone. He was so beautiful and at peace.

Another parent described what happened this way:

> I was holding him, and he started breathing in a different way, with a spasm, a catch in the exhale breath. We'd seen similar spells before and asked a doctor about them. He [the doctor] wasn't alarmed. He didn't know. But they seemed serious to us. This time I became alarmed and started for the hospital. He died, stopped breathing altogether on the way. Shaking him, CPR, nothing helped.

One couple was watching their baby sleep in the crib and whispering about the wonder of being parents when they realized their baby's skin had become pale:

> My husband picked him up, shook him; we called his name loudly, no response whatsoever. [He was] limp and very white. My husband began mouth-to-mouth in his arms and then on the floor. As I left the room to call the rescue unit, I looked back as my husband raised my son's head, and I saw blood trickling from my son's nose. He was deep blue. I knew he was dead.

These parents saw the breathing stop and made efforts to save their child, but they were unsuccessful. One small comfort for these parents might be that they were with the child when he died and there was little evidence of suffering.

One parent described how her baby lived through the apnea episode and was later monitored. We have mixed feelings about including this example here, for it is not our intent to leave parents with nagging questions about whether their child might also have lived if circumstances had been different. Nevertheless, it is important for parents to know that some babies do live, are later put on a monitor, and do outgrow the apnea episodes.

This baby stopped breathing at three days old while in the parents' bedroom:

At 10:30 he awoke. I tried nursing him back to sleep, but instead he had a crying spell for about fifteen minutes, which was unusual for him. Then he fell asleep. I had a terrible feeling that something was wrong but could not see anything. I sat up rocking him in the rocking chair in our bedroom. I did not want to go back to sleep as long as I felt that way. About fifteen minutes later I thought he stopped breathing and gently shook him and listened. Shortly, he did it again, and then he went limp in my arms.

I roughly shook the baby but did not get any response. I cried out to my husband to wake up and help me, quick: "The baby is not breathing!" I immediately knew in my mind that this was crib death but did not say so to my husband. He later told me that he thought I was being silly. When I handed him the baby, he realized very quickly that what I was saying was true. I kept saying, "Do something." My husband started blowing in the baby's mouth and gently squeezing his abdomen. We got dressed and ran to the car.

I drove to the hospital as fast as I could while my husband kept blowing and squeezing the baby's chest. We got to the hospital in five minutes, and during the car ride the baby did not breath on his own but was alert. He did have his eyes open and could move them from side to side. My husband ran out of the car at the emergency entrance. One of the glass doors was locked, and my husband hit it with his shoulder at a run, believing it would swing open. The jolt of being slammed between the door and his chest was enough to set the baby breathing and crying for his life. When he got into the emergency room he was checked out fine. In fact, the doctor on duty didn't believe that he actually stopped breathing because he hadn't turned blue.

We later met with a pediatrician in the nursery who checked the baby out and listened to us as to what had happened. He believed us, which was reassuring. At his suggestion we left the baby in the nursery hooked up to a monitor. The following night the baby was monitored. During that time between 1:00 and 3:00 A.M. he set off the monitor many times. My husband was holding him in his arms that night. We could have lost our baby that night if he hadn't had the monitor hooked to him.

The baby had one episode of setting off the alarm a week later while he was home but has had none since. The baby is now almost four months old.

The use of monitors will be discussed in chapter 12.

The Way the Babies Looked When They Were Found

Many of the flashbacks parents had of the death of their child related to how they found the child. They had vivid memories of how the baby looked and felt, whether the baby was blue or white, warm or cold.

Some parents found their baby limp and very white or blue:

"He was face down in the pillow! I turned on the light and quickly lifted him. He was like a pale rag doll."

"He was limp like a rag doll. He still had his color but was not breathing."

"The baby was limp and very white."

"I noticed she was warm and not yet blue."

"The baby did not look dead when I found him. He just looked as though he was sleeping."

"He was dead, newly dead, because he was still quite warm except for his hands, but all blue."

Other parents found the baby stiff and cold. Some babies looked bruised because blood had settled to the lower extremities after death. Others looked black. Some babies had vomit on the bed, and some had blood on their noses:

I picked him up and he was kind of stiff and cold. I shook him and called his name. Then as best I can remember I started to scream. I covered him up with a blanket. I remember thinking he might be cold.

She was cold and stiff, and her face was black.

I knew he was dead because there was a spot of blood on the sheets.

As I reached down I noticed what looked like a bruise on his jaw. When I picked him up, he didn't feel like a baby. The first thought I had was that one of the kids had put a doll here and it wasn't the baby at all. Then I knew it was, but there was no life in his body. When you pick up a sleeping baby, it stretches and moves and the movement is reassuring. His face was misshapen and distorted, and his eyes were strangely glazed.

He had a strange wetness all over him. I tried waking him while I changed his clothes. He wouldn't wake up.

His face looked splotched, white splotches.

He didn't seem right, so I touched his back. When I did, his head moved around kind of funny, and he looked kind of, well, not right. I went over to the wall and turned on the light and went back to look at him again. That's when I rolled him over and he had blood on his nose, and I realized he wasn't breathing.

I leaned over to pick him up when it hit me. His eyes were half open but not in a sleepy way. A look of death. Then I saw the blood-tinged froth from his nose and vomit on his front.

As I walked into her room, I noticed the underside of her hand was purple. Her head was face down into the covers. I picked up her hand, and her stiff body turned right over. She looked like she had been beaten.

The vomit or blood-tinged mucus from the nose or mouth result from the pressure change in the chest cavity after death. It is mucus discharge from the lungs.

Parents' Responses

The response on the part of many parents after they found their child was to attempt CPR (cardiopulmonary resuscitation). Some parents had no CPR training but still attempted to revive their child. In other cases someone gave instruction for CPR over the telephone, and in still other cases someone was available who had CPR training.

One parent said, "I tried my best to do CPR, but, of course, I didn't know a lot." Another parent said, "I tried to blow air into him, but I knew nothing about CPR, so I'm sure it was wrong."

Beyond that initial reaction of attempting CPR, parents had a wide range of responses to the death of their child.

There is no one way to respond to a tragedy, no one way that makes things better. It appears for these parents that losing a child suddenly is so shocking, so devastating, that the response may be unlike anything else they would do in life. We began this chapter by saying that the response to SIDS may be unique to this very painful time and place. What follows are descriptions of a range of responses that parents have had; whatever the parent's response to the death, it is normal, and quite possibly some other parent did the same thing or felt the same thing.

I remember going to a restaurant and not being able to stop eating. I couldn't fill up.

The paramedic must have read my mind because he said, "It's all over, she's gone." All I could think of was how long eternity is. How far away from us it is. And yet she was there. I couldn't cry. I just sat. Our family M.D. wanted to give me something, but I refused because I wanted, or needed, to feel the pain myself without my feelings being denied by a drug.

I remember sitting on our bed holding myself and rocking. I hit my head on our cast iron bed (hard) and thought, I'm going crazy and can't let myself do it.

It was a nightmare. We cried and hurt. We also moved the next day.

[After returning from the hospital] we went back to the house and packed up everything that was the baby's and put it in the trunk of my parents' car and then into storage. . . . We paid all the hospital bills as soon as they were available. We wanted to put it all behind us and get on with our lives.

[The next day] I went into the hills and burned the bassinet pad, sheets, and blankets he had slept in last.

The first night after she died was awful. I wandered around all night crying and looking for her. I didn't know where her body was: at the hospital, morgue, or funeral home. . . . The next night I slept better knowing where her body was.

We all three, myself, my husband, and my daughter, slept together that night and cried all night.

I just lay on the couch curled up until it was time to go to the funeral home. Nobody slept. . . . I think I smoked about two packs of cigarettes that night.

I wanted to kill myself because I thought I had suffocated the baby. I just wanted to die. . . . I was just like a caged animal. But my family was there, and they were good to me. It helped to be able to cry and yell and scream.

I couldn't keep warm enough. I constantly had a blanket wrapped around me. That night when everyone left, we were so tired, but we just couldn't get to sleep. My husband got up and wrote a poem to the baby.

[The day after the baby died] we went out that day and bought a brown teddy bear for our baby—something I had been wanting to do but kept putting off. Now it seemed the most important thing that I had to do. . . . The night of the funeral I wrote a poem to my son.

Clearly, anything parents do after the death of a child is "normal."

Holding the Baby After He or She Died

Most parents appreciated the opportunity to hold their baby and spend some quiet time with the child after it died. A few chose not to do so and in fact did not want to look at the child.

Some babies died at home, and the parents held the baby before the baby was taken away. One mother described how her child was pronounced dead and the family waited three hours for the mortician to come. During that time "we held and cried over him until they took him. That was very comforting."

One parent described how difficult it was to give the baby to someone else after the baby died at home:

At that point my mind snapped into gear, and I felt like the director of a motion picture. I remember saying that she [the baby] had to be gone before my husband got home. I attempted to get things organized. I said that we needed to cancel our garage sale that was slated for September 29. We needed to make arrangements for her cremation. We needed to make arrangements for her memorial service. I was still holding her. The coroner's wagon arrived, and I still wouldn't put her down or let anyone else have her. Someone said something that made sense to me, I don't remember what, and I let them have her. . . . I was running out behind him to see her for one last time. I stood at the funeral wagon for a long time and cried when they closed the door to leave.

Other parents held their babies in the hospital either after the child had been taken off life support or after the baby had died. One parent held the baby in the hospital after life support was removed and then again later, after family members had been called. "After about twenty to thirty minutes we let the nurse carry him away. I watched her take my baby away." One parent held her baby after they unplugged the life support equipment:

> I requested they unplug him, let me rock him, and leave us alone. My mom stayed. I remember being surprised at how limp he was. He lasted about two minutes and died in my arms. I also remember he went cold really fast, and I thought to myself, There goes his soul.

Another parent described the need to hold the baby:

> We went into the intensive care room, and I held him for a long time. I was so glad that they let me do that because I felt that I at least got to hold him for one last time. It was so hard to put him down, because I knew that I would never get to hold him again. He just looked like he was sleeping and would wake up at any minute.

The staff at the hospitals often encouraged the parents to see the baby before they left the hospital. One mother responded this way when asked by the nurse if she wanted to see her baby, although she did not feel the need to hold the child:

> I couldn't answer. I never imagined I would *ever* have to make such a decision. She told us that in her experience we should see him. So she took us in to where he lay. It was so real then to see his poor, gray, lifeless body. Still, so beautiful! I touched his forehead and my husband took his hand. He said, "My God, he's so cold," and we cried. I kissed his forehead and had to remind myself that his soul was gone. This was just his body left. But he was still soft and except for a slight gray tinge he looked like our child. Although I had never seen him entirely still before. We prayed together as we held his hands. I never picked him up—it was not necessary. We stayed a little longer, said goodbye, and left.

Other parents shared their experiences:

> The nurses showed us to a private room where we could have our son until the coroner arrived. We held our son close and also stared at his face, his every feature, checked to count his teeth again, opened his eyelids to see his blue eyes. I knew this would be the last time I would ever see my son. We were with him for two hours before the coroner came. The doctor came in the room and said just to lay him

down. Giving him up, laying him down, and turning my back and walking out of that room was the hardest thing I've ever done.

We were given time to hold her. The doctors seemed very disturbed by this, but the nurses were clearly recommending it. Our family doctor came in and told us he felt she had died of SIDS and gave us an opportunity to ask questions.

I asked the nurse if I could hold my baby boy one more time, and she said it would take a minute to clean him up. I held him, and all I could think of was, If I get him warm he will be okay. So I wrapped him up in his blankets and rocked him and it didn't help. . . . My husband and I passed him back and forth for two hours.

Generally the hospital personnel were caring and compassionate and made an effort to make the visual image of the child positive. However, some parents saw their baby with needle pricks and hooked up to tubes. Their memory of the time with their child was not as pleasant. One mother saw her child with "cuts and marks all over his baby skin from the tremendous effort to save him."

Some parents stated specifically that they did not want to hold or see their child after death. One parent said, "I didn't want to look at the baby any more than those few moments of trying to revive him." Another parent said the funeral home had called and asked if they wanted to come to see the baby, and the parent responded, "I didn't want to go." One parent said she did not hold her baby but wishes she had had that opportunity.

Guilt

Many parents expressed feelings of guilt even in those first few hours after the baby died. For some parents it was an initial response to realizing their child was dead:

He had been covered with a down quilt. So I thought he must have become overheated and he panicked when he pulled the crocheted cover over his face. I felt so guilty and he looked so awful, so ruined.

The doctor told us that he was dead. I could not believe what I was hearing. I thought I had suffocated the baby, and I told everyone in the hospital I had suffocated the baby. . . . I wanted to kill myself, because I thought I had suffocated the baby even though I had been assured that I had not. I just wanted to die. I looked into my husband's eyes and I saw all his pain. I thought I was responsible for causing all this pain, and I didn't want to live.

For other parents the feelings of guilt came later:

I agonized over the fact that I had left work late for lunch that day and if I had just gotten to him earlier he would still be alive. I was late because on my way out of the building I had seen an old acquaintance. One phrase that I had used haunted me repeatedly. We were discussing the trials and tribulations of parenthood, and I had commented that it was a big adjustment but that we weren't planning to send him back. The fact that somehow he was being sent back—maybe even at the moment I had uttered my complaints— caused intense feelings of guilt.

I sometimes thought that it was my fault because I thought he was taking up too much of my time.

I called my parents. My father answered. When I told him that the baby had died, there was a long silence. Then he said, "What happened?" I knew a part of his thinking was that as first-time parents we might have done something or not done something to cause the death. But all I could say was, "I don't know." It was the most painful, helpless moment in my life.

The first night my husband could not sleep. He asked me if I wanted to sleep with a murderer. He was talking about anything and everything. Finally we contacted a doctor to get a sedative for him.

The parents' role in life is to protect their children from harm. These parents were not able to do that, and because of the suddenness and unanswered questions about SIDS, an automatic response for some parents is guilt—because they could not protect their child from harm and death.

The Days After the Baby Died

Although parents typically remembered what happened when they found the baby or being at the hospital with the baby, the events of the next few days were a "blur" for many parents. They often did not know who made the funeral arrangements or who came to the house. Here are some of the ways parents described the few days after the baby died:

Most of the first few days melted into a sort of blur. I remember lots of crying and hugging, a constant dull inner pain, physical pain because I had been nursing the baby, and numbness to the rest of the world.

I can't remember making any of the arrangements. I think it was taken care of by relatives. The only thing that remains clear from hospital to funeral is having to call friends and co-workers to inform them of the death.

The first few days after that are a blur. I remember lying in bed not able to sleep, going to the funeral director's, the coroner calling to confirm SIDS, and people bringing food over.

I really don't remember much. I tried to avoid people. I just couldn't face people.

We lived in a complete fog until after the funeral.

I was numb for the next few days, then it turned to tears.

Our minister came over. If he helped any, I don't remember it. As far as I can remember, funeral arrangements were made over the phone and probably by my parents.

Other parents described in varying degrees of detail what happened in the days after the baby died:

That afternoon we went and made funeral arrangements. Then we went back home. We had a house full of people, and that helped a lot.

The following couple of days were *crazy!* But, on the other hand, I have to credit that for keeping us sane. We were so busy making arrangements for the funeral service, notifying friends and relatives, and preparing for their arrival, as well as "hosting" those who stopped by to see us or called, that we didn't have much time to have the whole thing "sink in." In a way, we are thankful for this.

The second day I spent on and off the phone with the funeral home, and with people coming and going. My husband and I would retreat to the bedroom in the basement and just sit. It's hard to remember everything that occurred. I think we were all numb with shock.

I said to my husband, "I can't believe we just left her there [at the cemetery]." One minute we had her, the next we were standing on a mound of snow and dirt with our little girl in a white box. I remember every detail of that day, even down to what kind of hat the undertaker wore. It's incredible. I can still feel the snow and the wind and see the faces of family members at the funeral. It was a day I never imagined would happen. It's a day I'll never be able to forget.

My father made the funeral arrangements. My mom gave me a black dress. I remember having to go for pills to stop the breast-feeding process. The only clear day is the day of the funeral. . . . I remember the people at my mom's house after the funeral started talking about when we were kids, and I started laughing. Then I felt I was the worst person in the world. How could I laugh when my son had just died? Because I am human, I know now. I had to, or die.

The day the baby died was an incredible experience for parents, family, and baby-sitters. We hope that this helps parents who have had this experience realize that they are not alone, no matter how unusual their responses may have appeared. We also hope that those parents who have not had a baby die have gained, to a very small degree, some understanding of that experience.

Testimony: Reliving the Death

This Louisiana mother was married and the mother of two other children when her four-month-old daughter died. It is almost four years later now, and she often relives the death but has few memories of her child alive. The family members never slept in their house after the night the baby died, and they moved to another state two months later.

"I woke up to the alarm, turned it off, went to turn on the shower, went to the kids' room for some reason. I put my hand under the baby's quilt, and she felt warm, but she hadn't moved. I felt vomit. I felt panic. I jerked her out of the bed and shook her. I stuck my finger down her throat and yelled for my husband. My husband tried breathing into her mouth, but we don't know CPR. We got my pediatrician on the phone. He said to give her mouth-to-mouth.

My husband punched a hole in the front door while waiting for the ambulance. The paramedics arrived, and she was taken to the hospital. They got her going for a while, but finally the doctor came out and said, 'We're sorry, she's dead. We think it's something called SIDS.' My husband dropped his coffee on the floor, and we held each other. He told me, 'We'll get through this.' Then he went outside, and I heard him say, 'No!' It was a scream, almost a wail, and it echoed. He came back inside and called his parents. While telling them, he dropped to his knees and pulled the arms of a metal waiting room chair out flat.

"My mother came, and she took us home. I opened a six-pack. I went into the baby's bedroom and ordered the crib taken down and taken out of the house. I picked up all her toys and put them in the playpen and told my husband and my dad to get it out of the house. Within a few hours all kinds of people started coming to the house. I was half drunk.

"That evening I listened to music to play for the funeral. I picked Jackson Browne's "For a Dancer," Bette Midler's "The Rose," and Wendy Waldman's "Private Ships." We had her buried in Louisiana where my in-laws live. We were at my in-laws' before the funeral. There were so many people there, and I went to the bathroom and just sat, to be alone. When we got to the funeral home everyone was sitting or standing around. In Louisiana a funeral is like a social event—everyone who thought they knew my husband's family was there, coffee cup in hand. When I started to walk in, everyone stopped talking. I think they hated to see it end. I stayed away from the crowds as much as possible, I sat outside or in corners, away from people. They were waiting for me to break. One thing I remember from the funeral is hearing my husband crying and saying, 'My baby.' He walked out of the service."

[How did others react at the funeral?] "The same old shit. They said things like 'She probably would have been retarded if she had lived,' 'It's God's will.' Some, like my in-laws, were devastated. Some looked at us as if we had killed her.

"When we got back home, the house was cold and empty. My husband called his cousins and asked them to come over. We played cards most of the night, and next morning we went to work. That night we moved in with my parents. We couldn't sleep in that house. Two months later we quit our jobs, uprooted our two other kids, and just left. We moved five hundred miles away to the state where she was buried. I drank every day until we moved.

"I have thought about suicide but have never attempted it. I just wanted out of it, but I wouldn't do it because I have other children to care for. I've also become terrified of death.

"My heart literally hurts at times, like there was a hole in it. It was hard to breathe. My stomach hurt so bad that I went to a doctor. It was physical pain. Emotionally, I constantly relived it." [What still hurts?] "Filling out this questionnaire hurts. Going to the cemetery hurts. I still can't look at her pictures. To alleviate the pain I go play with my other kids or go sit outside. Sometimes I buy a new tree to plant as kind of a symbol or gift to her, something alive.

"For a long time I wanted to dig her up. I'd go to the cemetery and just sit there, every day. I put away all her pictures. I guess that's the only thing my husband and I ever disagreed about. They're still put away.

"The death strengthened our marriage. He talks to me about almost anything concerning the baby. My son started having nightmares three years after the death when he was thirteen. We were lucky that he came to us and told us. We got him help.

"The memories I have of her are not memories of when she was alive but memories of that morning. I think of her at least every day. The memories come back whenever I start thinking about her. They come mostly at night when it's quiet, or in the day when it gets quiet. Flashbacks also begin when I get in the shower. I remember that morning when I was about to shower, and I think about going into the kids' room and checking the baby. Then the whole morning starts in my mind. One time I was at a red light and an ambulance was in front of me. I looked at the red cross on the back and I was back on the country road behind the ambulance following it to the hospital. Then I went through the rest of the morning. I came out of it still sitting at the red light and everyone was honking at me. That was three years after the death.

"I've learned that I'm a survivor. I've also learned that there are people who care about others. I wouldn't have survived without the SIDS chapter, my husband, my kids, and my in-laws. I try to help others who have lost babies. I watch the obituaries, and if I see an infant in there, I call whoever is doing the funeral and give them my name and number if it's SIDS. They usually give it to the parents. The parents usually call me, and I get information to them. I helped start a support group to give information to parents in my community.

"I don't blame anyone for the death except God, if there is a God." [Has your baby's death influenced your religious beliefs?] "Yes, I've been pissed off at God since she died. If there is a God, how could it kill helpless babies? Over and over again, let them die?"

Babies Don't Just Die, Do They?

Searching for the Causes of SIDS

Perhaps the most difficult aspect of having a child die of SIDS is that there is no tangible reason for the baby's dying. The definition of a SIDS death is

the sudden death of an infant or young child which is unexpected by history and for which a thorough autopsy examination fails to demonstrate an adequate cause of death.[1]

Part of our human nature seems to be that we must have a reason for everything. Sudden Infant Death Syndrome, therefore, creates so much confusion and frustration for parents because there is no "reason."

Thoughts about What Caused the Death

Because SIDS is not immediately evident when a child is found dead, many parents in our studies thought their child died from one of a wide range of causes. In the preceding chapter parents described how they found their babies: some looked bruised, some were white and cold, some had vomit near their mouths, and some looked like sleeping children. An important part of these parents' stories, then, is what their immediate thoughts were about the cause of death. For many parents, these immediate thoughts, although incorrect, stayed with them for a long time. For example, some parents who initially thought the death was due to their neglect still have those thoughts in the back of their minds even though they have been told over and over that it was not their fault.

More than one-third of the parents in our most recent study thought their baby had, in some way, suffocated and died from lack of oxygen. One parent thought the suffocation occurred because of a mattress that was too soft. One parent thought the baby suffocated because it was lying on a pillow. Another parent thought the baby had strangled itself in clothing. One parent said, "I *knew* I killed my baby because I laid him on my bed." Others thought the baby died from lack of oxygen caused by choking on vomit or spit-up food, since there was vomit by the baby's mouth. A parent said, "I thought I had not burped him well enough after his last feeding, and that he had spit up and gagged to death." One father said, "I thought my wife suffocated her."

Approximately one-fourth of the parents felt their child died of SIDS, because they had read about SIDS or had a child of a friend or relative die of SIDS. One parent had a premonition about SIDS during the pregnancy and before the baby died:

> All through the pregnancy I had a feeling he would die. I would often bring up the subject of crib death during the pregnancy and after his birth.

Another parent thought the baby died of SIDS as a result of stopping nursing. "I was afraid it happened because I had just stopped nursing." This parent had read somewhere that breast-fed babies do not die of SIDS.

Approximately 10 percent of the parents initially had no idea what might have caused the death. One parent responded, "At first I had no idea. I just could not think of anything."

Some parents immediately assumed they had caused the death through neglect of their child. When asked what they initially thought the cause of death might be, they responded in the following ways:

> "I felt I was the cause."
> "Neglect. He was choking on something due to neglect in feeding."
> "I had no idea. I thought it was my fault."
> "I was sure I had killed him!"

The remaining parents had a wide range of thoughts about the cause of their child's death:

"I thought that someone had broken in and beaten her up."

"I thought our cat could have done it. I've always heard that cats will suck the baby's breath out of them. I also remember putting the cat out before the ambulance arrived."

"I thought it had to be some terrible joke."

"I thought it was a punishment for what I had done and said to my husband."

"I thought it was because of the medicine I had given him for his cold."

"I thought it was because I let bottles sit on the counter after taking them out of the refrigerator."

"I thought it was caused by an accident or child abuse from the sitter."

"He was too cold. His room always seemed too cold to me."

"I thought he died from a flu."

It appears that when some parents find no obvious explanation for the death of their child, they tend to blame themselves even though there is no logical reason why they should be blamed. Or parents identify a cause that, again, is not logical, because of the great need to find *some* explanation.

Personal Theories about the Cause of the Baby's Death

When asked whether they had a personal theory about what caused the baby's death, approximately 40 percent of the parents said no. They accepted the diagnosis of SIDS. The remaining 60 percent, however, had a hunch about what caused the death. Often these hunches were related to the possible medical explanations for SIDS.

FORGETTING TO BREATHE. Approximately 40 percent of the parents had read or heard that a baby can just stop breathing and not start again. Some of these parents also knew that this "forgetting to breathe" was likely to be related to an immature brain stem that did not maintain regular breathing in a baby. One parent described the theory this way:

With an infant the breathing pattern is controlled by the lower brain stem. As she grows and begins to sleep through the night, the higher brain stem takes over. I think it is a short circuit in which *neither* is controlling the breathing, and she just *doesn't* breathe anymore.

Two parents described how they thought their baby's underdeveloped neurological system led to their baby's reverting to the pattern of life in the womb, when the baby did not breathe:

I feel that perhaps the major cause could be the brain stem theory. Maybe some babies' brain stems are just underdeveloped and they can't control the breathing. I think they almost revert to their life in the womb when they didn't breathe.

I always worried about it getting cold, so I kept the room about 80 to 90 degrees. Then I got to thinking that maybe he thought he was back in his mom's belly and didn't have to breathe.

Another parent thought the baby had a damaged brain stem because of unusually hard labor. Two parents explained in detail why they thought their babies forgot to breathe:

They say that SIDS babies never die when they're sick. I think when they get well they sleep so tight and easy, they forget to breathe.

Sometimes when I have a cold and I sleep at night, I can't breathe through my nose; I will forget to breathe and wake up with a start and my lungs hurt. Our daughter used to wake up crying a lot with a start when she had a cold. I think she forgot to wake up, or not in time.

OTHER THEORIES. Approximately 5 percent of the parents thought their baby died because of some respiratory problem such as a cold or pneumonia. One parent said the baby had a cold and had been inconsolable the night before he died. Another parent said, "Some kind of congestion caused the respiratory tract to malfunction. My baby had nasal congestion."

Approximately 5 percent of the parents thought their baby had been taken by God, or gave some spiritual-related reason for the death:

It was God's will for her to bless me and my family and friends' lives. She received her body for the resurrection. Her earth mission was completed.

God needed her to help him with his work in heaven more so than here on earth. Who was more innocent or pure than a child, so open, so honest. Who better to see the world through.

It's the Heavenly Father's way of saying, "You have a special child that has a special mission somewhere else."

God took her to spare her great pain later in life, perhaps childhood leukemia or something similar.

I believe that everyone is born with a book written by God describing how long their life will be, and my child's life was meant to be short.

They do their part and go like all of us do. Some just do it a little faster than others.

Another 5 percent of the parents felt their baby died because the baby was premature: "I believe her premature birth contributed to her death. Several theories relating to prematurity seem reasonable to me."

The remaining parents had a collage of responses for explaining why the baby died:

"Botulism."
"Pollution in the air."
"The baby wasn't fully developed."
"The baby had been circumcised and had an infection."
"The formula had no iron in it."
"From natural causes, just like an elderly person."
"Lack of attention."
"Hidden birth defect."
"A genetic metabolism problem."
"Got overtired and got exposed to something."
"Immunization shots."
"Suffocation."

One parent had been in a room with a kerosene heater during a power outage while she was carrying her child. When the kerosene heater was lit, a large cloud of black smoke resulted. This parent believed that this incident created a lack of oxygen for the fetus and that this caused the death. This parent went on to explain that she thought all SIDS deaths were related to some form of oxygen deprivation:

The underlying cause could be oxygen deprivation, but this itself could be a cause in a myriad of ways. In one case it could be a kerosene heater in winter; in another, a mother who smoked heavily at just the wrong time in her pregnancy; in another, a mother who played racquetball, which caused the oxygen to be diverted from the fetus to the large muscles.

When asked about her personal theory as to why her baby died, one mother exclaimed, "You wouldn't believe me if I told you."

In almost all of these cases an autopsy was performed and the diagnosis was SIDS—no known cause of death. Nevertheless, the majority of parents had some definite ideas about why their baby died. Although many of these ideas coincided with theories identified by research in the SIDS literature, some parents came up with reasons that had no apparent connection to the literature. We can only assume that parents carry these ideas with them for a long period of time, and the ideas that imply responsibility for the death on the part of parents are sure to create unnecessary stress in their lives.

When Autopsies Are Performed

Approximately 10 percent of the parents did not have an autopsy performed to provide them with an explanation for the death. One parent said, "I wish there had been one done. Maybe I wouldn't have these feelings of guilt." Another parent said, "We just assumed an autopsy would be performed and didn't realize until it was too late that one was not performed."

The results of most of the autopsies indicated that nothing was abnormal enough to have caused the death of these children. One parent, however, was told initially the autopsy indicated that the child died of choking. Later the explanation was that it was SIDS. This left the parents wondering why the pathology report was changed.

A vast majority of parents who had an autopsy performed were satisfied with the results. A few parents indicated, however, that even though an autopsy was performed and the result was SIDS, this was still not enough. When asked whether they were satisfied with the results of the autopsy, these parents responded:

I have to say yes and no, because I knew I could have other children without worrying about birth defects or disease. But not to know *exactly* why he is dead is a hard thing ever to accept.

I didn't get any answers to why he died.

It didn't explain why.

Healthy, normal babies should not just die for no reason.

They didn't show why he died. It wasn't an answer. It said a perfectly healthy baby died.

I was not satisfied with SIDS more than anything. Such a blanket reason. There were no answers to cause, prediction before death, and so forth. It did relieve us a little knowing we hadn't done anything to cause it.

As satisfied as humanly possible when told there was no reason for the death.

Four parents said they wished the autopsy had been more thorough. Two of those parents specifically indicated the need for an autopsy for research purposes, rather than just a routine autopsy, so that more knowledge could be obtained about SIDS.

The Theory of the Month

We asked parents how they felt about the media's coverage of new studies or new information about possible causes of SIDS. This coverage is often sensationalized, with headings such as "Cause of SIDS Found" or "New Evidence Linking Cigarette Smoking and SIDS." Often, this information is just a theory developed from small samples, with little conclusive evidence provided. The headlines, therefore, are misleading and usually offer very little information. We asked parents if this kind of media coverage helped them or hurt them, and we asked for suggestions about how to improve the situation.

Approximately half the parents felt the information did not really affect them. They just hoped there would soon be an answer so other parents would not have to suffer. Of the remaining 50 percent, about one-third thought it was not harmful and that at least it indicated research was being conducted. They gave responses such as these:

> I believe that researchers are just as anxious as parents to find a cure. In this age of technological advances it is highly unlikely that we wouldn't know the cause of something. All of the theories need attention, since it is still a mystery. I don't feel let down by these theories but pray for a cure.

> I am very interested in any theory. I read all I can. I have sent for studies on it. It helps me deal with it. Maybe the fact that I feel someone is trying to save our babies helps. But I don't think they really know what the cause is, and I feel that the cause is different in different cases of SIDS.

> The more research the better. Maybe someday we'll know for sure.

> This sort of publicity at least brings the subject of SIDS to the attention of the general public, but it also stirs up new feelings of guilt in SIDS parents and caretakers.

Of those who were affected by this media coverage, two-thirds felt it hurt parents who had experienced a SIDS death. The following statement is typical of those who felt media coverage was harmful:

> It bothers me that there is so much misleading information out. The media need to be more responsible about what they broadcast and print.

Some parents only believed press releases that came from the National SIDS Foundation. Many felt press reports often served to revive old feelings of guilt about what they might have done differently to prevent the death. The sensationalized headlines often created a hope that a real cause had been found; on closer examination, the reader found that it was old information or that the evidence was not conclusive. Another problem for parents is that friends and relatives will ask if the new theory explains their baby's death. One parent said,

> It hurt me to read about a study that showed parental neglect was the cause of twenty-three of twenty-four cases in New York. It upset me for a week that people might think that I had contributed to my child's death.

One parent said, "I sometimes wonder if the runaround isn't over some bizarre facts the scientists are covering up for. Who knows why." Another parent summed it up this way:

Any theory that I can relate to causes pain, but all the theories, causes, or whatever will never give my son back to me.

Research about Causes

Research about possible causes of SIDS is now readily available in the medical literature. Although this book is not about the pathology of SIDS, it seems appropriate to summarize what appear to be conclusions or the best understandings about SIDS to date.

SIDS probably includes several subgroups of differing causes. It is now believed that there is no one cause of SIDS but rather that SIDS is an umbrella term that includes several unknown causes. This may be the reason there are so many theories about what causes SIDS: a number of conditions or diseases may actually cause or trigger SIDS.

A second fairly consistent conclusion drawn by most researchers is that SIDS babies are not completely healthy at birth. As a group, infants who die of SIDS show structural and functional abnormalities, both through autopsies and during their lives which indicate that they are defective physiologically in some way.[3] It is suggested that these babies have some underlying vulnerabilities that originated during fetal development.[4] However, it needs to be made clear that none of these abnormalities in and of themselves can be used to predict or diagnose the death. The abnormalities along with various other trigger events such as infection or other stress may be the trigger that leads to SIDS.[5] This researcher has summarized what likely happens:

A growing body of knowledge indicates that these babies are not completely healthy before death. SIDS victims appear to have subtle defects of a physiologic, neurologic, cardiorespiratory and/or metabolic nature which interact with developmental and/or environmental factors resulting in sudden death.[6]

Cardiac or respiratory failure, or both, may actually terminate life for a SIDS baby, but how the chain of events actually results in death is still unknown.[7] According to another researcher, SIDS appears to happen when hypoxia or arrhythmia occur during sleep.[8] Hypoxia occurs when oxygen is not getting to the tissues of the body, and arrhythmia occurs when the heart rate is altered. The question then becomes, Why is the baby unable to recover from that state? The answer for many researchers is that there is an abnormal nervous system that may not itself cause death but may work with other triggers to cause the death. The abnormal nervous system may result from abnormal development of the brain stem or other aspects of the nervous system, or from the improper co-ordination of the nervous system.[9]

The goal of research is to find out what causes SIDS and, ulti-mately, to prevent SIDS from occurring. The parents who have contributed to this book and other parents who will grieve in the future deserve to have the answers that research attempts to find. One researcher puts it this way:

> Perhaps the burden of anxiety, guilt, shame, or blame would be dissipated by a knowledge of what went wrong, even though nothing could have been done in advance to prevent the occurrence.[10]

Testimony: A Father's Story

The father who tells his story here was twenty-five years old when his three-month-old son died. He reported that he has gone through depression, anger, guilt, and a lot of doubt since the death of his son.

"My wife and I left for work that morning, leaving the children with her older sister as we always did. We feel that Kenny's death happened between 1:00 and 3:00 that afternoon, although we did not find out until returning home after work. By the time we reached her sister's house, everyone was gone except my wife's youngest sister and her husband. They had come over to take us to the hospital. They said that Kenny had stopped breathing and had been taken to the hospital.

"Upon arriving there, we found that *everyone* from both sides of the family was already there. My wife went into hysterics and shock. I felt as if I were in a dream. I remember talking to the coroner and our minister. Most everyone was with my wife in a separate room. We were taken into a room where Kenny was. I kissed him. It felt like kissing a stone—so very cold. My wife held him for about a minute. Blood and mucus dripped from his nose.

"Most everything else is rather hazy until the day of the funeral. I can't remember making any of the arrangements. I think it was taken care of by relatives. The only thing that remains clear from the hospital to the funeral is having to call friends and co-workers to inform them of the death.

"The funeral was a very large affair. We did have a full showing and funeral. Most everyone we knew attended. I was quite satisfied. We had one of the last photos taken of Kenny placed above the casket during the showing. Many people reacted more emotionally than I did. Some with small children could not attend; it hit too close to home I think. The surprising thing to me was the number of people who stayed throughout the entire showing. I tended to worry more about how others reacted. I felt as though I had to be strong for everyone."

[Do you think having a funeral or some kind of service helped you and other people to cope with the death?] "Yes, definitely."

[Would you recommend a funeral to a friend who lost a baby?] "Yes. Initially our funeral director explained it was not customary to have a full funeral with showing for a baby as young as Kenny. But I firmly believe we made the right choice."

[What would you like others to know about how to help a person who is grieving over a baby's death?] "I feel that a SIDS death is unlike any other death because there is no apparent reason or cause for the occurrence. I hesitate to answer this question because it seems this question is generalizing infant death. As far as help in coping with a SIDS death, I believe that two things should be done. One, the spouses must communicate openly with each other, and especially just *be there* to listen if necessary. Otherwise, you wind up blaming each other when there's no one else to blame. And two, parents should contact and keep in touch frequently with a local support group. That's what they are there for, and they can provide some of the best therapy around in dealing with a SIDS death.

"The people who help me the most are the people who are simply *there* if we need someone to talk to. Also, the people who remember his birthday and death anniversary help too.

"Some try to tell us when we should stop grieving and get on with our lives. That, for me, was by far the worst. Others treat us as if we have some kind of disease that will affect their children. Many people also did not understand and criticized our use of an infant monitor on our subsequent child.

"Overall, a little more compassion by some of the doctors and nurses would have helped. But mostly, I wished people would not have been so scared to ask me what I felt like, what I was going through, and so forth . . . People tended to keep their distance as if they expected me to go into wild hysterics.

"My spouse helps me the most because, of course, she was directly involved like myself. Both of us were closest to our son from birth until death. SIDS support group members were *always* there if I needed someone to talk to. They were the greatest help, as far as outsiders can go, because they could relate directly to the situation. They were also great listeners and provided some valuable advice from time to time.

"I have felt personal guilt over the death of my son. Kenny had always been *extremely* fussy (cried *all* the time). I believe he was trying to warn us of what would happen. I should have held him more and tried to comfort him. Instead, I yelled at him to be quiet and go to sleep."

[Did you ever just want to go to sleep and wake up after the pain had gone away?] "Sometimes I still feel like it's all a dream: I'll wake up and Kenny will be asleep in his bed. Other than that, I really can't describe why. I think it's a very normal part of the grieving process to want to go to sleep hoping you will wake up and find out it was all just a dream.

"I think that our marriage was strengthened as a result of Kenny's death. With the exception of the SIDS support group, my wife and I are all we have. We need and have needed each other too much to let this come between us. We are each other's sounding board, counselor, and therapist.

"I think that my wife and I have different ways of coping with Kenny's death. I believe that there is a special bond between mother and child in which a father cannot be involved. There seems to be a special pain in my wife in knowing that the child she carried, nourished, and loved was taken from her. In a very real sense, a physical part of her has died that can never be brought back to life again.

"My parents are grieving in their own way. We do not see eye-to-eye on this. They expect us to grieve as they do and do not understand what we're going through. They do not talk about Kenny much. My wife's parents are very understanding. They also lost a son (by a different means) and can relate somewhat to our grief."

[Have there been changes in the way you care for other children as a result of the death?] "Our subsequent child was/is a little spoiled. I think subconsciously we tried to make up for some of the shortcomings we believed we had in caring for Kenny. We were also scared that we might lose her too.

"Our oldest daughter wanted to know where Kenny lived, and we told her that he lives in heaven with Jesus. She has had a few restless nights. She also will cry suddenly, saying that she wants Kenny back. She has a great fear of dying."

[Were your religious beliefs helpful to you in this crisis?] "Being raised in the church helped me in knowing that there was a purpose for what happened. I still believe in God, but since the death I have not been able to be in a place where people are worshipping. I feel as though I am at least owed an explanation, even though I sometimes realize I may not or should not expect one or question God's motives.

"The good things that I have learned about life are not to take everything for granted. About myself, I have learned that I have and will continue to survive the death of my son without blaming anyone."

[What will the future bring?] "A definite cause for SIDS and a reason for the death of my son. I hope. Most of all, I hope for another son."

"I'll Lend You for a Little While a Child of Mine," God Said.

Religion, Guilt, Punishment, and Blame

The children will return when the world is a good enough place for them to be.

—The Pied Piper[1]

Language is the foundation of our culture; it reinforces and sustains institutions within society. The English language, unfortunately, does not validate the death of an infant; this is a cultural taboo, as Therese Rando points out in her book *Parental Loss of a Child*.[2] A child who loses his or her parents is an orphan. A spouse whose mate dies is a widow or widower. There isn't a word, however, to describe a parent whose child has died. There are no social guidelines on how to answer the question that plagues bereaved parents, "How many children do you have?" Parents face a conflict every time the question is asked. A mother whose son died when he was one and a half months old explains:

> It hurts when people ask how many children we have. It hurts when friends or relatives avoid mentioning the baby. It hurts when we act like nothing ever happened.

To say one has this many children and that one of them died is considered morbid and also impolite. An accurate response forces the questioner to ask about the death of the child. It compels society to acknowledge that children die. As a result, mothers and fathers are left with the option of either denying the life of their child or committing a social offense.

Parents and society expect that children will be born, will grow up, become old, and die. The death of an infant, however, assaults the expectations of both parents and society. It is a culturally disturbing event. The surviving family members have to deal with their own guilt when a baby dies and with a lack of understanding from society:

> When my baby first died, a great many people would comment that I could have another baby and not to worry about it. They talked about the baby not as a human being but just a passing visitor. They had the attitude that he was just a baby and that I could go on to have another one to replace him.

Our culture exacts a price when a baby dies. Isolation and abandonment of surviving family members are the hallmarks of society's reproof:

> One month after my son's death, they stopped coming by. No calls on me to see how I am or if I need anything. If I need to talk I have to go to their home and call them to console myself. It seems like they don't want to talk about it any longer and as if I have some disease that they don't want around.

At the same time, grieving parents are punishing themselves for the child's death:

> I got it into my head that intellectually the cause of her death was [SIDS], but it took a long, long time for me to get it into my heart. I am fine now, but I found every possible piece of guilt I could before I could let myself be okay. One of my doctors made one day what I think was an offhanded remark about how I had done the best job he had ever seen of finding all the ways there were of being guilty. For me then I was able to let go of the guilt. I had done the best job of being guilty this man had ever seen, and for me it was okay to stop being guilty. I know it sounds so irrational today.

The guilt results from both a violation of a societal standard and the parents' failure to live up to their own personal expectations. Guilt sustains itself because of this dual trap of confronting the death of an infant. For parents, the primary duty is to protect children, so to fail in this primary responsibility of keeping children safe is reprehensible. Mothers and fathers have always taught health and safety rules to their children: "Look both ways before crossing the street," and "Don't play with matches." Inevitably all parents will fall short of the ideal, but most mothers and fathers have the opportunity to come to terms with this. SIDS is a symptomless, silent death without warning, and therefore it is unpreventable. When an infant dies suddenly and unexpectedly, the bereaved parents cannot even comfort themselves with the assurance that they did everything they could. There was no time to consult specialists to seek remedies, to find a cure.

Since the parents in these cases are faced with inescapable guilt, no one should tell parents they have nothing to feel guilty about. Many comments to the bereaved parents which are intended to help in fact do just the opposite—for example, "It's good he died young before you were attached to him," or "It's not as hard when the baby has not developed a personality." Telling grieving parents not to think about the death of their child perpetuates the belief that we can turn memories on and off like a faucet. Although this helps society with denial, it is impossible for the surviving family to achieve; society may cope, but the family feels further isolated. The implication is that the baby was not a "real" human yet because he or she was so young and therefore had less value. However, it is not possible to quantify the value of a human life by its length:

> People have made it more difficult who try to tell you that you don't miss a baby like you would an older child—or that it was better this way than being mentally retarded. It has made it a lot more difficult because after a few weeks there isn't anyone to talk to—people are very uncomfortable dealing with death, and they would really rather I didn't mention it or the child.

But parents begin to attribute personality traits to a baby even before its birth. A fetus that is active at night is going to be a night owl. A mother with heartburn may believe that the sex of the fetus is the cause. Once the baby is born, the parents search his face and behavior for the familiar: he has his father's nose or his mother's ears. Verbal battles are waged within families over the eventual eye color of the child.

Genetically as well as emotionally, children carry the future. The loss of a child so young shatters the illusion of safety, for infants are not riding their bikes in the street, swimming at the pool, or doing any of the other things that demand a parent's lecture on safety. Most of these babies died in their own homes and in their own beds. What offers more security than the picture of an infant sleeping peacefully in a crib? Almost ten years after her daughter died at five months, a mother shares her fears:

> My life has done a complete turnaround . . . The first few years after she died I could barely live through each day. It was a struggle to get out of bed. I was never afraid of anything, and now I can't sleep without a light on. I am scared of finding someone else dead.

It is even harder for the bereaved parents to be confronted by people who deny that life, no matter how long it lasts, is important. Devaluing an infant allows society to ignore the devastation caused by the death and to reinforce the illusion that children are not supposed to die:

> No one will talk about my baby as if he existed. I find myself bringing him up, and people look at me like I'm crazy. "He's dead," they say. "He's gone, forget him."

But to forget the child violates another social rule: that we should love and cherish our children. Caught in these complicated contradictions, families search for understanding. SIDS parents agreed almost unanimously that the people who were the most help in the crisis were those who had also had a baby die. Only with them could the SIDS parents find validation for their grief.

Some attempts at explaining the death of a child can be not only inaccurate but appalling:

> One dumb doctor stated, "Oh well, he just made room in the world for someone else."

Surviving with the grief of their child's death, parents struggle to cope with the loss of approval by society:

> [People] act like we have the plague or something because of our son's death. Often people won't talk about our son with me. There are a lot of times I'd like to be able to talk about him, but it seems to be a hush hush subject even with our own family. Sure, I might cry, but I find I need to relive those precious few days we had with

him. I want to relive the joy I had in having my son. I just feel sometimes that people think if you don't talk about the child you can pretend that it didn't happen, that it's not real. I think the most difficult situation we had was when our landlord refused to return our deposit because he said the baby's death depreciated the value of his house.

The meaningless death of a baby demands a search for meaning. Many parents, as well as relatives, friends, and professionals, turn to religion in an effort to solve this dilemma. Some individuals and groups prefer their religion concrete, believing that for every question there is an answer. Others believe in the mystical, the unfathomable qualities of spirituality. Given this diversity of faith, it is better to say "I'm sorry your baby died" than "God wanted your baby to die."

[People] tried to explain the death for us in their own spiritual terms— the baby wanted to die or it was her karma to die; God chose you to teach you something, and death is not sad, don't feel sad.

When parents can no longer blame themselves, human nature requires that this burden rest somewhere, and God often serves this purpose:

[I blamed] God. [My] question was, how could a loving, protecting, all-powerful God let this happen to an innocent child. The answer has come to seem that God's character is much different than I had thought.

Anger turned inward results in depression, and when a parent finally turns anger outward, a safe direction is at God:

My religious beliefs were really examined closely. I was also very angry with God. I had lived a good life and thought that nothing like this could happen to me. What a surprise. I finally decided that God had nothing to do with her death. He gave us our human natures and hers was imperfect and she just couldn't go on living.

In the absence of a logical explanation for the death of an infant, we seek the comforting rituals of religion. A mystery is used to explain a mystery:

Without the faith in knowing my daughter's in God's presence in heaven, I could not cope with her death and its finality. I need to know there is something more.

Religion is not without pitfalls. Many sects believe that every action is for a purpose, and some people attempt to explain God's plan. A mother of twins, one of whom died, explains:

> [People] made remarks that I felt were not appropriate, such as, "This is why God made twins," and "You're so lucky you have another baby."

If God is in control, then the death of the baby cannot be an accident. What then is this plan? The dogma in many traditional religions includes punishment for sin in this life. The interpretation implies that if you are a good person, go to church, and lead a good life, your guarantee of safety will protect you; the wicked, on the other hand, will be punished.

Parents and grandparents in our study reported that their beliefs had been both strengthened and weakened:

> To suggest there is a God sitting up there in control of this mess, actually planning the things that occur in our lives, is to suggest that he is a horrible sadist. And to admit the converse, that no one is in control, creates a sense of despair, depression, and hopelessness about life.

Babies are the beginning of the thread of our continuity in the world, not the end, so the end of life is the opposite of the birth of a child. Families, as well as society, lack a context in which to incorporate the death of a baby. In order to try to balance this contradiction, bereaved parents seek relief in a just and kindly God:

> I was raised to believe that life after death for a baby is life everlasting with God in heaven, which is a much happier existence than life on earth would have been for her.

Many parents in our study believe that God assumes the responsibility of parenting and that the baby is in better hands:

> [Even] for an infant I believe life still goes on. But who's taking care of her? I know God is, but am I right? Every time I see her picture, which is every day, I worry about it. I go to the cemetery almost every day and cry my eyes out and talk to her, and then I feel better.

To counter the concept of cause and effect, mothers and fathers often have to let go of the idea of a controlling God and a divine plan and become pragmatic in their beliefs:

I believe that if it is someone's time [to die], then they will die, and circumstances have nothing to do with God's will. I had to believe this or the guilt of not being home and being there for my baby would have destroyed me.

Death is abstract. Philosophers contemplate death, the religious extol the benefits of death, and yet life is a condition of battle against death. Living with these contradictions forces a justification and an understanding of life and death. A year and a half after her six-month-old son died, a mother shares with us:

I believe that everyone is born with a book written by God as to how long their life will be, and that my baby's life was meant to be short.

Parents almost instinctively search for a meaning for the death. Many need to believe the baby is spared the pain and suffering of life. Literature abounds with discussions of the peace of death; Charles Dickens put it this way: "It is a far, far better rest that I go to than I have ever known."[3] Death holds for many of the parents in our study a realization of a better existence:

[My religious beliefs were not] really helpful in the beginning. At first, I couldn't understand what I did to make God so mad at me. But then I realized that my son did not have to suffer and he would never have to worry about anything.

Conflicts between the magical thinking of one's childhood and the harsh reality of life take time to sort out. As children, we thought that if we really, really believe something, it will come true and anything is possible:

I did not immediately feel comforted by God or my religious beliefs. I felt abandoned and forgotten by God. It would have been such a simple thing for God to have intervened and gotten a baby to breathe. So I did feel anger.

Humans have a desperate need to blame someone when things go wrong. Current levels of litigation might suggest that there is no such thing as an accident; a careful search will produce the guilty party, and someone will take the blame. But when a baby dies, suddenly, unexplainably, the search is fruitless. The barren truth is that babies do "just" die:

The death was accidental. Not planned or caused by God. Not given to me as a test or punishment. The baby was not taken because God needed him more than the mother. We are all subject to disease, wars, accidents. These things just happen.

Blind, unquestioning faith is possible as long as the questions don't get very hard. A belief that God answers all prayers can be accepted until the answer is no. A bargain, ultimately, must be struck:

My faith has become stronger, but probably for the wrong reasons. I am afraid to doubt God or question the Bible or fail to pray often since my son died before he was baptized . . . I feel he is in heaven by virtue of being from a good Christian family. Could his eternal soul be jeopardized if I, as his mother, fall off or fall behind in my acceptance of Christ and my worship of God? Probably not, but why risk it? Now I cannot risk being anything less than a great Christian.

The death has to be important and must serve some unknown purpose. Senseless death is illogical and demands an explanation in an orderly society. Rather than live with meaningless death, people must apply some structure for understanding, and the rituals of religion provide that. However, the old adage that God only gives people what they can handle offers little comfort:

Nothing will ever be as it was before; it can't be, my baby is dead. He was on earth for three months, and he changed my family's life so much. We loved him so—I think in some ways we'll never be the same. People tell me how strong I am, that's why it happened to me. Well, I am not that strong.

Religious beliefs for approximately half the parents in our study were strengthened, which often brought a sense of peace and acceptance of the death of the baby. These beliefs were weakened for many, leading to a loss of belief in the infallibility of God. All the people in our study experienced a great change in their lives. For them, nothing will ever be quite the same again.

Testimony: A Spiritual Experience

A Florida mother believes there was a spiritual dimension to the death of her child. She had a dream that her baby was dead just before she found him, and she felt a presence in the room where he died. This religious experience and being able to talk about the dream has helped her cope. People think she is crazy when she tells them about the dream.

"The baby had been fed at 4:30 A.M., and I awoke at 7:30 A.M. and didn't hear the baby. My husband told me to sleep a little longer since the baby wasn't awake. When I awoke again, I noticed it was 9:00 A.M. I had just had a dream that someone was telling me, 'The baby is dead.' I was scared to go and look in on him. I noticed that my older son was up and watching cartoons in the living room, and he had to look at the baby before leaving the room since he had slept in the same room with him that night. Then my husband got up and rushed to the bathroom to shower. He ordinarily looked in on the baby also, so I figured that the dream was absurd. I went into the room to wake the baby for his feeding, since it was late. As soon as I entered the room I felt a presence. When I looked at the baby's hand I realized, or knew, that he was dead and that the dream was true.

"Now, whenever I think of him, I think of how I found him that morning. I also have dreams about it. It hurts so bad. Sometimes I feel like there is a knife piercing me with the sensation of his death. I feel like screaming that it is not true—he's alive. I even dream that it is untrue and that he is safe and sound. Then I wake up and find out that it is true and it did happen. I just want to go back to sleep and make up the death and make it untrue.

"God has been the source of my strength. Whenever I feel like I'm breaking down, I ask God to help me overcome it. I have two friends that have consoled me by rationalizing the fact that if God wanted him to die so young there was a good reason for it, and my baby is in the Kingdom of God. They have also helped me realize that it would not necessarily happen to a subsequent child, if I decided to have another child. The main ingredient for survival is faith in God. If there is faith in God, then all the hurt and pain can be overcome.

"When my baby first died, a great number of people would comment that I could have another baby and not to worry about it. They had the attitude that he was just a baby and that I could go on to have another one to replace him. I wish they had talked about him as a human being, not just a passing visitor. This made me angry because, to me, he had a personality. He was a person just like everyone else.

"Another frustrating aspect was the fact that everyone kept in touch, either by phone or in person, to an extreme. I wanted everyone to just leave me alone. It became unbearable. Then about one month after his death, they stopped. No one calls on me to see how I am or if I need anything. If I need to talk I have to go to their home and call them to console myself. It seems like they don't want to talk about it any longer. It's as if I have some disease and they don't want me around.

"For a time, I did have trouble functioning sexually, because all I could think of was conceiving the baby. I would freeze and break down.

"As for the future, I hope to have another child and spend time with that child. I have always been worried about finances, but now I realize that it is not a priority in life. A great deal of good things are taken away, and we must compensate for these losses by concentrating on other things around us. For example, I feel great knowing that I still have my husband and other two children and that our family has come closer due to this death in the family.

"It hurts not to have him around to enjoy his growth. I miss not seeing him develop as a baby. I overcome this pain by telling myself that God did this for a reason and that I should respect his reason and go on."

6

What Is Sanity When Life Is Crazy?

The Symptoms of Grief

The SIDS death is so socially unmentionable and personally devastating that the effects last for the lifetime of the bereaved parents. Research suggests that any kind of death involving a child constitutes a loss so profound it may shatter the life of a parent. Unanticipated sudden death, regardless of the age of the individual, also produces a formidable set of challenges to recovery. When both sudden death and child death are present, the grief work of the survivors becomes a lifelong experience.

> Who wants to face pain every day of your life? A cut or broken bone can be healed. How about your heart and soul? They say that time will heal all wounds. I have my doubts about that. I haven't had a day I didn't wake up and think about my baby.

Society creates many barriers to the resolution of the grief parents feel when a baby suddenly dies. When children do not outlive their parents, as everyone expects, friends, relatives, and professionals tend to distance themselves. Death before its time is considered reluctantly if at all by society, and general acceptance is difficult for the bereaved to find. The attitude seems to be: if it can happen to these parents, it could happen to anyone; it could happen to me, or to you, and any child can die, at any time. Most people find confronting this reality unbearable, and they therefore put emotional if not physical space between themselves and others who have suffered such a death.

Those whose babies die of SIDS have internalized the social value of orderly death, and consequently they endure chaos when facing a world where the natural order of things has been disrupted. Fears, nameless but terrifying, haunt these apprehensive parents, who find their lives filled with a constant sense of dread. Death for the survivors carries with it a tremendous price:

> [After four years it still hurts] that he died all alone with no one there to hold him. The empty feeling and the feeling that I failed my son, that I should have been able to do something for him. The loss is so great I never will get over it . . . that's my life sentence.

A woman's body has physically prepared not only to deliver the child but also to nourish it after birth: all the gears are engaged, the light's green for go. As the baby grows in the womb, so do the parents' thoughts of the future. This conditioning takes nine months, as nature prepares the mother and father to care for the infant after birth, to accept responsibility for a helpless, demanding baby. The day comes and a baby is born into a world of hope—the future stretches in front of the new parents.

Sometimes we do all the right things: prenatal care, diet, exercise, Lamaze, and fathers walking around with weighted Snugglys on to experience pregnancy. But sometimes, even when we do all the right things, a baby dies. Babies do not come with a set of instructions, and there are no guarantees.

Because of the suddenness of the death, the heart cannot comprehend what the head knows. Ambivalence results when parents find that at times they can still laugh, love, and feel; they may feel guilty that for a short period the pain has gone. Time can become distorted, and extreme levels of physical and psychological disorganization can follow the sudden death of an infant.

It is helpful at such a time to remember that grief is a process, not a product. It is not limited by chronological time. When has enough time for mourning passed? Emotional time, the time it takes for psychological processes to work themselves through, dictates the work of grief. It is not a problem that is solvable but rather an experience that becomes part of life:

> I have learned that time does indeed pass, that to some extent it can heal, and that actually time is neutral. It just passes.

Grief is a process that is ongoing, changing, at times more bearable, but for parents whose child has died grief may be forever. The loss of an infant is so profound that the grief these parents feel operates on emotional, not chronological time:

> I wish someone had told me that we all have our own timetable for grief. I went through a terrible period because I knew I wasn't healed after a year. I thought I must be exceptionally bad—or going crazy— because it took me two and a half years to really start living my own life again.

The timetable is one that only the individual will experience, and it creates its own special kind of insanity. Everything is familiar and yet not the same at all: the sun shines, the birds sing, and yet after the death of an infant they are unquestionably different. A mother of a seven-month-old baby who died helps us to understand:

> The age of the child does not diminish the impact of the grief. For one thing, the child has been an integral part of the parents' lives from the time it was conceived and often has been anticipated eagerly some time before that. Also, the loss of a baby leaves a tremendous void because of the twenty-four-hour-a-day care he requires. When a child becomes more self-sufficient, parents are not closely involved with him on such a constant basis. There are many empty hours after a baby dies. Finally, a baby is not any more replaceable than a mother or a grandfather. That baby is a unique human being with his own distinct personality. Having another baby may fill up your time again, but it will not fill the void left by the loss of your previous child.

One of the ways people experience the world is through the process of checking reality with others. This is not always possible, however, in a society that maintains its distance from families whose babies have died. The initial reaction of the parents when a baby dies is a kaleidoscope of emotions and physical reactions. A mother of a seven-month-old baby who died shares her immediate response:

> I cried out, saying I wanted to die. I began hitting my head on the wall, punching a hole through the wall, and pulling my hair.

Since the death is unexplained, the parents' reactions, in a vacuum caused by lack of knowledge, are normal. An infant's dependence on the parents and the parents' acceptance of this responsibility set the stage for protracted grief. The surreal sense after the death that the parent should still be caring for the child can turn into a feeling that the parent has abandoned the child. Sadly, these thoughts continue, as a mother tells us six months after the death of her baby:

> For a long time I wanted to dig her up. I'd go to the cemetery and just sit there every day.

Emotional paralysis sets in, along with bone-crushing pain, and many parents despair that it will never end. At this point, family and friends need to understand that this early stage of disorganization not be labeled negatively:

> I would put the milk in the cupboard and the cookies and canned foods in the refrigerator. I would go to the baby's room and put my head on his crib. I didn't wash the sheets for two months after he died, because they smelled like him. I would be talking about something and forget or just go into a daze. People kept telling me I needed professional help.

Suicidal Grief

Over 42 percent of the parents in our study (47 percent of the mothers and 17 percent of the fathers) considered suicide because of the death of their baby. The unbearable pain of a cancer patient is understood by society, but the unrelenting anguish associated with the death of a child is less well appreciated. Thoughts of suicide, rarely spoken of aloud, remain hidden because the person knows about the effect of death on surviving members of the family. Six percent of the mothers and six percent of the fathers in this study attempted suicide. It is not known at this time how many suicides do occur after the sudden death of an infant, but it is known that these families are at extremely high risk. Perhaps the danger of potential suicide would not be as great if the culture allowed the horrific grief these families feel to be expressed. Caught in the grip of the pain of loss, survivors are often told to go have another baby. This is not a helpful response, as the real suffering of this mother makes clear:

> Not only [have I thought of suicide]—I have also considered killing my remaining child to spare her the horrendous pain life seems to

inevitably hold for her. I see the future as continuing to get worse instead of better. My marriage is disintegrating. I can't put my mom through the death of her child, especially an intentional one. Unless I kill her first—but then there's my dad, and my grandmother, and where would it stop?

Seeking Professional Help

Professional intervention can be helpful, but only when the parent is ready to engage in her or his own healing. Some parents in our study sought help almost immediately; others never did. Grief and mourning are not symptoms of mental illness, neither in degree nor length. Extraordinary events create extraordinary responses. Like people who have been under anesthesia, which impairs short-term memory, a bereaved parent may be unable to remember simple things like a phone number or how he or she got to the store. Intervention is indicated when either chronic or life-threatening situations occur. The evaluations must be done by someone who understands not only the work of bereavement but also the unique process of mourning the death of a child. Not remembering a date three months after the death is normal; not remembering after three years may be chronic. Short-term drug or alcohol use is common among those trying to numb the unrelenting pain. Long-term use is a sign of abuse and will only exacerbate the problem, delaying the resolution of grief.

Physical symptoms are real, and a heart breaking cannot be described but only felt. The inevitable guilt process that follows the sudden death of an infant is much more complex:

> Sometimes, shortly after the death of my baby, when I would walk into the bedroom it would feel like I was suffocating. When I left it would stop.

Other senses continue as if the baby were still alive. Arms can literally ache to hold a baby, breasts still produce milk, and the mind does not forget:

> I kept thinking that I heard him cry, especially at night. My arms would ache with no one to hold. I would be in the store thinking for a fleeting second that he was a baby that went by. Looking at baby clothes when I no longer had a baby. Finding myself in the

aisle with the baby foods and formulas. Not being able to get the sight of him that morning out of my mind and hearing his father scream in my dreams. It is hard to remember simple things.

Feelings of anger and rage surface as if part of a dream that slowly, painfully becomes reality. Anger alternates with depression as parents experience emotions out of control:

> Sometimes [there were] the thoughts and preoccupation with hating other people with babies, hating their babies, hating pregnant women, hating happy people. These thoughts would overwhelm me. I wondered what was wrong with me for having such bad feelings. I hated myself for wishing disaster on them. I became abrupt, cold, distant, aloof, and overly melancholy. It lasted well over a year.

Since a baby represents the future, his or her unexpected death does not allow for any sense of closure on that brief life. There isn't time to prepare for the death, time to think and plan. The grief work for these parents often consists less of mourning experiences and memories, and more of mourning what could or should have been. The passage of time does not necessarily bring a sense of peace; sometimes new conflicts occur:

> I want the pain to pass, but the further I get away from when he died I panic because I might forget little details about him.

These parents' lives have been irrevocably altered, and they can never return to life as it was before. Their values undergo a permanent change. Parenting is not something that can be turned on and off. However, the death of an infant does not end the parenting in those families where there are surviving siblings, but it can be difficult for a parent to develop balance while exploring the pain and guilt of death:

> I sleep with my dead baby's blanket. Sometimes I want to shake my other children when they whine about stupid things and scream, "Well at least you're alive." Then I forget everything. I forget phone numbers, dates, times. I can't even make small, everyday decisions. I feel the need to tell everyone I meet what happened. It's crazy when other people ask me what's wrong and why I am crying, and what's worse, some act like I never had a baby at all.

Should we expect these parents to be perfect parents to their surviving or subsequent children? Of course, no one can live up to the idealized image of the perfect parent. Instead, mothers and fathers try to find some equilibrium while they feel suspended in air. Two years after the death of her son a mother shares these thoughts with us:

> The parents will not become model parents forever after just because they have lost a child. We are still human. We will still get tired and short-tempered. There will still be times when we remember with longing the carefree days before the responsibility of child-rearing was pervasive. It is entirely possible we will sit and grinch with all the other grinching parents occasionally. That certainly will not mean we have forgotten to love our child dearly or that we have forgotten the wounds of losing another. We are just being normal.

Guilt and anger are inextricably intertwined: guilt leads quickly to anger, and then to guilt about being angry. Caught in a closed loop, many parents expressed anger that some children seem to survive in spite of their parents: child abuse in any form thus becomes intolerable to them. Ironically, the best efforts to care for a child are not insurance against that child's death. Two years later, a mother expresses the guilt and anger surrounding the death of her son:

> [Since my baby died, I have gone through] in a word, hell. I've gone through self-doubt, wondering if I had been a good mother to my son during his short life, and wondering if I could be a good mother to my surviving child. Guilt over the times I had gotten upset with my son. Guilt and self-hate for hating those who still had their babies and didn't care for them the way they should. Anger that it was my baby who had died, and lots and lots of depression.

A "Formula" for Grief

Our society establishes a formula for grief, and decides when it is time for people to shake themselves off and get back to business. Many parents shared perceptions of impatience from others who felt their grieving had gone on long enough. But telling a grieving parent that it is time to get back to work or to have another baby is unhelpful and upsetting:

> Now I know people mean well, but some things that people say made me very angry and hurt. [Some of the remarks were] "It's been

six months now, you must be over it," and "You can have another baby," or "At least you lost your child when you hardly knew him." Another said, "Look at all the people who can't have children. At least you had one."

Grief reactions are as varied as the people responding to our surveys. We found that grief cannot be described as a procession of stages. Rather, there are many different responses, all of which are normal in the unnatural event of a baby's sudden death.

The parents' first reaction when a baby dies is that of shock and numbness. They felt so overwhelmed that they recoiled from the experience. Attempting to make sense out of a senseless event, these mothers and fathers express bewilderment. Many wish to retreat physically and emotionally to the time before the death. Others wanted to go into a deep sleep, to awaken when everything would be all right again:

> The pain is very intense, and it is with you always. In sleep I could avoid the pain, and sometimes when I woke up, before the realization of what happened would come to me, for a few minutes I would almost forget it happened.

The clichés of life are supposedly based on some fact, but for those parents whose baby has died, the comforting words so often heard are not true. Time does not heal all wounds—some must be lived with. Life may go on, but part of life remains forever frozen in time:

> It hurts that our shared future is gone—I'll never hear him say "Mama," never see him run to my arms, never see him on his first day of school, will never see him graduate or marry. It hurts most when [I see] a child of the age he should be. I don't try to alleviate the pain—I go with it and let it run its course. To deny the hurt in my mind would be to deny my son, and I won't ever do that.

Lifelong Grief

Our research indicates that parents can grieve their entire lives for a child who has died. Events of different kinds remind them of the death: Christmas, other holidays, birthdays, the first day of school, graduations—all lead to a lifetime of wondering what that child would have been like.

As I watch my youngest get ready to start school next fall, I feel those moments that were lost to me six years ago. I know that I have to set aside what's past and make the most of today.

In accepting the gift of a new life, a parent accepts the responsibility for that life. Reassurances that the baby's death is "not your fault" and that "there is nothing you could have done" are empty words and fall on deaf ears:

I feel I've hurt my children and husband somehow. I was responsible for my son's total well-being, so I also feel the same about his death. I feel I kind of let this happen and so I've let everyone down and hurt them. They loved him so. I'm more wary of everyone, and I don't seem to like as many people as before. My family and I have been so devastated that I'll never let anyone hurt them. As far as I am concerned, no one could hurt me now, nothing could touch this pain I feel.

This mother shares her thoughts just three months after the death of her son, and yet the unrealistic expectations about being a perfect parent are clear. Mothers and fathers often define parenting as always being available and protecting their children from any harm. SIDS parents and grandparents live with the idea that they should have been able to do something, that somehow they should have been able to prevent the death of their baby.

Eight years after the death of her two-and-a-half-month-old son, a mother writes:

It's been so long, in some ways it's hard to remember and yet in some ways it's as clear as if it happened yesterday. What I remember most is feeling as if I had failed miserably as a mother and as a person. I felt somehow I should have known my son needed me when he was dying that I should have instinctively been able to save him. I had given him life and should have been able to keep him alive . . . For a long time I felt that my whole life was out of control; if my baby died even though I had tried so hard to be the perfect wife and mother, then anything could happen.

Perceived sins of omission and commission also play a part. The truth of practical parenting falls short of the idealized image. For example, for a parent to bury his or her head under a pillow in hopes that the baby will go back to sleep is common. Moreover, feelings of irritation and frustration are part of raising children, though these are forgotten as the child grows and we focus on the positive aspects of parenting. When the baby dies suddenly, these thoughts and actions are not resolved, and the bereaved parent often focuses on the smallest and most negative memories. The resulting guilt leads to a painful process of letting go of each memory, one by one:

> Perhaps the biggest change in me has been the change in my attitude about what is possible. I have gone from thinking, That sort of thing only happens to other people, to It can happen here. Taking things for granted has become an attitude of the past. Perhaps in time I will find the happy medium between worrying over things I cannot change and being prepared for the unexpected. Right now I am stuck in the worry mode. Perhaps in time I will sleep through the nights without checking on my children several times to see if they are still breathing. But I hope I never get over taking time to watch my children play and appreciating every moment I have with them.

Parents report intense suffocating pain after the baby's death, physical sensations of the heart breaking, darkness, fear, and chaos. As time passed these feelings became ones of disorganization, physical and mental tiredness, depression, and anger. Those parents who responded to our surveys several years after the event reported that the grief had taken on a bittersweet quality, with intense periods of pain when times, places, or even smells triggered memories. Many events mark the passage of time, and some of these will always bring with them a reawakening of grief for these families:

> I read the newspaper differently than I did before. When I read headlines about death and destruction I think of those families left behind. When I read the obituaries, I look for more than just familiar names. I look for details about that person's life and death, and I reflect on how those left behind have been affected. The funny papers don't amuse me as much as they once did—death is not funny, nor is hurting people and disliking children. I've become a tough audience.

In spite of the tremendous task of learning to live again after a SIDS death, these parents do acknowledge, nevertheless, a new sense of purpose and meaning in their lives:

> [Life] is not what one plans, but is not necessarily bad. One must somehow accept life as it comes, and be thankful for what we get and for how long we have it. Never take things for granted. I thought

that a baby was just a baby, always taking and never giving, but our son gave me so much love in four short months. I'll maybe never be able to list all the things I learned from an infant.

Most of the parents expressed surprise that they had survived the experience of the death of their child. They found a level of strength that none of us want to test, and they know now that they can handle anything:

> I'm not afraid of dying anymore, maybe because I'll see my son again. I now have a special feeling for all kids, especially the very young and helpless. I would not wish this tragedy on anyone, but I feel I know much more than those who've not experienced such a tragedy. Like someone said, we who have lost a child have entered a twilight zone—we're different.

The greatest task for these parents is finding the help they need to learn how to forgive themselves. Somehow they need to know they are not bad people, and that sometimes, even when we do it all by the rules, sometimes . . . a baby dies.

Testimony: An Attempted Suicide

This Florida father told us his story three years after his five-week-old baby died. Not long after the death he tried to kill himself on a number of occasions. Today, with the help of a counselor, he is doing much better and is thinking of helping others at a suicide prevention center.

"My career completely fell apart after the baby died. I changed jobs several times and was finally laid off work. After the death, I felt numb or dead inside for several months. I didn't want to do anything. Everything I ever believed about raising a family or working seemed to be turned upside down. It was hard just to go to work.

"I felt guilty because I had not wanted the baby and encouraged my wife to get an abortion. It was devastating when the baby died.

"Our marriage has suffered from the stresses. I want to make it clear, however, that I am not sure if the baby's death 'caused' or is directly related to some of these events. We had just relocated in Atlanta at the time, and we were experiencing many, many changes.

I sort of look upon the baby's death as the straw that broke the camel's back.

"I found myself increasingly unable to control my emotions at work and at home after coming out of this numb feeling. I lost my temper at work so badly that for the first time in my career I was threatened with being fired. My boss indicated in a letter to me that I had been given enough time by the company to get over Susan's death, and so on and so forth.

"This only made me more bitter, and it influenced me to start looking for another job. This started a string of changing jobs. I must have changed jobs four times in two and a half years.

"Karen and I were unable to help each other. We seemed to lose total control of our lives. Our financial situation became a serious problem. Karen stopped working part-time, and this added to the burden.

"At the one-year anniversary of Susan's death, I was in a serious automobile accident. Fortunately, the accident was not at all my fault, and even though the car was badly damaged, I was not hurt. I wondered, however, if things were just fated to become worse and worse.

"It was shortly after this that I changed jobs again. I became increasingly depressed and made a serious suicide attempt around Thanksgiving. I tried to gas myself but fortunately failed. Again, I came out of it all unhurt.

"I'm skipping a lot, but I want to focus on a turning point. A little more than two years after Susan's death, I again lost my temper at work. I really almost completely lost total control. I was screaming at this guy. He was actually acting like a jerk, but my response was totally inappropriate. I remember screaming at him that I had lost a daughter and was tired of dealing with "assholes" like him.

"I was almost fired for this one. It was at this point that I sought out therapy. It was a turning point.

"I am presently working again and feeling much better. The third anniversary [of the baby's death] was tough but not traumatic. I am much more in control of my emotions. *Control* might not be the best word, but I am better able to accept them.

"I don't know if the marriage will continue, but there is hope. (There is hope at work, also.) In fact, today I received an excellent review from my current employer.

"I hope this gives you a feel for some of the things that took place. I wonder, if Susan had lived, if these things would have happened. That's the real mystery."

[You have come in contact with many people who in some way or another have influenced your grieving. What things have people done during the time since your baby's death that have been helpful to you?] "I am very *bitter* on this issue. No one in the family has helped in any meaningful way. It seems like a totally taboo subject. If I ever talk about Susan's death, people become silent and look very uncomfortable. I was not allowed to grieve by those around me. It was like, you should go back to work and be normal after two weeks. Karen and I tried to help each other, but her mom was a major source of conflict for us. No one, after a couple of months, seemed to understand my lethargy and depression. It was five months after the tragedy that I met a person who understood. The only person I can talk to openly about Susan is my counselor. Most other people think I should be over it.

"People made comments at work after a few months that I should be over it by now. My wife's mother made comments about my not keeping the house up; even my wife questioned my motivation. I had always been a hard worker, but life had lost all meaning.

"As I've stated, people just want to push the issue under the rug. I was not allowed to grieve. Remarks like 'You have two other children' so somehow it's okay, or 'At least it's not your first one.' None of these remarks helped at all.

"If Karen and I could have been on our own and not living with her mother, it might have helped. Perhaps if SIDS parents had contacted us or visited us immediately after the death . . . We were surrounded by people who just couldn't help us. We had experienced every parent's worst fear. We had lost a child.

"[With my counselor] I am accepted for what I am. I am treated like an adult. Deanne helps me understand and accept myself. She has taught me how to relax, both physically and emotionally. She does not judge my feelings or behavior. I can talk with her about my deepest feelings and thoughts. Communication is direct, to the point, with no games being played. She has also helped me to start loving myself."

[What would you like others to know about how to help a person who is grieving over a baby's death?] "Do not make snap judgments about the person. The comments about how it wasn't your first or it only lived a short time are totally inappropriate. Others should understand that it may take years for the grieving process to unfold. Allow the person to talk about the death, even if it tears you up by just listening to it. Be supportive and non-judgmental. At times, just leave the person alone, but also be honest with him or her. If you don't understand what a person is going through, tell him or her in a decent way. Again, comments like 'You should be over it' and 'Get back to work' are totally inappropriate.

"Karen found the baby at 9:00 A.M. on Memorial Day. I got up first, and since everyone was sleeping I took a swim. When I looked up from the pool and saw Karen, I somehow knew Susan had died. I went in the room, and it was the most shocking and horrifying thing I have ever seen. It was like seeing part of yourself torn out and thrown down. I lost total control for a couple of minutes, crying like I'd never cried before. Karen got the children upstairs with her mother. I called the paramedics. All I can remember is the paramedics, police, and fire department coming. I had to show them where the baby was. Before they came, I went back again and stood for quite a while looking at Susan. My heart bled for her. The undertaker came and asked for baby wipes to clean her up before taking her. This disgusted me. We then made the funeral arrangements.

"I never had any thoughts on it [what caused the death], to be honest. She had an eye infection and her navel was inflamed. The first thing I saw was mucous around her navel. I assumed she died of an infection, but this was later. This may sound crazy. I always wondered, or wonder, if Susan somehow could have picked up my not wanting her. I know it sounds crazy, and it is. I truly loved her.

"An autopsy was performed. We never received or were told of the results. It was just classified as SIDS." [Personal theories?] "I did not want the baby, before she was born. And I also wondered by taking the transfer to Atlanta and putting Karen through all the stress while pregnant if this didn't contribute to it.

"Frankly, I wouldn't mind seeing some information about SIDS splashed across the papers. I don't think the public is aware of the extent of the problem. It does not receive enough publicity at all. This might result in increasing the research funds for SIDS.

"No SIDS group contacted us. We talked to a priest, but he talked more to Karen than to me. Both of us felt very lonely, closed in, and isolated. We had just moved to a new city and did not know anyone.

"I think a counselor called, but we needed someone to come over and not give us the chance to turn down any offers of help.

"Some neighbors brought over some food, and this helped lift our spirits. Everyone we met seemed very uncomfortable around us. Our doctor contacted us. He was upset and really was not of much help. At the time I questioned his treatment of Susan. The funeral director, the guy we bought the stone and grave from, was totally insensitive.

"No relatives came to the funeral because we had relocated. Karen's mom was there. The doctor did not come. It was very lonely and sad. We knew no one in town. We were in a room with Susan, and it was almost a relief when our two children acted up. I was shocked and numb. I wanted to go back to Florida. I felt bitter. When it was over we went outside the church. Everyone stood around for Karen. I stood off to the side with the children alone. No one said a word to me. I had a feeling that a long and difficult path lay ahead. A lonely one.

"The funeral didn't help me. To have to go public with something like this just doesn't make any sense to me. It is just too private a thing. I hated the funeral. It was like being on public display.

"It is so final. I wonder what she would have been like. It's the lost opportunity for play and to see her crawl, walk, and talk. The hardest fact in my case is that I didn't want her, and by the death I'll never have a chance to make amends for that fact.

"[I think of her] a lot. She would be three now. I see other girls her age and I can see her with them. I wonder what she would have been like. I don't ever want to forget her. Her life was meaningful even if only for five weeks. She taught me the value of my other children and the value of human life in general. I owe her a lot.

"My father committed suicide. It was very rough. It was eight years ago. The two events are similar in a way. One thing with my father is that I had memories of our past together. With Susan there really aren't a lot of memories of times together to draw upon. The two events are similar in that I can't really talk about them to anyone except my wife and my counselor.

"We're in the process of selling the house now. I don't think our move is related to the death. I was laid off and could not find a job in Atlanta. I'll be honest, however. I will not miss being in the house where Susan died. I just see her lying in the playpen. It was a grisly, terrible image. I will never forget how she looked. I once had a nightmare about my son dying. It was so real that I woke up and cried for a long time."

[Could you describe anything you have done that made you wonder sometimes if you were going crazy?] "Constant preoccupation with suicide. Changing jobs and total loss of my temper at times. A feeling of not having control of any area of my life."

[Did you ever just want to go to sleep and wake up after the pain has gone away?] "It's obvious. Who wants to suffer all the time? To see your life completely fall apart is a devastating experience. The worry that you'll walk in and find another one of the children gone was overwhelming for a long time. If the pain cannot be dealt with, I would rather not wake up.

"It's an individual's choice [regarding suicide]. If the pain is so severe for a person, he or she should have the right to end the life. It's an individual's choice. Sometimes more harm can be done by one being forced to live than being allowed to die. I have come a long way since my last attempt two years ago, however. I feel I am rebuilding my life. I can be an effective father for my children. I want to help other people. I can't do that if I'm dead!

"The death weakened our marriage. For the first time we both could not help each other. We were suffering too much. We lost sight of our future and created more problems for ourselves. My wife chose to deal with the death totally on her own. She took some time off work and took care of our children. I sought out a counselor connected with the SIDS group. My wife opposed this, and after many fights I quit going. It was later that I went to another counselor and have continued going despite her lack of support. Karen chooses to deal with it on her own. I was like that at first, but I now believe you have to reach out for help.

"I went back to work after two weeks off work. Karen would not work and stayed at home.

"I have considered divorce. Not due to the death itself. We have grown apart. My wife's opposition to the therapy has been a problem. I believe the family needs to be opened up to different influences. My relationship with Karen's mom has deteriorated very much. I feel she was nonsupportive and extremely insensitive to my situation after Susan's death.

"I'm a little more cautious now with the other children. Checking on them a lot at night. Billie was one at the time, and I would nudge her at night because she would sleep so quietly. We called the doctor more often for minor things. Justin was four at the time. He wanted to know if he would see her again. He loved her. I told him that she had died. We would not see her anymore. I don't think he understood. I told him that we all will die and this is nothing to fear.

"Billie, one year, was unaffected. Justin went into a shell. He was not as much of a leader as he was at one time. He seemed troubled. It was only after reading about SIDS and children's grief that I realized he was grieving in his own way. I worked with him, and he's doing fine now. I do not feel it is in Justin's best interest to bring up the baby's death.

"They attended the funeral. They acted up in the funeral home, which was a pleasant diversion. It seemed to really bother Justin at the cemetery. Hell, it bothered all of us.

"Believe it or not, I had had a vasectomy two days before her death. We had decided not to have any more children before the death.

"My religious beliefs were weakened by the death. I can't understand how any divine being, and so forth, could allow this to happen. I know it sounds illogical, but that's how I feel. I still go to church when I feel like it, but I am very angry at God. (I guess I do believe.) The death makes no sense to me in religious terms.

"The priest suggested counseling for me. He was very helpful with Karen.

"I just attended one support group meeting. They showed a film of the show Phil Donahue did on bereaved parents. It was a gut-wrenching experience. Parents in the room cried. I didn't feel good after the meeting. There was no facilitator present who could make any sense out of what we had just seen. There was no attempt to integrate or synthesize the information. The show seemed in poor taste at times.

"[Three years after the death] I still feel bitter about the way others treated me after the death. I am in therapy, and this is helping. I should say that it hurts when people say you should be over it or forget about it. It really hurts. It sort of denies Susan's existence.

"I've learned to enjoy my children more. That our time together is precious and it could be shortened. I learned how to cry again. I can cry freely now. Before, I couldn't. I will never put my career ahead of my children. My children are number one.

"I've learned I can survive just about anything. I have great inner strength. I'm giving my time in volunteer activities working with children. The greatest therapy is in helping others. I've learned that I'm not all that bad and that I can and must build a new life.

"Divorce is a possibility. The family situation is not good right now. I am going to continue pursuing opportunities to help others, especially children. I will do everything I can to be a strong and effective father for my children. My career is on the rebound.

"When I feel I'm ready, I want to work at a suicide prevention center. Let me close with an example. A woman down the block had her husband apparently leave her. Sally had been grieving over the loss of her mother, and I knew she needed help. I dropped by with a religious book. (This is what she liked.) She was in terrible shape. She cried and was hysterical at times, and I was scared because I was never in this spot before. I stayed with her, and she cried on my shoulder. I only left when I was convinced she was okay. She later thanked me and said, 'While the neighbors gossiped you came down and helped.' To me this is what life is all about. It may be truly what Susan taught me: to get involved with others, and that life is truly precious."

7

Marriage and Sudden Infant Death

"I don't know that you really care that much," Sarah said. "Do you?"
    Macon said, "Care?"
    "I said to you the other day, I said, 'Macon, now that Ethan's dead I sometimes wonder if there's any point to life.' Do you remember what you answered?"
    "Well, not offhand," Macon said.
    "You said, 'Honey, to tell the truth, it never seemed to me there was all that much point to begin with.' Those were your exact words."
    "Um . . ."
    "And you don't even know what was wrong with that."
    "No, I guess I don't," Macon said.
    "You're not a comfort, Macon," Sarah said.
    "Honey, I'm trying to be."
    "You just go on your same old way like before. Your little routines and rituals, depressing habits, day after day. No comfort at all."
    "Shouldn't I need comfort too?" Macon asked. "You're not the only one, Sarah. I don't know why you feel it's your loss alone."
    "Well, I just do, sometimes," Sarah said.

                                                    —Anne Tyler[1]

Men experience life differently from the way women do, emotionally, cognitively, and physically. Society has different expectations for men and women. Through social conditioning, men tend to be more externally oriented. Their sense of self is often based on what happens outside themselves, and in concrete expressions: for example, through the work ethic, ambition, physical power. Women are more often trained to be internally oriented and base their sense of self-worth on more abstract constructs, such as relationships and nurturing. These different ways of dealing with the world can complement each other or cause discord. When a couple is faced with the death of their baby, these differences can lead to a crisis. One woman explains after the death of her baby seventeen years ago:

> He was macho and kept it all in. He only cried once, at the cemetery. He thought I was going crazy.

Another woman, nine years after the death of her son, clarifies the differences between her and her husband:

> I am verbal, he is a worker. When our son died, I sat around thinking, analyzing, observing, talking when I could. My husband planted long rows and rows of corn. I am involved with trying to make things better for SIDS families based on all the analyzing, thinking, and talking I have done. My husband is raising his sheep and working in his office. I am filling out this questionnaire; he probably won't.

Marriage is a difficult state to maintain nowadays. Gone are the days when people depended on each other for their basic survival needs, both physical and cultural. Today, many of the interdependencies in marriage have been replaced with an exploration of independence. Balancing the journey toward self-actualization and trying to accommodate someone else at the same time can have devastating results. Excessive individualism, or selfishness, without connections or commitment, asks, "What do I get out of this?" and "How are my needs getting met in this relationship?" rather than "What will we have and build together?"

Death is an enigma to us all. But when clearly defined social roles, expectations, and rituals are absent, the death of a baby can add considerable strain to the marriage.

In this context, it is not surprising that over 90 percent of the 127 people answering the questionnaires in our study said that their marriage was affected by the death. Almost 93 percent of those responding said that their way of coping was different from that of their spouse.

Women completed 109 surveys, writing in all the available space. They attached extra pages, sent poetry and journal entries. By contrast, men filled out 18 questionnaires, rarely answering beyond a simple yes or no. The few questionnaires we received from men seem to bear out that what women report is true: that men tend to be less communicative when it comes to expressing grief. Most of the information in this study came from women who reported on their feelings and actions and on the feelings and behaviors of their spouses. As a result, our study is basically about women and their responses to the death of their child.

One difference we found concerned the idea of emotional strength. Women felt that they had to be strong for others. Men, on the other hand, said that they needed to be strong for themselves. The majority of women reported that their husbands got busy: they went back to work and resumed "normal" activities. This woman helps us understand:

> He had to go back to work to help make life seem real to himself again. He knew he must in order to help me.

That so few of our questionnaires were filled out by men suggests that many American men still feel they need to be strong and silent. But when a baby dies suddenly, these men experience a clash between the need to remain strong and in control while seething with turmoil inside. Cultural expectations for men delay their grief, as this father, whose two-month-old baby died, explains:

> Three years after [my daughter's] death I went to a psychiatrist who helped me unlock my grief. It took me those three years to finally let myself grieve the loss of my daughter. No one's fault but mine. Everything was done that could have been done.

The role of the family provider also gives men the opportunity to deny and delay grief:

> I didn't want to think about it so I started working twenty, sometimes twenty-four hours a day so I didn't have to go home.

However, remaining stoic and in control leaves the individual father further removed from his emotions. His role as problem-solver and fixer of things also leads to unresolvable conflicts, for death is not something that can be fixed or solved. Frustrated by these conflicting demands on him, one father described these differences in the ways he and his wife coped following the death of their child three months earlier:

My wife has been much more open about her feelings and grief, whereas I seem to remain, at least outwardly, unemotional. Sometimes I wish I could just let it all out, but it just won't come.

Our society determines one set of behaviors for men and another for women, with the result that although we may on an intellectual level encourage a man to express emotions, we then become uncomfortable with a man who actually cries. Breaking through social learning can be extremely difficult, especially in times of high stress, when falling back into known roles feels like the only way to make it through. This father shares what he did after the death of his child:

I buried myself in my work to hide from my feelings. The normal world of my work was comforting in itself.

We should not assign a good or bad label to how people cope with their grief. In many cases attempted strategies allowed them to minimize or deny their grief. These coping skills, while allowing them to remain "manly," were not seen as helpful either to them or to their partners. A mother whose six-month-old son died explains:

I need to talk, talk, talk about what I'm feeling at the moment. I need to share my thoughts and feelings, and I need to be hugged when I'm crying and in pain. My husband, rather than needing to be around someone else, tends to go off by himself. To be alone with his grief, to keep it all inside. I sometimes resent him for keeping it all to himself, for not sharing with me, and he resents me for blabbing about it all the time and wearing my heart on my sleeve.

Women are encouraged from an early age to be more expressive; their verbal, intuitive, and nurturing skills are positively reinforced. Men are encouraged to compete, to win, and not to let a little pain get in the way. One man whose son died at the age of two and a half months puts it succinctly:

Being organized creates stability, stability creates control, control maintains calm. If you lose one, disorganization and trouble are the result.

So how do marriages survive the assault on both the relationship and the individual when a child dies? We found that 26 percent of the people in our study considered divorce. Two percent indicated that they had separated because of the death, and 4 percent stated that they had in fact divorced as a result of the death. A careful reading, though, of the anecdotal material provided by the respondents presents a different picture. When asked "Did you divorce your spouse in the aftermath of the death?" 4 percent said yes. Many others, when adding additional information, pointed out they did later divorce the spouse they were with at the time of the death—one may assume that they did not consider this to have occurred during the "aftermath" period following the death. It may also be true that these respondents do not want to blame a dead infant for the end of the marriage. We have to be careful about drawing conclusions when we compare the statistical data with the anecdotal; nevertheless, a full 35 percent of the men and 22 percent of the women reported that their marriages were weakened by the death of their baby. Twenty-four percent of both men and women reported that their marriages had been both strengthened and weakened as a result of the death. Fifty-one percent of the respondents in our study said their relationship had been strengthened. Two and a half years after the death of her daughter, a mother explains:

> The pain was so intense for both of us that we couldn't even deal with our own pain, let alone deal with each other's. It seemed like we just didn't have anything to give anymore, and when you're not giving in a marriage at all times, that marriage can quickly fall apart. Time does heal, and with time we did deal with our grief and then learned how to give again and deal with each other.

Sadly, it seems that at a time when the two people need each other most, they are kept apart by differences in learned behavior of which they may not even be aware.

The need for intimacy, for closeness, is such a basic human need that babies can die from a lack of it—consider the infants diagnosed with the malady "failure to thrive." Women tend to express intimacy through touch, conversation, and presence ("just being there"). For men, however, intimacy, closeness with another, is expressed sexually. For women, sex after the death of their child is a reminder of the conception of the dead child, and the resulting gestation and birth.

> Instead of thinking about my husband or what we're doing [sexual intercourse], I think about the baby. I think this is how his life started and how could it be over already. I always want to cry.

Not surprisingly, then, over 52 percent of the participants in our study said that their sexual relationship changed after the death. Five and a half years after the death of his three-month-old daughter a man explains:

> My wife has lost her desire for sex, and I find I need the physical release more now than ever before. Our sexual relationship is very frustrating.

Since a man often feels required to perform sexually, rejection of his sexual overtures by his partner denies his desire for intimacy and questions his ability to perform adequately.

These misunderstandings regarding the fulfillment of individual needs act to divide the couple further. As they struggle to balance personal needs against the need to maintain the relationship, they usually are not understanding or communicating basic differences in their needs for intimacy. Because sex is used in some relationships as a quid pro quo, refusing sex can be an expression of anger, as this woman makes clear two years after her baby died:

> He can sleep—that made me mad. I was up all night for months. He withdrew from sharing his feelings. I withdrew physically, sexually, mentally; anger came out.

At best the arrival of children always presents complications and difficulties in any relationship, but when the child dies, the family becomes high risk for personal and emotional struggles. Five years after the death of her baby a mother helps us to understand:

> Anything that was wrong [with our marriage] before was augmented one hundredfold; all our energy is spent trying to cope with the death, and we have nothing left over for each other. My husband became more workaholic and sportaholic and wanted me to get pregnant again right away. I needed to cry and talk and talk about it over and over and over. I felt I needed to get over it better before thinking about another pregnancy. I had a total lack of desire for a sexual relationship. My husband felt an increased desire as a way of venting emotions and became very sexually aggressive.

Information about the divorce rate among families experiencing SIDS is contradictory and, as our study found, unreliable. Many clinicians assume a high divorce rate, but the research does not bear this out. It appears that the divorce rate for families experiencing SIDS is no higher than the national average rate for divorce. A possible explanation for the discrepancy between the answers in the survey and the anecdotal information may be that these parents cannot blame the death of their baby for their divorce; to hold a dead infant responsible feels morally reprehensible, and the parents would be likely to find other reasons for the divorce. But comparative suffering is an exercise in futility. The loss of a job may be the catalyst for divorce in one family, yet it cannot be compared to the pain of the death of a child. All the same, resulting stresses to that relationship at that time and place are not bearable. Ultimately, relationships are often difficult to maintain in the best of circumstances, and that they deteriorate in the worst of times is to be expected.

Love cannot overcome all the crises in people's lives. Feeding the flames of love when a bereaved parent is doing well to be able to get up in the morning and tie his or her own shoelaces requires fuel that is not always available. Commitment and communication can become impossible when the pain of an infant's death has reduced the parent to a basic level of survival. At best the complicated requirements of the marriage must wait until the mother and father find enough energy not only to heal themselves but also their relationship.

Testimony: "When Is It My Turn to Cry?"

A North Dakota father writes of how difficult it is both to grieve for the loss of his baby, Jennifer, and at the same time to "be strong for his family."

"All of us have heard of how one event or another will turn a person's life around or how a tragedy will disrupt the lives of many people. With little or no warning, the lives of several people can be changed, overturned, or redirected because of one fateful event. This is exactly what happened to my wife, family, friends, and me on a Sunday three months ago. In a matter of seconds our cheerful, gay vacation supper turned into a tearful struggle to bring life back into our young daughter's body.

"Immediately following the discovery of Jennifer's lifeless body, the tears that flowed were of horror, fear of the truth, and disbelief. My tears as I tried to revive our baby were a mixture caused by total confusion between a fear of disbelief and a fear of not wanting to know what was evident before my eyes, lying in my arms. As we accompanied Jenny to the hospital and held her for the last time, the tears and statements were directed to her but were really spoken selfishly for each of us. Being religious enough to believe God had Jenny with him and she would have a greater peace with him than we could ever provide, each of us was crying for our loss, the loss of a beautiful baby girl.

"Throughout the next few days we were protected by our families from intrusions and problems that the arrival of many friends and acquaintances can bring. During this time, however, we insisted on making the decisions for Jennifer's funeral and appropriate arrangements because she was ours. So together Chris and I decided what dress Jenny was to be buried in, what type of casket to purchase, where we should plan and purchase our family plots, and similar decisions that seemed to go on and on. These were decisions I had never thought about before which were difficult to decide on then and hard to think about now.

"Finally Jenny was buried, with the blessings of family, friends, and parents. Everyone had to regroup in their own special ways so that they might continue to live productive lives. For days after Jenny's death we were visited by people who wished us well and extended appropriate sympathy. Slowly the tears seemed to disappear as our natural defense mechanisms came forward to push the despair down deeper so as to allow for self-preservation.

"Our return home to Minot was tearful and somewhat frightening as the loneliness was reinforced and reality's cruelty became terribly apparent. Friends and colleagues trying to be kind or simply to protect themselves would ignore the subject of Jennifer and the entire situation concerning her death. This natural tendency for everyone to ignore the subject for fear of bringing up tender memories created hostility in both Chris and me. We loved Jennifer while she was with us, and we continue to love her though she is no longer with us; ignoring her was insulting something very important in our lives. I was hurt then and to some degree criticize this action now; but, more than three months ago, if I were confronting a friend who had lost a baby, fear of saying something wrong would probably have kept me from talking of the subject also.

"Those people who would comment about Jenny's death would say how sorry they were and then ask how my wife was. This concern for Chris was appreciated, for she was terribly shaken by Jennifer's death. Along with concern for Chris's well-being came words of wisdom or advice as to my conduct or how to handle my wife in this situation. People advised me to handle Chris with great care for this was a loss like nothing she would ever have encountered before. 'Show her great patience, more than ever before, be kind to her, and be extremely understanding.'

"The needs of my wife were well known to me during this ordeal, and I felt I was prepared to follow through with my obligation to stand by her and help. Suddenly, however, just two weeks after Jennifer's death, I realized that for some reason I was expected to be the strength of our relationship. I was supposed to provide great amounts of support for my mourning wife and show her greater patience and love than ever before. Everywhere I turned I received this same advice. Only two people mentioned concern for me during this period. This feeling began to bother me after a while for it seemed that I was either supposed not to show any emotion about the death of our daughter or I was simply supposed to be able to go through this ordeal without having it affect me, thereby not needing the period of mourning that was afforded my wife.

"Strong feelings surfaced: Doesn't anyone care about me? Jennifer was part of me too, you know. When is it my turn to cry? I became sensitive.

"I sensed people were telling me it was all right for me to have cried immediately following Jennifer's death, but now my mourning must stop and I should be able to repel those strong emotions and be a man for my wife, family, and society. My wife was allowed a period not to be herself, but I was expected to go back to work upon our return and function as though nothing had happened. My tender defense emotions quickly turned into a feeling of hostility toward society in general as it somehow told me I couldn't really be myself, I couldn't cry anymore, I must be strong, I must be a man.

"In dealing with Jennifer's death I could and can cry with my wife in the security of our home and feel only a slight bit of embarrassment, since crying is unusual in my family and opposes my basic nature. My basic manly nature is not to be one to show much emotion, but I still can cry and release those strong emotions within the confines of my home. Nowhere else have I encountered such freedom.

"Following Jennifer's death, I saw my father cry for the first time in my life. Her death shook this pillar of strength to an emotional state I don't believe he ever knew before. My father felt badly about this emotional state, and the afternoon before Jennifer's funeral as we stood in our front yard, he apologized for not being stronger. He was truthful when he said, as he sobbed, how he expected and wanted himself to be the strength and resolving force to guide us through this tragedy, but he just couldn't. He had never experienced such a helpless feeling, and it was hard for him to accept that feeling.

"I recall telling my father that I could expect no more out of any father than for him to be himself. Jennifer had touched everyone who had known her with the special love that was unique to her, and my father was expressing his loss of that love with his tears. This conversation and display of emotion was a unique experience for both of us, and I doubt if we will ever find a situation where we will freely discuss our true emotions with each other again. For even now I know I have allowed my defenses to build up and protect me and not allow me to talk totally freely, even with this very special man.

"When is it my turn to cry? I'm not sure society or my upbringing will allow me a time to really cry, unafraid of the reaction and repercussion that might follow. I must be strong, I must support my wife because I am a man. I must be the cornerstone of our family because society says so, my family says so, and, until I can reverse my learned nature, I say so."

8

Grandmothers and Grandfathers: The Sadness in Our Soul

All too often we forget that many people make up a family and have different needs to be addressed. In this chapter we will look at the importance of remembering some others who are also intimately connected to the death of a baby to SIDS, who share in the immense process of grief—the grandparents.

Specifically, we will look at what grandparents go through after the death of their grandchild and how they reach out to the baby's parents.

Children are not supposed to die before their parents and certainly not before their grandparents. This is the "normal" evolution of life, right? Sometimes not, as you will hear in the responses of the eighty grandparents in our study.

What Was the Hardest Thing to Deal with When Your Grandchild Died?

You are not only dealing with your grief, you are trying to help your own child through a horrible experience. The parent's pain is your pain too. It is very hard to watch your child suffer and not be able to "make it all better" as when they were little.

[The hardest thing?] No one to cuddle and be proud of.

I found it heartbreaking to see my daughter's empty arms and swollen breasts.

How to take it, because I think people don't think about the grandparents when it happens. They put all their time into the parents, and they need to help the grandparents too.

She was our first grandchild and the most beautiful little girl I ever saw. It is hard to treat the subsequent children in anything like a normal, relaxed manner. And our son and daughter-in-law's pain was most difficult.

When you get to be middle aged and know you can't have any more children of your own, the hope for the future is in your grandchildren. We had just adjusted to being grandparents and then he was gone.

Not only losing a grandchild, but seeing your children grieve. It's like a "double whammy."

The grandchild represents your immortality, in a sense, which is now gone. Also, your own children hurt so badly—and there seems to be nothing you can do to ease that agony.

Trying to understand or find a reason, "Why this baby?"

[The hardest thing?] That people don't think it hurt as much as it did and still does. People don't believe he was healthy—they think he had to be "sickly."

In my case, the loss of a future "grandpa" relationship.

Experiences of Grandparents

For anyone who has never experienced the death of a child or who might not realize who besides the parents is affected, the grandparents in this study can certainly offer some insight. They willingly and at times painfully described the effect that the death of their grandchild had on them personally. The following are just a few of the feelings experienced by surviving grandparents:

This has been a devastating experience. I had dealt with death before, but somehow this was different. Because it was a child, the son of my daughter, flesh of my flesh. There is a sadness in my soul. I'm having a hard time overcoming this sadness. Most people are not aware of my pain. I try not to burden others. I do not think my pain is abnormal or that I need psychiatric help. I just hope it will get better as time goes by. It was the potential that was lost that bothers me. My daughter is over thirty-five years old and now feels she wants to try again to have a boy. It worries me that she is older. How many more pregnancies will she have in order to have a boy? What if she never has another boy?

I have experienced sorrow, anger, doubt in the doctor's decision to leave the baby in the mother when it was so big and the mother is small. She was two weeks overdue. I also wish we lived closer so we could be there to comfort our daughter and son-in-law. There were a lot of whys. Why couldn't their baby have lived? They wanted it so much. Why do people who really don't want children seem to have them without any problems? It just seems so unfair. Why didn't the doctor induce labor two weeks earlier when the baby was kicking a lot?

Whenever my thoughts turn to my grandchild, I am filled with sorrow, grief, and regret. Sorrow because I do miss his presence, grief for me, but especially for our son and daughter-in-law, and regret that I didn't spend more time with him.

Finding our beautiful granddaughter dead in her crib was by far the most devastating thing that has ever happened to either one of us. We visit her grave, look at pictures, and talk about her frequently. I shall never forget or cease to treat her as part of our family.

[I feel] sadness, grief, and a little envy when my friends have a new grandchild. I worry about my daughter and the loss she is having to deal with.

Unbearable heartache, disbelief (it didn't really happen, it was only a bad dream), crying spells, insomnia, the feeling that there's nothing to live for, extremely sensitive feelings, loss of appetite, longing to hold the baby. Having a helpless feeling, not being in control. A terrible hurt at seeing our son and his wife suffering—not being able to take away the pain. Feeling a distance between us. My husband and I are so devastated at losing our first grandchild this way. We each are grieving in a different way and cannot comfort each other. I feel so alone in my grief so much of the time. I worry about my two sons and daughter-in-law (even my dog) more than usual—their health and safety.

A lot of heartache and tears. It seems like everything you see and do can relate to the baby. He will never know the joys of brothers and sisters, of eating candy, birthday parties, a little swimming pool, riding the cars at the fair, holding a puppy or baby pig, and holidays. But I guess he is happier in heaven.

My first reaction was, of course, disbelief. Then having to "be there" for the parents. The feeling of wanting to be strong for them, but wondering if I could somehow have prevented the death. Now, accepting her death and being grateful for the love I could give her if even for a short time.

At sixty-four years, you begin to think of death, *but your own.* It's hard to take the death of your own children or grandchildren before yours. You *expect* to die before them. I try to keep his death way back in my mind and try not to think about it as it makes me sad and depressed.

At first I felt that God had taken the baby for no reason at all. I was bitter—I couldn't understand why my grandson had to die when he had so much to live for. I felt as if there was no God. Why? Why? Why?

Immediately after my grandchild's death my brother and I had to work with our own mother to overcome her grief and despair. She had lost a child, her firstborn, and the death of her great-grandchild brought it all back to her. She found it very hard to accept. We never succeeded. My mother's health deteriorated rapidly.

For a long time, when I sat in the recliner in which I held him, I could (seemed to) feel his body on my shoulder. Time heals a lot of wounds, but the one-year anniversary of his death brought a rerun of the events in my mind.

First, a sense of personal loss—"it cannot happen to me" reaction. Then a shifting toward reality and a feeling of support to our daughter and her husband, doing what we could to assuage their grief, and all their problems of "why." Realizing that their problems were far more complex and fundamental than our sense of loss, ours became basically a supportive role. We had made all the baptismal arrangements as requested by our daughter. The most tragic act personally was canceling the baptismal ceremony with the church.

There has been a great amount of reflection on the last visit—the day of death and before. Of course we cried then and many times since. I still want to look at all the pictures we have to remind me of those beautiful days we were together. One event has been special to me that I cannot explain, but then I really don't care if it is explained. About one month to six weeks after my grandson's death I awakened suddenly to feel, see, experience his warm, glowing smile. It was to say, everything is all right now. It wasn't spoken; it was just communicated. I really felt the stress of the events leave. This did not allow me to forget, or to stop wondering why.

The grandparents revealed many different emotions:

Jealousy of others who have new grandchildren.
Bitterness because of the loss of their grandchild.
Irritation at others' thoughtlessness.
Regret at not having more time to spend with their grandchild.
Pride in the way their adult children "handled" the situation.
Exhaustion from grieving.
Anger at God for taking their grandchild away from them.
Resentment toward other parents who have children, but don't seem to want or care for them as well as their own child had cared for the lost baby.
Sadness because of the loss of a future relationship with this grandchild.
Optimism and hope for better days ahead.
Anxiety about the future.
Concern about their adult children, grandchildren, and even pets.
Frustration that there are no definite answers to explain the death.
Disbelief because of the out-of-order sequence of the death. The old are supposed to die before the young.
Doubt in doctors.
Depression, helplessness, sorrow.

The grandparents were asked to describe how the death of their grandchild compared with other crises in their life. Does it compare? Their stories explain:

My father died less than a year before my grandson was born. My father's death was easier to accept because he had had a long, happy life; he died instantly, which is how he would have chosen to die. My grandson was named after my father, so his death opened wounds for all my family which had just begun to heal. My grandson was to carry on the family's name.

My mother's death was sudden and unexpected, and I must admit that it hit me much harder. Of course, she had been in my life for thirty years, and we were very close.

Even my husband's cardiac arrest didn't have the emotional impact of this. There was an explanation and a recovery. I feel if we survived this SIDS, we could survive anything. It was devastating.

Nothing can be as traumatic as losing a child and not knowing the cause.

[My] three divorces were difficult, but they were nothing compared to this. I thought I knew what pain was then, but when my grandchild died I found out I really knew nothing of hurt. It was weeks, or more likely months, before I could get a hold of myself.

Deaths of my father and older sister were easier to accept than that of an innocent baby.

I had cancer but survived. No comparison with the finality of the baby's death.

How Do Families Survive?

How does one's life take on meaning and direction after one has experienced such a tragic event as the death of an infant? Is it okay to talk about the deceased baby? How do you talk about the baby with surviving parents and siblings? What events help in the healing process? Do memories fade over time? Do religious beliefs help or hinder the healing process? Do support groups aid in the grieving process? And if you ever feel "crazy," how can you be sure that you are not? These are a few of the questions that our grandparents were willing to discuss with us.

They also told us how they found hope in what felt like a hopeless situation, how their personal strength and the strength of other family members guided them on their journey to a sense of acceptance, and how time passes and hurt becomes less intense but the memories never die. These grandparents were able to survive, and in this section they will share their stories.

Reaching out to others was a helpful way to work through personal grief for many grandparents:

I have written numerous letters [to other SIDS grandparents] sharing my experiences and grieving in an effort to let them know that they are not alone. I also visited some and talked with them.

I have attended graveside services. I've sent sympathy cards and have taken food to the family.

I just try to be there for them if they should want to talk or need to know that someone does care.

By praying for them and trying to be supportive to them when it is needed.

Talked on the phone. Wrote them notes and just offered assistance when needed.

I sent cards and suggested they come to the support group. I am going to volunteer my services to our local group and help with whatever they need me for.

Grandparents and Parents Together

The following are thoughts from those (68 percent of the grand-mothers, and 31 percent of the grandfathers) who believed that it is a good idea to have support group meetings for both parents and grandparents together:

"[It is a good idea because] the parents and grandparents can share the pain and subsequently the healing."

"It might have helped us avoid some of the pain we unthink-ingly caused our children early on."

"Feelings of both [grandparents and parents] need to be aired and shared for good communication."

"I think it prevents guilt feelings from setting in."

"If more understanding can be achieved, it should be done."

"The loss may be felt differently, but the loss was a part of you extending through the parents. A better sense of the depth of the loss could be realized in such a group."

For others (32 percent of the grandmothers, and 69 percent of the grandfathers), the thought of having a joint support group for both the parents and grandparents to attend together was not viewed favorably:

I do not find support groups to be very helpful. I have tried them on other problems and have decided that I prefer to find my way alone and with the help of people I love.

Separately would be all right. The loss of a child creates a nervous tension in the parents and in-laws. Going to the meetings very often together might create a situation for trouble. I want to get along with my son-in-law.

Our needs are different. Only other parents who have suffered the loss of a child can truly empathize. The rest of us can only sympathize.

"Going Crazy"

We asked the grandparents if they ever thought that they were "going crazy" after the death of their grandchild. Here are some of their responses:

Yes, I did. I am a very outgoing person, and now I didn't want to see or talk to anyone.

I really don't think I felt I was going crazy, but many times it was difficult to concentrate on the daily routine things that needed doing.

I went to work after three or four days, but by the time my lunch hour came I would just run to the car and cry. I would just be ready to scream. I had a hard time keeping my mind on what I was doing, and I know I did a lot of things that I wouldn't have otherwise.

[I suffered] loss of memory about some things. Not remembering what I said to people.

I just cried easily.

I didn't realize that I was hyperventilating because of the stress and fear, plus doctors kept telling me I was depressed; therefore I thought I was completely out of control and going crazy.

The death changed what seemed to be a nightmare into reality.

No, I couldn't "go crazy." I had other children to care for and console, and a mother to care for. This kept me busy and allowed time to heal the wound. My mind was kept active on other things.

Feeling Guilty

In regard to guilt, 29 percent of the grandparents stated that they had felt personal guilt over the death of the baby, while a few others (9 percent) blamed someone else for the death. The following are some of the grandparents' feelings about the reasons for their own guilt:

I am a cigarette smoker, and I felt, in searching for a reason, that I could be at fault.

I felt that I should have been able to detect a problem.

I had put a little honey in one of his formula bottles and then, later on, heard of the botulism theory of SIDS. This was two or three days before he died—I have been assured this probably was *not* the cause.

[Feel guilt?] Doesn't everyone?

Yes, I wondered if I could have prevented it if I'd been there, especially when I hadn't wanted to leave when I did. And I wondered about the little hat I had put on him to keep his head warm, as it helped him sleep better. It did have ties under his chin, and these were loose when they found him.

I felt guilty because of the impersonal rearing of my own four children.

Funerals

Most of the families (94 percent) said that there was a funeral for the baby, and 57 percent reported that there was an open casket. Many found the funeral to be a healthy experience:

It was good to see the baby, to say goodbye, to experience the love and sympathy of others.

It was a healing experience. Seeing our other grandchildren being so loving and thoughtful toward their cousin and uncle and aunt and us was especially helpful.

The minister gave a very nice, short sermonette about the baby just being loaned to us by God for a special mission of his and needing him back with him. He compared him to all the little angels of his and that there must be a very special reason for his taking him back, one maybe we would never know or understand.

The funeral helped me come to grips with the reality, and prepared me to begin with the rebuilding.

We needed to say goodbye. We needed to do something for him as a loving tribute. We needed the support of our friends.

A funeral is important to the grieving process. It is a completion of the death—a ceremony to see the little one on to his new life.

I thought an open casket would be horrible, but it helped to say goodbye. Seeing him in the first moments was unbearable. But I think it was a wise decision made by my son and daughter-in-law.

One grandmother expressed disgust with the funeral director:

The director was unbelievable—*no compassion!* He told me the day I was there to make arrangements that this was "only a baby." I wanted clothes put on the baby, and he said that it was foolish as it was a closed coffin. He had made no arrangements to transport the baby to the cemetery, so he put the casket in the back of a station wagon. Also, he asked the people to bring the flowers.

We asked the grandparents how they reacted at the funeral:

I was very upset, and the night following the funeral I ended up in the hospital with pneumonia.

All I can remember is that I couldn't stop shaking or crying.

It was very moving to see others cry because I found it so hard to cry myself. There was no need to be ashamed of the tears.

I blocked out the fact that he was dead. I did not want to upset my daughter by breaking down, and they needed me to be strong. I had no one to hold me up.

[I was] bitter toward God.

It was hard for me, as my elderly parents needed so much support.

[It was] very sad. Baby's sisters released balloons at the site signifying their release of him back to God. Very touching for adults, very symbolic.

Dealing with Painful Memories

How does one erase painful memories that continue to come back? Our grandparents did not have the definitive answer to that question except to say that painful memories do fade over time. Many (51 percent) experienced flashbacks of the death. Some (42 percent) just wanted to go to sleep and wake up after the pain had gone away. Some of the grandmothers (5 percent) had thoughts of suicide after the death of the baby. And for some (42 percent), the clarity of the memories faded over time, while for others the memories remained perfectly clear.

Flashbacks, sharp and often painful images in the mind's eye, can burden a grandparent for months or years after the death:

> I was at work when I got a call, so now whenever I get a call at work I start to shake, thinking Is this a bad call? I also have a hard time when a phone is ringing at work; it makes me very nervous if it rings too long.

> I see my daughter-in-law coming into the front room carrying the baby—dead. Her [the baby's] arms are straight out lying to the side. I see the hospital picture with her [the baby's] hand up. I used to think she was waving hello; now I think it is goodbye.

Some grandparents did not experience flashbacks, much to their chagrin: "Now I get angry because I can't remember how he looked."

Other Memories

Grandparents shared a wide variety of thoughts on memories:

> [Memories fade] just a little, but I will never get over the shock and grief. He will always remain in my prayers and thoughts even though we had him for such a little while.

> There is healing power in time.

> The memories remain, but the hurt has faded.

> No, memories have not faded. I will see him until the day I die.

The pain is not as intense or right on the surface all the time, but it takes little for my tears to flow, and the details are etched in my mind and heart.

I just can't get him out of mind. He was the first grandson.

Many grandparents said that they sometimes wished they could just go to sleep and wake up after the pain had gone away. A sampling of responses follow:

"It hurt so bad and I didn't think I could bear another day."
"[I hoped if I slept] then the heartache would be over."
"[It was a] normal desire to escape from unpleasant circumstances."

Religion

A majority of the 80 grandparents (90 percent) stated that their religious beliefs were helpful to them in this crisis. Many (46 percent) thought that their beliefs were strengthened because of the baby's death; some (32 percent) thought they hadn't changed at all; and a few (5 percent) thought that their beliefs were weakened.

STRENGTHENED BELIEFS. Many grandparents felt that their religious beliefs were strengthened as a result of the death:

"We felt we now have an angel in heaven."
"Maybe because I could *blame God.*"
"I believe that God will not send us more than we can stand or take."
"It has made me more believing in another life where I shall perhaps meet our baby and be happy with her."
"I believe in a life hereafter and know that our baby is with God. It is the only way I can cope—to have faith."
"I was able to find solace in the belief of life after death. It gave me a handle to hold on to while I searched for a reason for the death in my mind."

WEAKENED BELIEFS. Others felt that their religious beliefs were weakened as a result of the death:

"What justification is there for God suddenly taking a normal, apparently healthy baby and bringing such misery?"

"I simply couldn't understand why this had to happen."

"I become very irritated when someone says that this is God's will. It's man's lack of knowledge, and we have to keep trying."

A WIDE VARIETY OF RELIGIOUS BELIEFS. The grandparents were extremely diverse in their thinking with regard to the religious implications of the baby's death:

The Lord giveth and the Lord taketh away. But he is always with you and understands your anger over a death.

Who ever said that life is fair?

I feel that God did us a great injustice.

I believe in a personal God who always will see me through any adversity. Sometimes we don't understand why things happen, but he is always there to care and help me do the right thing.

I talk to God a lot more now and say, "Thy will be done." Always before I would tell God what I wanted done.

The first thing I did after the death was go to the church that morning and get out my frustrations with God. In telling him what I thought was unfair and getting some anger out, it made me feel closer to him.

I just couldn't understand why God took him so young. Even though I know not to question God's work.

At first I was irate—"Don't tell me there's a God and he lets this happen!" Weeks later my attitude changed.

I believe that no matter what happens in life beyond our control, it happens for a reason and because of it some goodness will emerge in some way.

On Marriages

Some of the marriages of our grandparents (32 percent) seemed to be affected in some way by the death of their grandchild. Of that

32 percent, most thought that their marriages were strengthened (90 percent); others thought that their marriages were weakened; and others just were not sure. Another insight that they shared regarding their marriages was that most (52 percent) found that their coping strategies differed from those of their spouses and that they needed to find ways of accepting that.

STRENGTHENED MARRIAGES. A few thoughts from those who felt their marriages were strengthened:

> We shared a terrible experience and were able to understand what the other was going through as no one else could.

> To see how God brought our family together and erased old wrongs and helped us work out problems has made all of us a stronger family, and because I saw us cope with the death I know we can handle life's crises.

> I think we were brought closer together due to the realization of the fragility of life. Plus, we must enjoy the time we have together because we saw firsthand how abruptly it can end.

WEAKENED MARRIAGES. Others experienced weakened marriages:

> If I must face things as big as death alone, then I should have my freedom and not be tied down to one person. This was very one-sided. He said that his reason for not going to the funeral was that he "hates" funerals. As if everyone likes them.

SOME SPOUSES WERE UNCERTAIN. Some grandparents were uncertain whether the marriage was strengthened or weakened as a result of the death:

> We had some very trying times. I'm sure during the hardest times [the marriage was] probably weakened, but now I hope it's stronger.

> I don't think it has either strengthened or weakened our marriage which has always been a good one. But I know that neither my husband nor I can talk to the other about our grandson's death as we both get too emotional and it doesn't do either one of us any good.

VARIED COPING STRATEGIES. Most grandparents reported that their personal coping mechanisms differed from those of their spouse:

> My husband's answer to any problem is, don't talk about it and it will go away. I am the opposite.

> My husband doesn't talk about his feelings but takes flowers once a week to the gravesite.

> I tend to hold back grief. My wife tends to cry and let grief out, and that's perhaps better.

> My wife was much stronger.

> My husband did not talk about how he felt, but he worked out his grief by "doing for" the parents. He helped in the arranging and paying for the funeral. I have to talk out and cry out my grief, and it helps to be able to help other SIDS parents in their grief.

> His attitude was, it's done and there isn't anything we can do about it. Pick up and go on. I'm sure he hurt as much as I did, but he had a hard time showing any emotions.

> I am much more outward. He never talked very much about it but was willing to listen.

> I tend to put it out of my mind. My wife cried more.

> I am inclined to "bottle things up," while my wife is more inclined to share and "let it all hang out."

Personal Theories

Even though with Sudden Infant Death Syndrome the cause of the infant's death is not known, we asked the grandparents if they had a personal theory that they thought might explain their grandchild's death, and 34 percent stated that they did. The personal theories ranged from medical reasons to family reasons to religious reasoning. The theories aided some grandparents in their understanding and coping, but for others the theories just added more questions. Here are a few of the theories:

> I do know they gave her oxygen at birth, and that has been on my mind.

I believe that it could have been caused by the DPT shot the baby had a couple of days prior to her death. When she was in to see the doctor to get her second shot, he said that she was in perfect health.

I think something in the baby's nervous system hasn't developed as much as the rest of his body has grown.

I think the brain stops giving messages to breathe.

Death due to accumulated stress on an immature or weakened system.

Allergy maybe? We have many in the family.

I think God needed a little angel.

Surviving Grandchildren

Many of our grandparents (68 percent) noted there were surviving siblings in the family, and 55 percent of those reported that they did talk with the children about the death. The following are some of the ideas that these grandparents shared with the surviving siblings:

We have tried to explain fully what happened and what is being done today to try to prevent this from occurring in new infants.

The conversations with the two-year-old are when she sees the picture of her sister. She will say, "My baby sister is with God. She is a pretty baby." We agree with her.

I talk to him only when he mentions her. This is not an easy situation for an adult to try to explain to a small child who wants answers to everything.

I tell them Jesus wanted those two little boys to play together, and someday we will see them again.

We tell him that the baby lives in Jesus' house now.

We talk about him being an angel in heaven.

When Danny's name is mentioned, we talk about him whichever way the discussion turns. If death, I talk about his being with Baby Jesus up in heaven.

We have talked to John about little Patrick, what he looked like, how he played with him, what happened to him, where he is now, how it all happened, and answer truthfully and calmly any questions that he [John] might ask and reassure him that it is all right to cry, that little Patrick has gone on to another life, but that we miss him and that is all right too.

Helping the Parents

The grandparents are survivors after the death of an infant. The siblings are survivors, as are the parents of the baby. We asked the grandparents to comment on what they did to help the baby's parents cope with the death of their child:

I call my son more often just to talk and let him know I'm here if he needs me.

How much can you do but accept it and love each other?

We talk about him at every opportunity. They say that helps so much. Parents don't want him forgotten by us or by anyone else.

Be there for them when they need me and butt out when they don't.

Someone, I think it was the funeral director, advised us to let our children make as many of the decisions as they could. A parent's immediate reaction is to try to ease the child's burden by saying, "Don't worry, we'll take care of everything." We let them know that we were available if they needed our help. If they found it too difficult to pack the baby's belongings, we would do it for them. They appreciated our support but took care of everything themselves, and it was good for them. They shared their grief and tears together. They made the funeral arrangements on their own and as a result felt they were adults and good, caring parents who took care of their son from beginning to end.

[We] paid for the funeral expenses.

[We helped] by not pushing suggestions on them.

Talk to them—hug and hold them.

We planted a tree in our grandson's memory, and we often let them know how well it is doing and how it will be strong and beautiful as a constant reminder of him.

[We helped] by being close and by seeing them often. We would take our cue from them. Generally, we left our life open for them to enter and stay as long as possible or as they wished.

How Parents Help Grandparents

Many grandparents shared how the baby's parents helped them deal with the death of their grandchild:

My daughter and I talked and cried and hugged.

They don't get upset when I still cry at times, and they honor the feelings I have for my grandson.

They are very considerate—they include us in their lives and plans.

They like to have me help with their new daughter. They always make me feel welcome. They're always doing nice things for me such as getting my lawn mower ready for the lawn-mowing season, giving me a tomato plant, and so forth.

By jointly meeting their own responsibilities and developing their own program of mutual support and understanding.

[They] express gratitude for the support and understanding we provided during the crisis.

Other parents were just not able to be of much support to the grandparents. "Were you able to help the grandparents in any way?"

"Not much."
"Nothing."

What Still Hurts?

Even after the support has been given and time has passed, pain remains. We asked the grandparents, "Today, what still hurts?" The passage of time tended to lessen the pain, but many grandparents said that the hurt was still very real months and years later. Here is a sampling of responses:

There is no real pain, just a dull ache. It hurts more when we fear for our new grandchildren, wondering if it will happen to them. Mostly we try to remember the happy times.

Our memory of our grandson is what still hurts. It hurts on his birthday and on his death anniversary. Also, when I see little boys about his age, I wonder what he would look like. I try to keep busy and take care of my other grandchildren, love them, do things for them, and thank God for giving us others that we hope and pray are healthy and stay healthy.

It hurts to think we lost a grandson who would have had such potential and who was such a joy to be with. The new granddaughter is a big help in getting over the grandson's death, but still . . . there are moments of sadness to have lost such a sweet little fellow. To alleviate the pain, I think that my little grandson would not want us to be sad forever about losing him. Yes, he wants us to be sad for a while because losing him was a great loss, but he wants us to realize we have to get on with life. We will see him again. He would want us to be happy again.

When I get to crying so hard, I think of my little grandson saying, "Don't cry, Grandma, I am so happy here in heaven."

The Good Things

It has often been said that good things can come out of sad events. So we asked the grandparents, "What good things have you learned about life?" They told us:

Although life is fragile, every day can be exciting if we let love flow through us and touch the life of someone else.

It's not a good idea to take life for granted.

There are many blessings, even when tragedy strikes. Life goes on, and you do too. Worrying about things is a waste of energy—the things you worry about probably will never happen.

I know that hope is always here—that while we may not always be happy, we can have an inner joy from knowing that God is in control and that there is life abundant for us if we commit our lives to God and his purpose. He will give us strength for the day and purpose for tomorrow. Life is good!

I can't honestly say that I've learned any good things about life since my grandson's death. I am still too bitter about it. I, of course, am grateful for the blessings that we do have, but this is by far the most awful tragedy that has ever happened in our family, and I hope that none of us ever has to go through it again.

You must enjoy life to the fullest because we don't know how long we have on earth.

Enjoy! Enjoy! Life is fragile; carefully consider how you use your time.

[I have learned] to make the best of all trials and disappointments, and to try and keep a positive attitude and things in life will go much better.

Life is precious. Live each day to the fullest. Treat each person as I would like to be treated.

Enjoy every moment and never hold a grudge.

That it [life] does go on; that hearts mend; that we truly don't "lose" a baby or a husband. They continue to be a part of you.

That life can end as fast as it starts. But I'll never understand why. I guess I have learned that God has his reason for taking babies so young. But there are good things in life. Just go out and look for the good life.

I have learned that life is what we make it.

There are a lot of caring people.

Even when at times you feel like giving up, there is always a reason to go on. There will always be the good and the bad. It's best to enjoy every minute you can have with the little ones because you never know when sadness can strike again. All of the grandchildren are bright spots in my life.

I've learned that life is unpredictable and can be very short. I've learned to try to make the most of each day as we don't know about tomorrow. Pain is part of life, and maybe it strengthens us somehow.

At age sixty-nine, I would say that in time of tragedy most people are great. What happens to us in between?

[The good things?] That medical examiners are honest and straightforward in their reporting.

That every day is a good day. It's just that some days are better than others.

We are placed on this earth for a brief moment: to love, to serve, to rejoice, to die.

The Good Things about Yourself

We asked the grandparents who had endured such a crisis, "What good things have you learned about yourself?"

I think I've learned to care more about people and their problems and to try to "count my blessings."

I am stronger than I thought I was.

Only that I can cope with a lot.

I have learned to accept the will of God and to take life day by day. It will be God's way.

I have learned that with God's help, I am stronger than I thought possible. I have learned that I can be of help to other people, and daily I am learning to be more sensitive to those around me, and I pray that I may continue to be so for the rest of my life.

That I am but an instrument. That grief experienced enlarges our capacity to understand someone else's grief.

That I love my daughter so much.

I guess I have more "backbone" than I apparently thought, even though it is arthritic. I want to be available to help our family if and when they need me.

That I can bounce back from something I considered to be the worst thing that ever happened in my life, and can give more of myself to my wife and family.

I learned that I could "handle" such a situation and still be human. I could cry and feel the loss and yet reach out to my children. I also learned that I had given my children strength to handle tragedy and go on with life.

We continue to have strong resources and strength to call upon.

What Will the Future Bring?

We posed this final question about the future to the grandparents, and it yielded an interesting variety of responses:

Who knows? We'll live one day at a time and roll with the punches.

I don't know what the future holds, but I know who holds the future. God is in control, though it may not seem so. And sometime there will be an answer as to why SIDS has claimed the lives of so many little ones, and these lives will then be safe. The world is getting better and so are the people, though some days may seem very dark.

Hopefully [the future will bring] new perspectives in other people.

I don't have much hope for the future. I will be very paranoid with any subsequent children. I am afraid the same thing will happen. I'm not looking forward to more grandchildren now.

Some pain—some joy.

I have never forgotten the song in the back of my heart. Hopefully [the future will bring] more grandchildren and the song.

I don't worry about it.

More of the same—plus aging for my dear, intelligent husband and myself. I want to be a *"nice* old lady."

Happier days, I hope, but with the raw realization that it can happen again.

My crystal ball is broken.

[What will the future bring?] The unexpected.

Testimony: "My, What Is This?"

This Nebraska grandmother told us her story six and a half years after her six-week-old grandson died. She was able to hold him when he was about an hour old. And she remembers him looking around as if to say, "My, what is this?" At these times she finds it hard to deal with his death.

"I went to visit some friends after I got off work, and then I stopped by the friends of the baby's mother, a couple, who were caring for the older child. I asked about the family, and they said, 'You didn't know? They're at the hospital.' When I got there, they told me that the baby was dead. It just didn't seem real, though I knew it had to be or they wouldn't have said so.

"My son explained that he had heard a noise earlier but hadn't thought much about a baby making a noise. Since they were visiting with friends, he didn't think too much about it until he went in to check on the baby and then he knew something was wrong. I'm not sure exactly what he saw (even though he has said), but he said that he knew right away the baby wasn't right.

"They called someone who got them to the hospital. I don't remember what they said they did. The next couple of days are a blur. The usual things were done that needed to be done. I do not know of any single person who was not understanding and supportive.

"[At the funeral] the church was at least half full. The baby was dressed all in white like he was going on a journey. He was a beautiful baby.

"At the funeral I cried most of the time. I told my son-in-law that crying was not a thing to be ashamed of. I showed my friends the baby and tried to help where I could.

"All I can remember about the funeral service was that my mother was 'up there' telling the baby that everything was okay.

"The finality of death is a hard thing to accept, especially in one so young. I'm sure a person tends to shut out the hurt as much as possible. That is part of the reason things seem such a blur, even though in thinking about the baby, I still have some pain."

[What have you gone through since your grandchild died?] "I have felt a sense of loss, of course, but it also seems like in some ways he was never born. However, since I got to hold him when he was about an hour old, I still can see him looking around like, 'My, what is this?' The memories of that moment make it hard to forget the pain. I also think about him on his birthday, on the day of his death, and sometimes at family get-togethers. Also, knowing (wondering) how his parents feel since his dad found him. My heart aches for them when I think about it, but life does go on.

"I feel that I have been very fortunate during this most difficult time." [What things have people done during the time since your grandchild's death that have been helpful to you?] "They have allowed me to talk about him. It is not brought up often, but I have been fortunate to be around people who have felt free to talk about him when the subject does come up.

"During the first six months following the death of my grandson, I just wanted to go to sleep and wake up after the pain had gone away. I thought, how can I handle life after the death of a child that young? When I was talking with the baby's father, he said that the thought of suicide had crossed his mind following the death of his son.

"My religious beliefs were helpful at this time of crisis. I felt that I had something stronger than myself to help me. God gave life and he gave 'death,' as we call it, but I feel it is just a stepping stone to the next phase of learning, so life continues."

[Have you gone through any other major crises in your life, and if yes, how would these crises compare to the death of a baby grandchild?] "I went through a divorce both as a child and as an adult. With the death of my grandchild, the death was final, but there are happy memories. With the divorce, the happy memories are overshadowed by the hurt of the unhappiness that caused the divorce. And the divorced people are still around, which makes the hurt last longer.

[What would you like others to know about how to help a person who is grieving over a baby's death?] "Don't feel ashamed or scared to talk about the child, what happened, or why. Even though I've experienced this tragedy, I still feel scared to talk about the event with other people."

[What are the hardest things of all for a grandparent to deal with when a baby grandchild dies?] "How do you comfort the parents, especially your own child?"

[Now, today, what still hurts?] "Not having him here to watch him grow up." [When does it hurt?] "When I seriously get to thinking about him and know I will never see him grow up, and when I get to thinking about his dad finding him dead." [What are you doing to alleviate your pain?] "Thinking of God and knowing there had to be a reason for his death. Like the baby's mother said, 'God needs those little angels to keep him company.' "

The Community Response: Friends, Relatives, and Professionals

Neighbors bring food with death and flowers with sickness and little things in between.

—*Harper Lee*[1]

For families whose babies have died, there are no immediate solutions or seven easy steps to the successful completion of mourning. The grief of these families cannot be managed in a "how to" manual for friends, relatives, and professionals. Rather, we offer an exploration without an explanation about what happens when babies die without any reason. Without fanfare of trumpets, warning, or struggle, but with a whisper and a sigh, their lives are over.

Answers from the scientific community regarding the cause or causes of SIDS are still remote, and faced with a crisis in uncharted waters, the best that friends, relatives, and professionals who work with bereaved families can do is to accept the contradictions of life and death.

Nevertheless the response of those friends, relatives, and professionals is vitally important to the family whose baby has suddenly died. Most people want to do something, say something, anything that will ease the pain they encounter. It is not always easy to tell, however, what really helps these mothers and fathers.

Since the death is so hard to accept, high levels of denial are present in the minds of the family members. The position of helper is fraught with complications, for there is no one right way to proceed. The only clear-cut helpful response would be to return to these families their babies, alive and healthy. So instead we must try to reach out to these families, touch them, and allow their grief to touch us, while bearing in mind that what may be comforting at one point may not be at another, and that what may seem considerate to a mother may seem intrusive to the father:

> You don't have to know the right things to say to the parents. It is important to let them know that you care about them and you want to continue to be a comfortable companion, but you really don't know exactly what to do. Tell them you are willing to wade through all this mire of grief with them and that you won't be offended by them telling you exactly what you neglected to say or shouldn't have said.

The sudden, unexpected death of a healthy baby is hard to understand, and it compels all of us to seek some kind of order out of the confusion. "Seek and ye shall find" has a concrete meaning to it, and so parents turn to pop psychology in search of answers. Theories flood scientific journals and the mass media with the subtle or not so subtle message that all problems can be solved. But death is not a mathematical equation that has a simple solution. No matter how hard we try to push death away from us—into hospitals, into funeral homes—death is a constant part of life. We need to recognize that what is not said by the bereaved parents is felt with pain and anger: that there should be rules, that children should outlive their parents, that babies should not die without reason. We seek logical answers to explain why a baby dies. People also experience irrational thoughts—for example, the baby "decided" not to breathe, not to live—and because this is so offensive to the survivors as well as to others in society, such thoughts remain unspoken, only heard in our hearts:

> Someone could have been there to listen. Someone could have been there to give me a hug. Just to know someone cares, instead of making me an outcast. Someone who would have let me scream, cry, yell, and ask anything I wanted to get off my chest. Someone who would have let me blame myself, blame doctors, blame God, wonder what I could have done, should have done, wonder what wasn't done. I needed someone who would have let me do that.

This anger comes out in all of us at times. The mothers and fathers are angry at the doctor who failed. They express anger at the religious person who mouths meaningless clichés about "God's will" and a "grand plan." They are angry at a friend who says, "You're young, you'll have more children." They are angry at a family member who talks about her friend's baby who was revived. But avoiding the reality of death through anger denies the support and understanding these families need to survive. Friends, relatives, and professionals may disavow their own anger and pain at the death of a baby by retreating, putting distance between those whose babies have died and those whose haven't, thus creating a false sense of protection:

> Some [people] have never acknowledged the death at all. As long as possible they avoided us so as to avoid the issue, then they took up where they left off discussing work, sports, weather, and so on.

To allow the bereaved parents into our lives forces us to realize we are all the same and that the same thing could happen to our children. We must be helpers, healers, lovers, and friends, and must face a test no one should ever have to take.

What to do? When we asked the families whose babies had died, they gave us a contradictory list of responses. Still, there are some important things anyone can do. Initial contact is essential, if only to say, "I'm sorry for your pain." Continuing communication is also very important. A mother whose seven-week-old baby died seven months ago shares this:

> Don't talk too much, but be there to listen. Don't ask if you can do something; the person won't know what to say. Pitch in if you see some way to lighten their load. Take their laundry home, offer to baby-sit, ask if they need something from the grocery. Drop off a bucket of chicken or something to eat. Invite them for dinner or dessert, meet them for lunch. Don't tell them to call if they need to talk: call them. Talk about the baby if you knew him.

Talking about the death of a child does not in fact make it harder for these parents. Trust that they remember very well, and they need to discuss the baby's birth, life, and death:

> When we talk about things our baby did, we are not trying to pretend he is not dead any more than other parents talking about things their grown children did as babies are trying to pretend their children have not grown up.

For friends to stay away from these families because they do not know what to do or say can only make the pain worse:

> It is not easier for the grieving parents to not see or talk to you. The sight of you or something you say may bring tears, but that is all right. Loneliness brought on by widespread avoidance only exacerbates the pain of grief.

Faced with the unspeakable, friends are forced to confront their own mortality, their own worst nightmares, and still be of help to these families. Two years after her three-month-old daughter died, this mother tells us what may be of help:

> Your caring may have to be a little less conditional than adult friendships usually are, because, unfortunately, the parents often cannot know exactly what their needs are. It is a time when reacting is the only coping mechanism. Anticipating is difficult and sometimes impossible. But it does help to know that they can express their feelings in a nonjudgmental atmosphere. The parents may react to the same comment or situation in a totally different way from one day to the next. They may be unusually outspoken, sometimes to the point of being blunt, or withdrawn. Patience is the ultimate virtue in companions.

We cannot develop or apply any test to determine what would help any particular family, for people differ and have diverse needs. All the same, not doing or saying anything has the effect of screaming, "Leper, unclean," at these families. It is better to attempt something than to do nothing:

> Remember the baby's name and use it. It makes us feel good that others are willing to keep our child in their memories. We certainly don't want him erased from ours, and it is pleasant to share those remembrances we hold dearly in a relaxed and natural way.

For the long term we have to accept that these families are changed and will never be exactly what they were before. We cannot expect them to get back to normal when what was reasonable is no longer:

> After two or three months the novelty of what had happened was in the past for everybody but my husband and me and our other daughter. We were expected to carry on, stop hurting, act normal, and go on with our lives like nothing had happened. I think if I had

been allowed to grieve longer or had not been expected to be so strong for everyone else's sake, it would have been better. I got so tired of hearing how strong I was . . . or how well I was taking it. I felt that I wasn't allowed to have bad days—or at least nobody understood if I did. I think being told how strong I was made me feel that I had to live up to everybody's expectations of me, and I tended to bury my feelings instead of dealing with them.

Time, patience, and acceptance: these are the things parents told us over and over in so many ways that they needed from those around them.

Rating the Professionals

Those responding to our survey were asked to rate the professionals they dealt with at the time of the death on a scale of 1 (excellent) to 5 (poor); they were then asked to comment on their rating. Not everyone who answered had contact with all of the professionals listed in the survey.

Many of those who were on the front line—usually emergency medical technicians (EMTs), fire fighters, law enforcement officials, physicians, nurses, and other hospital personnel—were rated. Generally speaking, all state governments have developed procedures to be followed in the event of a sudden death; many, however, are protocols for homicides. It also appeared that the professionals' need to follow the routine and the standard procedures when a baby dies can sometimes outweigh immediate concern for the surviving family members. Because of a heightened awareness of child abuse, many professionals receive training to help them recognize physical trauma and resulting death, but surprisingly, they do not recognize characteristics of SIDS, even though it is the single leading cause of death for infants between birth and one year.

Survey participants tended to agree that overall, EMTs, law enforcement, and fire fighters did a fine job responding to the crisis when the baby died. Many of the parents or others who were caring for the baby had attempted CPR, and they expressed frustration that their lack of skill and knowledge prevented resuscitation of the child. Many had received CPR instructions by phone before the EMTs arrived. Emergency personnel did a uniformly excellent job in reassuring the parents that they had done everything possible.

Even with the most sophisticated equipment in some of the best hospitals, these babies do not survive. Emergency personnel, first on the scene, not only managed the medical situation, but generally also found the time to be supportive and helpful to families.

Those who were usually involved next were hospital personnel. Of 114 surveys, 95 rated physicians, who, overall, received the greatest number of low scores. To understand this phenomenon, we need to remember that in our society physicians are seen by many people as "givers of life." Death is the enemy, and medicine is the battleground upon which physicians strive to emerge victorious. When the small patient dies, this is the ultimate failure for the doctor, as well as for the parents. For both it inspires rage: "What do mean there's nothing we can do?"

As a result, physicians were often judged most harshly. Because of the general perception of doctors' power and control, which leads to expectations beyond the capability of any human being, criticism is bound to be severe. Low ratings may also reflect the unrealistic expectations that some physicians have of themselves, and their apparent sense of defeat is communicated by what they say or do.

In their criticism these families did not, in the end, blame the doctor for the death of the baby. Usually they had found their infants lifeless and recognized on a basic primal level that they faced death. What they really objected to in the doctors was a lack of human warmth. Adjectives such as *cold, detached,* and *distant* were used to describe the physicians who received poor ratings. Explanations by the parents of their ratings included comments that the physician was "just there to do a job," and "not educated, as lost as I was," or there was "limited contact, what conversation did take place was business-oriented only." A physician who lacked emotion, or some sign of human compassion and caring, usually got poor ratings. On the other hand, those doctors who expressed some kind of personal grief were rated higher: "The physician trying to revive our son had tears in his eyes as he told me our baby was dead." Another family shared their experience:

> The doctor did an excellent job because we were in a different town
> from where we live so that doctor at the hospital was not our doctor.
> He truly acted like he cared and did all he could to make us feel at
> ease. After he heard the preliminary results of the autopsy, he called

us to let us know what he found out. He also called our own personal physician who in turn called us and talked to us about what happened.

Follow-up is also an important factor in determining these parents' satisfaction with the physician:

[The] pediatrician arrived immediately and gave me SIDS literature, assuring me it was not anyone's fault. [He] came back later that day to check on me. He called and made sure I received an autopsy report.

Death is a very personal event and should be handled in a personal way. "Our pediatrician was extremely supportive, called every day, came by for a visit"—these and other efforts seemed to touch the families deeply, leaving them with a sense that the physician cared:

The hospital staff was incredible; the doctor and the nurse were great personally and professionally. [The] ER physician was very gentle in explaining our daughter's death. He did not act rushed. He spent a lot of time with us.

Sensitivity is really the key to the comfort people felt with all the professionals they were involved with. Although this was not stated directly, in fact the emotional response of the professional indicates to family members a sharing of the death. Feelings of isolation were expressed by those families who were met with an indifferent or unsympathetic response.

The presence of a nurse can be of great solace, as one mother reported: "The ER nurse was comforting and sincere. She stayed with us and talked to us as we held our baby for the last time." Another family described a different experience: "I have never felt it was necessary shoving papers in my face while waiting in the ER. I feel it could have waited."

Professionals should be aware that their own requirements for organization and routine are simply a strategy for minimizing their own feelings of sorrow. But is it really "professional" to remain stoic, particularly in a situation that demands a different response? As one family reported, "The nurses were really special, truly, because they cared. They stayed with us in the waiting room and tried to make us feel as comfortable as they could." Another family whose son was kept alive for a few days on life supports said, "[The nurses were] very sensitive, I was touched by the dignity with which the nurses treated our comatose son. They changed his diaper frequently, massaged his legs with lotion, and were very caring."

These gestures express love for a baby who has died, and this is the ultimate tribute: it says that he or she lived, died, and was important. As this parent put it, "The nurses were very helpful; they let me hold him and say a goodbye prayer for about twenty minutes."

The importance of the last time with the baby after death cannot be minimized. All the parents in our study emphasized the significance of that moment. Those who had not held their baby one last time expressed regret that they hadn't. Some, after given the choice, did not hold their baby. But others were not given the option, or, as this mother said, "The nurse wouldn't let us stay with our son and rushed our time with him." At times the professional reaction was insensitive to these parents who wanted to spend time with their dead infant. Some professionals treated the parents as if their desires were morbid and unhealthy. If physicians, nurses, or others could quantify how much time it takes to say goodbye to a baby—how much time it takes to let go of all the heartfelt expectations of lives together—then we could say to a grieving parent, this much and no more. But of course professionals haven't a clue. When allowed to take as much time as they needed, parents didn't stay for long periods of time but left the baby when they were ready.

> I should have been able to spend time with my baby alone at the morgue. Instead the medical examiner just stood there till I was ready to leave. He didn't let us have private time. He just stood there and made me feel like we had to hurry up.

Many doctors and nurses offered medication to help alleviate the parents' grief. But medication, although accepted by many, was not felt to be helpful. It prolonged the pain and added an even more surreal quality to the nightmare of death.

Coroners and medical examiners were often singled out for high praise. In their narratives, families expressed their gratitude that someone explained what little is known about SIDS—these families are hungry for information and want all the facts. Parents who had an opportunity to sit down with the coroner and go over the results of the autopsy described a sense of satisfaction that they know all there is to know at this time.

It is important to remember that since coroners work with death on a daily basis, they should be better at explaining death than most professionals. Many parents wanted and received copies of the autopsy report. Although many had an opportunity to go over the report with a doctor, others did not and wished they had. The autopsy report will be able to state an actual "cause" of death: SIDS by definition is death without a known cause. The hardest part of the autopsy and resulting report is the lack of concrete "reasons." How do you respond when an "otherwise healthy baby" dies? Once again, families are left with the inexplicable: the baby died and no one knows why.

Religion promises so much: "He that believeth in me, though he were dead, yet shall he live; and whosoever liveth and believeth in me shall never die." Most of us learned lessons like these at an age when magical thinking prevailed. We carry over into adulthood, however, the deep-rooted yearning for the power of miracles, for the absolute control of God. For bereaved parents, finding a balance between the mystical thinking of childhood and the concrete reality of the death of a baby can be a terrible struggle.

Religious professionals noted in the study included ministers, priests, one rabbi, and several nuns. The religious professionals received many "excellent" ratings and few poor ratings.

For many people, spiritual beliefs have the power not only to generate guilt, but also to absolve and forgive, releasing families from their guilt. "Your baby is in heaven with God" and "She's in the hands of God" are two examples of statements that were comforting for many believers.

Many families, regardless of their religious orientation, find that they simply have to believe in a concrete interpretation of God, in heaven, in angels. It all has to be true for them, for the alternative is too horrible to imagine: that the little baby is in a box, in the ground, cold and alone. There has to be something beyond the pain and grief of death. Life, short or long, must hold some kind of meaning. We can only feel, hear, and taste death; its meaning is unintelligible to us. One day perhaps we will know the truth.

Funeral directors received the highest number of excellent ratings. This should not be surprising, as the vocation involves working with death and grieving families. The stereotype of a greedy, insensitive profiteer was replaced by the reality of the most caring, concerned individual many of these families had contact with. "Compassionate, understanding, and efficient, knew what to do at the right time," one family reported. Another family shared their experience:

> Our funeral director charged us only the cost of the casket; he went out of his way to make our funeral beautiful and appropriate for a child. They allowed us to spend as much time with him as we wanted.

Social workers and counselors had the fewest contacts with families, in our study. This was unfortunate because they could be a great deal of help. Some states now require public health nurses to be knowledgeable about SIDS and to contact families. From the surveys it would seem that hospital staff need to learn more about SIDS, and should be able to provide information and phone numbers for these families so that they can contact support groups that meet in their areas.

SIDS support groups and Compassionate Friends, a national organization for bereaved parents, perhaps provided the most support and help to these families. It is important to have someone there who really understands, someone to listen and know the experience. Many of these families have maintained contact with their support groups for years, have become SIDS contact persons themselves, and have started new groups. They feel that if the death of their child is to have any meaning, they need to help other families find peace with the world and with themselves.

After the cards and letters have stopped coming, when the phone is silent and the last casserole dish has been returned, a stillness descends on these families. This is the time bereaved parents really need to have other people around. Death is not a short-term event for these families; they need ongoing, long-term support and care. We must not attempt to force them back into what we perceive to be reality. Rather, we need to listen and talk about death with them, and talk about the baby. It's essential to talk about the dead child. After all, a dead child is no mystery to these parents. They know all about it.

Testimony: "We Really Are Parents! He's Going to Be with Us a Long Time"

When this mother shared her story with us, it had been nine years since her son died at the age of one month.

"We moved from a large urban center to a farm in a very rural area when we had been married eleven years. We were in our early thirties. As planned, I was soon pregnant with our first child. I did not seek work, knowing I would want to quit in a few months to stay home with the baby. My husband was a traveling salesman, home two weeks, away two weeks at a time. We knew no one in the two closest communities and didn't have any family close by. My pregnancy was a healthy, full-term one. My son was born on Easter Sunday. He died the evening of Mother's Day that same year.

"We had put our son in his crib that night. He cried for a while and fell asleep. I went to bed soon after and checked on the baby as I went. He was in the corner of his crib. My husband came in and moved him to the center. He remembers that he could feel the baby breathing deeply and regularly. It was a warm night—no blanket, no sleeper, just a T-shirt and diaper. As we stood whispering above him (We really are parents! He's going to be with us a long time.) his skin became pale. My husband picked him up, shook him; we called his name loudly—no response whatsoever, limp and very white. My husband began mouth-to-mouth [resuscitation] in his arms and then on the floor. As I left the room to call the rescue unit, I looked back, and my husband raised his head, and I saw blood trickling from our son's nose and mouth. He was deep blue. I knew he was dead. It took a total of thirty to forty-five seconds. He was DOA at the hospital.

"We decided on a memorial service and cremation. The service was necessary but difficult, the beginning of bearing up, being strong, putting everyone else at ease. Very few there had even seen our son alive and this increased the loneliness. The memorial service was socially, for me, very unpleasant. Spiritually, it was very important, encouraging and affirming of our son's life on earth and in heaven, and an expression of our faith in God, our source of strength to go on living, and our hope in eternal life.

"Individuals who were the most helpful during this time were those few who were able to accept our son's life and death as part of our lives. They remembered us with a phone call or just a few words in passing at Easter and Mother's Day. They are willing to listen with interest and a lack of obvious discomfort if our son's name or SIDS comes up in a conversation.

"Other people were less than helpful, and there seems to me to be two extremes. The first I think of as mushy, drippy sweet. 'You poor dear,' they would say, and 'You deserve happiness.' But they don't ask questions or listen, they don't make themselves available. The other extreme is the cool, cerebral type. If you are mature, intelligent, or spiritually right, you keep your pain to yourself, grieving for a few months privately and then putting it behind you. To speak the child's name is not only unnecessary but melodramatic. And to speak of it publicly is a neurotic need to make a career out of a private matter, like talking about sex or worse.

"After the cards and letters stopped coming, I was ready to receive them. I wish the supportive things done the first month could have continued the whole first year: food, visits, cards, phone calls, general sensitivity.

"Three months after our baby died, my husband was ready for another baby. He said, 'Our son lived, he died, it's in the past, let's move on.' But I was only four months from giving birth, three months past breast feeding. I was fat, out of shape, and still involved with letting our son go. I wanted to be a mother to that child, not another. I wasn't ready.

"People said, 'You're doing so well.' They seemed surprised I was able to smile, to walk, to talk, to function. No one asked how I felt, how I slept, what I thought. If you are not tearing your hair out, you're okay: 'You're so strong.' People were relieved. It became my job to put people at ease, to make them comfortable with me. I would be letting them down to show pain, confusion, sadness. Even so, women would not talk about pregnancy, babies, or children in from of me. The subject was changed when I joined a group. I wanted to share my first pregnancy and delivery experience. The one close friend I had made since we moved was so upset by my son's death that she only came to see me once more. I never saw her again. Only one friend included me in mother talk. Occasionally she would simply ask, did I use disposable diapers, and so forth—she recognized my motherhood.

"The only other supportive experience outside our marriage during the first two years after our son died was attending a regional meeting of the National Sudden Infant Death Syndrome Foundation. Five months after the death of our son, I met other SIDS parents for the first time and heard their stories. I even found that my experience was helpful to them. They were intensely relieved to hear that our son had not cried out or struggled as he died. One mother cried as she told her story in our motel room, eight years after her baby died. I thought possibly then it was all right that I cried once in a while.

"Generally during this time I was alone, and eight months after the death of our son, I went into a depression. I didn't move for a month. My husband made supper most of the time. I couldn't feel anything. I probably needed professional help at that point, but neither my husband nor I knew what was wrong or what to expect. Was this normal grief? I thought of the mental health clinic. What would I say if I went there? I'm not an alcoholic. I haven't attempted suicide. I just needed to talk about my baby. Do people go to a mental health office because they have no one to talk to? I didn't know. Besides, I am an intelligent, educated person; I should be able to handle this, I was taught self-sufficiency early. Also, as a Christian, isn't my faith supposed to be enough? Don't I have enough faith? If I do, and I thought I did, I should find God's strength sufficient. If I don't, where do I go with that answer? Somehow, I came to realize that I had to grieve, my own way, no matter what my husband, family, or the world thought. I cried hard and loud. I told God how painful it was, that I wasn't strong at all, that I missed my son. I wrote about it. I talked to the paper. Gradually, I began to feel again, move again. Energy and ambition returned. I think my husband had been holding his breath, hoping this would pass quickly. Friends helped him understand that I needed acceptance from him, time, and patience. He was great and has been very supportive ever since, listening mostly.

"One year after our son died, I told my husband I was ready for another baby. The next week I was pregnant. This time I was confined to the house and even bed with severe vomiting, constant bleeding, and early contractions. I prepared to lose another baby while praying for him to live. Our second son was born almost six weeks early, but after ten days in the hospital we took him home without complications. He was behind in development the first two years, as most preemies are. My biggest fear was not SIDS—that was the second biggest—it was retardation. It wasn't until his first year in kindergarten, when he came home with a 100 percent or 'excellent' across the top of his paper that I felt sure he was really all right.

"I was aware early that I wasn't giving myself to my second son as I had to our first son. I loved him but from an emotionally safe distance. One morning when he was two years old, he was playing on the dining room floor. I glanced at him and a thrill went through me. He's mine; he's my child. An unadmitted, unconscious fear was released, and I felt for the first time the joy that I had known for our first son from the first moment I saw him.

"We had wanted three or four children, and time was running out, but, fearful of a third difficult experience, we did not have our next child for four years. After recharging myself during this time I was again eager for another baby. I ordered a normal baby this time, please. I wanted to relax and enjoy a new baby this time like other people do. I was very involved with SIDS work, church activities, and farm-related projects. I would take this baby with me everywhere. This time I was an experienced breast-feeding mother who wouldn't be isolated from important work and friends. I had an uneventful, full-term pregnancy, the easiest birth ever, and a healthy baby who was breathing quite well, the nurses and doctor said. As knowledgeable as I was, however, I couldn't responsibly ignore the new screening process for SIDS siblings at the hospital. We were convinced that the tests would simply reassure us that indeed we had the normal baby we had requested. We were shocked when we were told that our new son had shallow breathing and periodic breathing, that he was in danger of dying, and he needed medication and a monitor immediately. When I asked some questions, the response was, 'You don't want another SIDS baby do you?' What was I supposed to answer to that!

"So, for nine months we lived with a monitor and an abnormal baby. People still ask how our 'SIDS baby' is, or how our sick baby is doing. He's now almost three years old, and still they ask. Again,

I had to deal with the public's insensitivity and discomfort. The same people who had cuddled and played with our second son were afraid to hold this baby. Those who wanted to hold him didn't understand the restrictions of time, distance, and skills should he require emergency aid. Some assumed we were overreacting to our first son's death by having a monitor. They treated us condescendingly. A new pastor said, 'All parents wonder if their baby is breathing.' And others said, 'Be happy you have the monitor.' There were echoes of 'Be joyful, your baby is in heaven.' Others had to tell us of every baby they ever heard of who had stopped breathing but was revived by an alert mother who knew enough to shake her baby in time. Simple, huh? All the while we were answering mostly false alarms as if this could be another life or death moment, another DOA.

"This baby did not go everywhere with me. 'The monitor doesn't need to change your life,' a technician had said. 'You just can't drive alone with him to get groceries.' Living as we do, five-and-a-half miles from town, without available neighbors or family, this was more than a minor restriction. We also had to make sure that our four-year-old understood that the monitor was important enough not to be touched, without alarming him. Even during my pregnancy, he had been asking, will this baby die too? My husband and I didn't go out alone together until our baby was ten months old. And again, I faced the reserve, the renewed guilt. If I'm exhausted and don't want to answer the third alarm between midnight and 4:40 A.M., does this mean I don't love my baby enough? You don't want another SIDS baby, I told myself. And more if onlys, why mes, and will I handle it well if this one dies too? Will I even survive it?

"I had never been aware of much anger toward God, people, or whatever. A lot of frustration, loneliness, guilt, but almost no anger. It puzzled me: anger is on the list of grief symptoms I describe in my talks to SIDS parents. Six and a half years after my baby died, I was watching a movie, when the son in the movie admitted he was angry at his brother for drowning. I burst into tears. Movies never make me cry ordinarily, and I realized I was angry with my baby for dying. By then I was finally convinced that I really had been a good mother to my baby. I was not to blame. I did my part. My baby's part was to live. He didn't. I cried for only five minutes or so and felt enormously relieved and amazed. I suppose it was such an unthinkable thought to blame a four-week-old baby for anything, especially his own death, especially by his own mother, and I had shoved these thoughts, way, way down.

"One of the most perplexing qualities of grief during these years has been one of balance. At times I have wanted to assure people that the period of time even immediately following a death is not necessarily all heartbreak. It is possible to find positive developments along with the negative. Remembering our baby who died is sometimes painful, often warm and loving, even joyful. But while expressing those positive feelings, I am afraid of denying the depth of pain, and vice versa. Sometimes the joy and pain are exactly one.

"In the first years, this duality made it difficult to explain, even to myself, what I was experiencing. Should I be humming along with the radio as I water plants and enjoy a sunny morning just four weeks after my child has died? Why am I hearing cries that aren't coming from the nursery anymore? Why am I sitting here sobbing and aching in pain when I have just thanked God for the wonderful gift of eternal life for my baby? How can I laugh at a joke when I feel so empty, numb with sadness? Joy does not deny pain; pain does not deny joy. Now, mourning my child does not mean I am not absolutely thrilled to have two living children. My emotions, joy and sadness, exist side by side."

10

What Should I Say to a Grieving Person?

People grieve in many different ways. Some isolate themselves from others, some become overly involved in others' lives, some turn to alcohol and drugs as a way to cope, some try to kill themselves, some just cry, and some stuff their emotions deep down inside and hope that the pain will somehow simply disappear.

Mourning the death of a loved one is expressed in many ways, just as the attempt to express comfort is shared in various ways. Some people avoid the subject of death and grief out of their own discomfort with the topic; some try to address the issue of death by sharing what they believe to be reasons for the death and by saying that it happened for the best; some act as if the death never happened; and some send cards and listen and just share their presence with the grief-stricken survivors.

What can you say to a bereaved parent or grandparent? What can you do to help? It is difficult to generalize. What might be helpful for one person could provoke anger in another. The response often depends on the individual personality, on the setting, and on the time and place.

For example, one woman pointed out,

> Nobody can know exactly what to say to a grieving parent. Things that at the time may seem right can be very wrong. But a simple "I'm sorry" can mean so much. A hug or tear also helps the parents to realize that the grief is not totally his or hers.
>
> I didn't like my mother-in-law's attitude of martyrdom. She acted as though she was the only one who cared. My parents couldn't understand her attitude, and they were truly grieving also. She wanted

to know how we could think of replacing Timmy. She can't understand that Timmy can never be replaced.

In this chapter, we will look at what parents and grandparents thought was helpful and also what was not so helpful as they journeyed through their own grief after the loss of their child or grandchild.

How Others Helped

They listen and try to see things from my point of view. They truly care and are sympathetic. They know I'm hurting and let me know they love me and will be there when I need them. Hugs and squeezes of the hand sometimes mean more than words now. The real friends do not try to minimize my grief by telling me about something worse.

Just being there to talk with or getting me out so I don't dwell on sad thoughts.

We share feelings and then we find things to laugh about, anything, nothing in particular, maybe just a silly situation. I find laughter helps as much as tears, when shared by someone who cares.

[They] attempt to find positive aspects of the situation.

They offer factual information.

They just listen.

Just assuring us that it wasn't our fault. That these things do happen sometimes.

Mostly—just being there. No one can ease your pain; only time does that. But friends and family who support your "down days" and share your "up days" really help. We used the SIDS support group only for information, but knowing they were there and caring was a help.

We had some masses said for us. I have a dear friend to talk to, and my sisters and an out-of-town friend were so good to drop a card and letter [to me] about once a week.

Most people expressed their sympathy; some brought desserts.

They have been there for us. They would keep dropping in and bringing food and cakes and things so that we didn't have to worry about cooking for about six weeks after the baby died.

Our neighbor lady met me on the street by the store one day in town shortly after the loss of my grandson, and she handed me a written note telling me how she felt. This was my friend whom I had forgotten to call. She took time off from work and came to the service at the chapel, bringing a plant for the baby's parents. She came early to be able to put her arms around me and to console me for a while. This meant a lot to me. And young adults are good today, not like some people think they all are. The parents' friends came and shared their grief as well as happy times, standing by their side through it all. They also gave my husband and me both a hug.

Just listen to me talk about her death—that's the most important part of helping me.

Mention my grandson to me.

They let me talk about it.

People do not talk about it now. The subject of the loss of my grandchild never comes up. At first, however, everyone was here to share the immediate grief, funeral, and so forth. I don't know what I would have done without that help. But after the first week everyone avoided the subject.

Many phone calls saying that if I want to talk about it that they are there. Some friends still ask me if they can help and ask how I'm doing.

They came to the funeral, called, or sent cards. It showed me they cared. Some friends came to visit or took me to lunch or tried to get me out of the house. The death of an infant breaks even the coldest heart. The people that cried with me and said that they cared and listened when I wanted to talk were the most helpful.

[They] stopped comparing other siblings to the dead baby.

Others have allowed me to talk about it. They were sympathetic without being morose.

[I appreciate it] when they keep expressions of sympathy short and don't get overly carried away.

If people would simply listen. We had so many friends who were just there for us. They would put an arm around us or would cry with us or talk.

A rally of friends, including a co-worker who had experienced the same tragic loss a few years before, which I had not known about. Realizing that such incidents can and do happen in an area previously unknown to us helped greatly. It seemed as though a broadening vision of life materially helped us to "cope."

They have shared with me the grief they experienced when their own child/grandchild died.

It is evident that a person's presence is important to those who are grieving. What the person says does not have to be particularly profound, for who knows, really, what to say?

Some people tend to keep you feeling upset because they avoid you, because they don't know what to say or do. Some people act like they don't believe that SIDS exists. They want you to give another reason why she died so young. People have also said things like, "I guess it was better she died so young because you would have been more attached to her later in life." Others have said, "It was God's way of punishing us for our wrong way of life."

Most people want to be helpful and not add to the pain. Sometimes it can be difficult for even family members and friends with the best intentions; one woman describes her own confusion:

Everyone from doctors, friends, relatives, and ministers all were so helpful. We have many beautiful and loving people in our lives, and they did and have done everything possible for us. The main thing is no matter when or where I needed someone to talk to there was always someone there.

The only thing that might have bothered me is sometimes I would need to be alone to think things through, and then a houseful of company would come that I could have done without for the time being; but they had no way of knowing I was feeling that way at the time.

What Would Have Been Helpful

Many parents and grandparents said that they had a strong support system to help them through their time of grief. These people spent time with them, listened to them, talked with them, and remembered the child after time had passed. Other parents and grandparents stated that they wished certain things had happened after the death of the baby which didn't. Their insights follow:

> We were visited by a representative of a local hospital two days after we lost our grandchild. Their visit was a comfort, but our minds were in such a state of shock that a follow-up visit in about six weeks really would have helped.

> After the first few weeks following the death, people seem to fade away and I found that I was alone a great deal. A little more companionship would have been appreciated.

> Everyone pitched in and did everything for all of us during those first few days, but we could have had help the second week too.

> I wish someone could have helped us understand how these things happen.

> Friends could have prepared the food for after the funeral. The grandmothers and great-grandmothers had to do it. I couldn't think of food at a time like that. It was hard, and I resent having to do that.

> I wish someone could have found the time to call and talk or just send a card and say that they were sorry to hear the news of my grandson's death.

> I needed a reasonable, logical explanation of the death, rather than "We don't know."

> Our names should have immediately been forwarded to a SIDS group. Instead, we had to find one and make the contact several weeks later ourselves.

> We needed more communication from the medical profession. The infant's mother commented about no effort being made to permit a postmortem examination.

How to Help a Grieving Person

For parents and grandparents to get to the place where they can rejoice for the time they did have their baby is a slow, painful process. These parents and grandparents cannot necessarily speed up the process of healing by having or not having another baby. The process is not helped along when well-meaning friends or relatives remove all signs of the baby from the grief-stricken home, unless it is done at the parents' request. Friends and family members who allow parents and grandparents to express doubts, to cry, to vent all the bottled-up emotions of hostility and anger without rejecting them or denying their pain help the parents and grandparents put their confused worlds back into order.

For some specific advice, we asked the parents and grandparents to comment on what they would like others to know about how to help a person who is grieving over a baby's death. The experts speak:

> Let the person suffering the death talk. I know myself, I need to talk. I don't want other people to forget Sara. I need to know that other people remember her too. I have to tell people how I feel, I need to know that they really want to listen and not feel that I'm going crazy because I need to tell people about it.
>
> Some people get upset when I mention the baby's name. They tell me to forget about it. I will never forget.

> If the grieving person wants to talk, cry, or scream, let him or her do it. Just be there to listen, not to judge his or her actions.

> Acknowledge the hurt and give them a hug.

> Be available to listen to what they have to say. Be someone they can show their anger to in the beginning.

> Don't say how fortunate they are to have the other children.

> Say you care. Be willing to listen. If rejected, call again later—even a year later.

> Be patient—it's hard to understand why.

> To talk about the death is the best possible thing to do. Don't ignore the situation.

> Listen to them and don't forget them after a couple of weeks.

> There is a need to talk, without trying to give reasons. No reason is going to be acceptable when you hurt so much. A hug, the touch of a hand, an expression of concern, a willing listener were and still are the things that have helped the most.

Be willing to talk about the child who was and still is a part of the family.

Let them grieve. Do not make them feel guilty. There is enough guilt already.

If you feel like doing something, don't hesitate and wait for them to come to you. They never will. Don't give up after a first attempt if they don't respond the way you think they should. It will take time. Everyone reacts differently. Cards and notes—send lots of them just to let them know you care and are still thinking about them. People not close to the baby will forget in a few weeks' time, and that is when you really need to know someone still cares. Talking really does help. Don't be afraid to cry with them. When someone can shed a few tears with you, you know they really care.

Don't infer that because a baby was so young that the loss is insignificant or that one is "lucky" that one didn't have him [for] several years before he died. I think prayers, thoughtful notes, and listening if people wish to talk about the baby all seem to help.

Just be with them and make them feel you're always available when they need someone to talk to.

People need to know that it hurts a long time.

Nothing can be said to ease the hurt and pain; only your sincere presence and actions [can help].

Realize what an impact a baby has on our lives. They are the "ultimate high" when they are born—the center of the family's attention. Why don't people understand that their death is not trivial? Many think, It was only a baby. People should just say, "I'm sorry." Why do they all try to explain it?

What works in one situation might not work in another. One mother felt great comfort to think that her baby was an angel; but another mother rejected this notion angrily, saying, "I didn't want an angel, I wanted a baby." Statements like "At least the baby didn't suffer" can sometimes trigger a living nightmare of thoughts: "Did he cry out and I didn't hear him? Did he struggle and suffer alone? How will I ever know?" Many of the parents and grandparents in the loneliness of sleepless nights often remember and microscopically examine what relatives, friends, and professionals say to them.

Although there is no simple formula for "what to say or do for a grieving person," there are some things that we communicate verbally or nonverbally which can help restore some peace of mind. It's important to say, "I care," "I will be here if you need me," or "Let me do those dishes" (or make beds, or whatever you can see that needs to be done). The family might really need you weeks later, after the company is gone and the last covered dish has been returned. A call—"Come to dinner," or "Let's go to a movie"— can help move the family into interaction with others which they have been avoiding because they just do not know how to start again.

We must be prepared for outrage, anger, guilt, as well as other responses as we try to comfort a bereaved person. Most of the parents and grandparents felt that they were able to discern the difference between those who were honest and caring and the more self-righteous, unusually self-serving individuals. If we genuinely care, it will come through no matter how we fumble along. It is okay to cry because they will feel that they are sharing their grief, and not that they are making us feel bad. It is perfectly natural to feel bad when a baby dies, so leave the stiff upper lip at home. Follow the cues given by the family members and do not insist on entertaining them with stories of other tragedies, unless you also have directly experienced the death of a child. It is essential that we explore our own feelings about death and come to terms with what we are comfortable with. Our genuineness will come through.

The parents and grandparents in our studies gave evidence of great wisdom, honesty, and compassion. They described the importance of friends who would listen, allow them to be who they were at the moment, and not judge. They wanted to be able to talk about their lost baby because this child will always be a part of their family. The grandparents wanted people to think of them too because the hurt is very real after such a great loss and they also need support. The parents and grandparents suggested that others phone, stop by and visit, send notes and cards, and take the time to show they care—not just immediately after the death, but weeks, months, even years later because the memories last a long time. To others who experience such a loss, these people who have "been there" recommend that they allow the grief to occur and that they not rush it.

The death of an infant to SIDS is a thoroughly devastating experience for parents and grandparents. As with any loss of a loved one, we must find peace within ourselves. This often requires great time and energy as we strive toward better understanding of a complex situation. There are no right or wrong answers, no "proper" ways to mourn, no foolproof plans, and there is no correct time frame within which to complete one's personal journey through the mourning process. Grieving is indeed a process—a lengthy life experience—and not a single moment in time. Grief is a very normal, necessary, and individualized element of the healing process which can have many positive results in terms of personal insight and growth. At this sensitive time, one's life either falls apart or falls in place, or both in turn. One important point that many of the parents and grandparents emphasized was that they realized they had more inner strength than they had originally given themselves credit for.

Testimony: "All I Need to Do Is Talk about It"

This father lost his daughter to SIDS five years ago, and he is still engulfed in pain and sadness. He knows he needs professional help but cannot seek it out because he feels it would be socially and professionally unacceptable. The relationship with his wife has deteriorated because of the stress associated with the death.

"I have been told that normal grief lasts about two years. If that is so, I'm not normal. I still grieve. The guilt I feel is tremendous. I blame myself for not being there when my child needed me the most. My wife and I have grown apart from each other, and I don't even care anymore. I am resented by my son because I am overprotective. I can't sleep at night. I want another child, but I can't physically father another. I know I need help, but I can't get it; I would lose my job. My friends were a great source of support, but my wife has forced me to move away from them, and I now have no one. Contact with my friends only creates problems with my wife. If society had not attached a stigma to seeking the kind of help I needed, I would have been much better off, and maybe my marriage would not be falling apart now.

"My wife found my daughter when she checked on her in the morning. She had died during the night while sleeping on her stomach. Postmortem lividity had set in, and her face was distorted and black. I ran in when my wife screamed. She held my daughter out to me, face first, and told me, 'Do something! Hurry!'

"I have investigated enough deaths to recognize that she was gone. I took her and laid her back in the crib and then went to the phone. I called 911 and told them to send the coroner and the duty sergeant. Then I put my fist through a wall. I couldn't even think. Most of the first few days are kind of lost in a nightmare. But I do remember my son asking what was going on, and my telling him all I knew was that his sister was dead and we didn't know why.

"I have probably had five hundred or more flashbacks, too many to really count. In the flashbacks I see the blackened face of my daughter being shoved at me and the constant, repeating scream saying, 'Do something!' "

[What other major crises have you gone through in your life?] "My father figure (grandfather) died when I was fifteen years old. My mother was murdered four years before my daughter was born. All of the things that I have really loved in my life have been taken away suddenly and without reason.

"For a while after the death I drank pretty heavily. There was also a lot of fighting with my wife. It was mostly yelling, nothing physical. We did separate for a while after the death. The arguments reached a point where physical violence was the next step. I chose to leave before I reached the point of striking her. My wife has feelings that she tries to articulate but can't. So she turns these feelings into anger and accusations that are usually directed at me. I have a lot of guilt about the death that I keep inside simply because it is no one else's fault but my own. So why bother others with my personal problem?

"My wife is really trying to be close to me. She is beautiful and loving, and desirable to most men. Yet I feel as though I don't want or need her. I have often thought that I must be crazy not to want our relationship to grow.

"My wife has lost her desire for sex, and I find I need the physical release now more than ever before. Our sexual relationship is very frustrating.

"I think the death has raised a question in us about our capabilities, and I doubt that either of us is really what we thought we were. My wife has let me know that I am not the person she wanted to marry. There *are* things that I can't control or *make better*. I am less of a man than she thought, and I let her down in a way that is unforgivable. We have seen in each other a different person than we saw when we were first married, and we don't like what we see. We think we made a big mistake.

"The funeral was helpful. We needed it to say goodbye, and we found that we had more friends than we had thought. My son was seven at the time, and having to answer his questions helped me cope with the service. If he hadn't been there I would have lost my mind. I think I was in a daze. I babbled a lot. I just wanted to run away from it all.

"The funeral director was very helpful with factual information, and he knew how to listen. The pathologist contacted us as soon as he had his results (in twenty-four hours) and answered what questions I had. I will never forget his kindness and concern. The doctors, nurses, and priest were sadly misinformed about SIDS. My sister came over and started taking my daughter's clothes (to get them out of the way). I threw her out, physically! My best friend took me out of the house and away from all the people to a cornfield, and gave me what I needed the most—a place to scream!

"The people who are the greatest help to me are not judgmental. It's most helpful when people understand that all I need to do is talk about it and that this is part of the grief process. They just need to let me pour my heart out to them, in confidence, and let me know they are there to help out in any way they can.

"The hardest thing is that I don't have a little girl to hold anymore. I let her down. The memories are hardest on her birthday, the date of her death, Thanksgiving, and Christmas. For some reason Easter is hard, when all the little girls are dressed up in their Easter dresses."

[What good things have you learned about life?] "I wish I could answer this. Right now my life isn't so good. Maybe the only good thing about life is that life goes on. The future? Divorce, probably.

A continued closeness with my son, a reunion with my friends, and a search for companionship. I don't want to make the same mistakes again, and I don't want to hurt my wife any more than I already have."

11

What Do I Tell the Other Children?

The grieving process parents go through when there is a SIDS death is so extremely painful that the loss felt by the surviving children in the family is often forgotten. In our most recent study we explored the experiences of children by asking parents: if the way they cared for other children was affected by the death; what kinds of questions children asked; and whether the children's behaviors changed. We also asked parents to complete a short interview with each of their children and report their responses.

It became obvious very quickly that siblings of the child who died also suffered in their own unique ways. Children wondered whether they had done something to cause the death. They wondered whether their brother or sister had a bicycle in heaven. They wondered whether they would ever be happy again. Some children became more sensitive and caring after the death of their sibling; others became disruptive and rebellious. Many families were involved in family counseling and addressed some of the concerns of the remaining children with professional help. Other parents said they just tried to answer their children's questions as honestly as possible. Parents also expressed frustration at having to answer questions for their children (such as "Why did my brother die?") when they themselves did not know the answer.

The questions the children asked and the thoughts they had about the death help us understand that the death of a child truly affects the entire family. This chapter may help parents and professionals as they try to meet the needs of grieving children.

Caring for Other Children

The parents in the study were asked if there had been changes in the way they cared for their other children as a result of the death. Parents described how their care changed for children already born, as well as children who became part of the family after the death.

Approximately 90 percent of the parents who had other children at the time of the death said they changed the way they cared for these children. Most of the parents said they were more protective of their children and took extraordinary measures to make sure they would not lose another child. One parent said, "I cling to her night and day."

These parents were especially concerned about their children during sleep, since that is when SIDS occurs. Many parents said they would check their children while they were sleeping, even children who were teenagers. One parent said,

> I check all the kids during the night. I should say, my husband does. I've been afraid to.

Here are some typical responses from parents:

> When they were babies, I'd jump up every little while, day or night, to check on them. I remember times I'd check on them and I couldn't tell if they were breathing, and I'd grab them up and start shaking them, and they'd awake and cry. And then I'd feel awful for waking them.

> A crib death is something you never get over. My poor second baby, the times I have jerked him out of the crib (he was asleep) thinking he wasn't breathing. Sneaking into his room at night to feel him—having him sleep with me so I could feel him "alive"!

> I had a subsequent premature baby, and I stayed up nights until 5:00 or 6:00 A.M. the first three months.

> I always worried about their safety. I *always* check on them at night, and my oldest is nine! But it helps me sleep better knowing they're okay. I have also put off putting my sixteen-month-old in another room. I just feel better knowing he's by me. I often find myself lying in bed at night listening to him breathe.

Many parents who had subsequent children put those children on monitors, which seemed to give them some sense of security.

One parent said, "Any subsequent children *will* be monitored." Parents would also have their children sleep with them, as a way of trying to prevent another child from dying. One parent said it was difficult later getting the child to sleep in her own bed. Another parent said, "I did not leave her for at least a year, and she slept with me for the first three months of her life."

Some parents said they spoiled their children. One parent explained that although her husband was very conservative in his spending, he tended to go "overboard" when it came to the children as a result of the SIDS death. Parents also said they were more permissive, and one parent said she had a hard time saying no.

Parents also expressed fear of any sickness and would be more likely to call the doctor, day or night. One mother said she would panic every time the child got hurt. Many parents also seemed to have a different appreciation for their remaining children—they saw them with a different set of lenses after a child had died of SIDS:

> "I am more careful and pay more attention, because they could die anytime."
> "I am overprotective, and I love him more. I feel I love him more than any other parent loves her child."
> "We treat our child as if we may lose him."
> "I think we have more expectations of him."
> "Every day is celebrated!"

Some parents said their priorities have changed: "I can leave the dishes and read a story first, or take a walk with them." Many parents said they spent more time with their other children. One parent said, "I hold her more, take more pictures of her. I'm afraid it will happen to her."

One parent explained how her own grieving affected how she treated her child: "I am inconsistent. Their life isn't stable because mine isn't stable."

One mother said she did everything differently from the way in which she did things for the child who died of SIDS. For example, she and her husband monitored the subsequent baby and bought all new furniture (they had borrowed furniture for the child who died). She said, "I wanted this baby to be permanent. I bought *everything* new, even though I knew I wouldn't have more children."

These parents' responses indicate that most parents become more closely attached to remaining or subsequent children. A small group of parents, however, described an inability to become close to other children:

> I have a hard time dealing with our older daughter who is now six years old. It has gotten better with time, but at first I just didn't have any tolerance for her at all. I pulled myself away from her at first.

> For a long time I was scared to take care of her. When I finally did bring her home, I was constantly shaking her awake to make sure she was alive.

Some parents described an initial inability to bond with a subsequent child:

> I was less willing to "bond." It took weeks to bond to the last child. I was worried sick about bringing him home and was full of anxiety about the delivery, hated the doctor, and felt bitter, although we wanted to have this last child.

Questions Asked by the Surviving Children

The great majority of parents said their surviving children asked questions about the death of the child from SIDS. Parents also described how very difficult it was to answer these questions because of the age and intellectual ability of the child, and because the parents themselves did not have the answers. The most difficult question was probably "Why did the baby die?" The parents described their own frustration as they repeatedly searched for the same answers.

One parent listed a wide range of questions that her children asked about the death:

> Why is he dead? Where did he go? Why did they put make-up on him when he was in that box? When will he come back? Why did they put that box in the ground? Is that how babies grow—you plant them? Why didn't he open his eyes? Isn't he going to get hungry? Shouldn't we feed him? Can we go see him, wherever he is? Why can't Daddy get him back? He is our baby, isn't he? Why is everyone crying?

As we consider the list of questions with which this one parent was inundated, we can begin to realize the difficult responsibility parents have in trying to explain the death to surviving children in the family. These questions concern the difference between a spirit or soul and the physical body; the finality of death; the logistics of a funeral; and why parents cannot solve all problems. It is also clear that even if we could provide all the answers, a young child's mind is not mature enough to comprehend those abstract answers.

The question most frequently asked by children was "Where is the baby?" Or, put in other ways, "Where did she go?" "Where does she live?" Most parents said the baby was in heaven or with God. One parent said, "He is in the spirit world." Another parent said, "He's an angel. The brightest star in the sky is his star!" One parent simply said the baby was buried in the ground. Obviously, young children would have difficulty understanding abstract terms such as *heaven* or *spirit,* and yet there do not appear to be simpler answers.

Another question frequently asked by children was "Why did the baby die?" How does a parent answer this for a young child when parents are supposed to know everything? But of course even experts do not have the answer. Parents most often simply explained that they did not know why the baby died. Here are some of the other answers parents gave:

"He died because he was sick (or had a disease)."
"He quit breathing."
"It was time for her to live with God."
"God wanted him because he was a very special baby."
"God needed her more than we did."

Another question often asked by children was "Will I die, too?" Parents usually responded by saying the child would not die of SIDS because only babies died of SIDS. They would often add that people usually die when they are old. Children would sometimes follow up with questions like "Will you die?" "Will my sister (or brother) die?"

Although these are the most frequently asked questions, children are capable of asking almost anything. Parents should be prepared for a full range of questions. Here are some very complex questions that are difficult for many adults and people in the helping professions to answer:

"Why was he taken?"
"Can we go there too?"
"Did our baby love us?"
"Is he in the ground or is he in the air?"
"Does he miss us?"
"Will I see her again?"
"How did he get to heaven?"
"What does a soul or spirit look like?"
"Will we ever be happy again?"
"Why didn't God save her?"
"Why didn't he look like himself at the funeral?"
"Why did they put make-up on her?"
"Why was she put in a box?"
"Can she see us?"
"Why didn't the toys go to heaven?"
"Does he have a bike in heaven?"
"Will he still be a baby when I get to heaven, or will he be grown up?"
"Will she always be our sister?"
"Is she with Grandpa in heaven?"

A few children asked questions that indicated they felt some guilt over the death of their sibling:

"Was it because I wished her dead?"
"Was it my fault?"
"Did I kill her?"

The children asking these questions will probably need to be assured many times and in a variety of ways that they were not to blame for the death of their brother or sister. When we consider the guilt parents feel because of the death of their child and add to it the guilt some children feel because of the death of a sibling, we realize that the theme of "guilt" is an issue that must be addressed by professionals working with all members of the family.

How do parents answer these questions? The answers vary as much as the questions. A common response on the part of the parents was that they tried to be honest. Their responses often reflected religious beliefs—for example, when children asked, "Will we see her again?" parents' responses differed depending on their religious beliefs. Some parents said, "Yes, we will see her in heaven." Other parents who did not believe in an afterlife said, "No, we will not see her again." The great majority of parents in this most recent study—approximately 80 percent—did have a religious belief that affected their reactions to the death.

There are at least three possible approaches to the problem of what to say to the children after a baby dies:

1. If we do not really know the answer to questions surrounding the mystery of death, we should be honest and say so.
2. If we do not really know the answers, we should tell a comforting story, kind of like a Santa Claus or Tooth Fairy story.
3. If we think we do know the answers, we should tell the children what we believe.

In our opinion, the first and third approaches are acceptable, the second unwise. Why? Because children need comfort in the face of death. They need comfort from adults who can openly and honestly give it. In regard to the first approach many adults are not certain about what happens after death, but they are comfortable with their uncertainty. Children will take their lead and also learn to be comfortable with uncertainty.

If one takes the second approach, however, it could easily backfire. Children are quite adept at "reading" adults, and it is likely that they will find out sooner or later that the trusted adult is really not trustworthy when it comes to talking about difficult subjects. The child could come to believe, especially in adolescence, that parents are guilty of sugar-coating the truth. This can lead to uneasiness: "Is she telling me the truth now, or just making me feel good again?"

The third approach seems quite reasonable to us. If an adult honestly thinks he or she does know the answers to questions about death, it makes sense to give those answers to the child. It also can be helpful to point out that not everyone believes this way, that good people who love each other can have a variety of beliefs. Husbands and wives in successful marriages do not necessarily have the same religious beliefs. And families are often torn by religious controversies when some individuals try to impose their beliefs on others. Tolerance of differences is the key.

Helping children talk openly and honestly about their thoughts on death and religion in general can have great benefits for families, creating an atmosphere in which open communication can lead to solutions to life's dilemmas. Parents do not need to know the answers to all the terrible questions life poses. We only need to be able to face these questions honestly with our children and help them find a way with us out of the wilderness.

Changes in the Children's Behavior

More than two-thirds of the parents said there was a change in the behavior of the remaining children after the death of the baby. Many parents realized that their own grief kept them from being as attentive to their children's needs as they had been before the death. And this is okay. Sometimes it is enough just to get out of bed and remember how to tie your shoes. Many parents indicated that their children regressed in their development. Children began wetting the bed or they went back to using diapers when they had been toilet trained before the death. One mother said,

> She seemed to regress in bed-wetting and in the need for security items such as a blanket and a pacifier. We had just gotten them away from her before the death.

Another mother said, "He started pretending to be a tiny baby again." Parents also said their children became "clingy"—they stayed close to their parents, when previously they had been secure enough to play independently and spend time alone. One parent said the children "had new fears, were more frightened of being left alone, of losing another family member."

Several parents said their children had trouble with sleep. It is unclear whether the children were associating their own sleep with the siblings' dying in their sleep. One mother said her eight-year-old was afraid to go to sleep. Other parents described their children's difficulties with sleep:

> He would never let us close his bedroom door at night or turn the light off. He still needs to have a hall light on as well as a night light.

She became afraid of the dark. She still is afraid two years later.

Our daughter still needs reassurance at night that we'll stay upstairs until she's asleep. For at least a year she would not spend the night away from home.

He would wake up at night and scream for one to two hours. The lights would have to be on. We are predominantly over this now. Thank God!

Several parents said their children became harder to discipline:

She got harder to discipline and acted up more for attention. I think this was my fault, because I was so wrapped up in myself that I didn't give her the attention she had been used to. But time heals, and with time we have learned things all over again. We just have a different relationship.

She was extremely active, almost out of control.

She was more moody, more disorderly. She tried harder for attention.

Three parents with older children indicated that their children had trouble at school. Two of these parents said their child had difficulty concentrating at school, and that the grades suffered (this response was mentioned by many other parents). The third parent said the child became a behavior problem in school after the death.

A few parents said their children became more sensitive and co-operative as a result of the death:

They all (five boys) matured. There was a greater sensitivity, more compassion for others, a deeper understanding of life.

He seemed to be more respectful of our feelings. He seemed to open up about his own feelings. He would talk to us honestly about other matters that concerned him.

Parents also said their children would reenact the events surrounding the death during play. A parent of children ages two and four said,

They play-acted things with their toys that they had heard concerning the baby's death and things they saw at the funeral.

Another parent said,

They do not like to see babies, either in real life or in pictures, but they do play with their dolls a lot and sometimes name them [the dead child's name] or talk about their baby being sick. But they always get better.

Some children make connections that would only make sense to children. One parent said her child was "terrified of men in uniforms." The child had seen the paramedics who took the baby away and did not bring him back. Another parent said,

> He thinks helicopters have a direct line to heaven and back. The last time he saw the baby, she was rushed from the sitter's to the hospital by helicopter.

Although most of the problem behaviors as seen by parents were difficult to deal with, especially since the parents were doing their own grieving, they seemed to be the kinds of behaviors that would go away with time. In three cases, however, there were more severe reactions on the part of siblings:

> When our daughter [a child of three and a half] sees other babies, she will tell the mother our baby died. She is very demanding and naughty, almost all the time. She has been potty trained for almost two years, and now she has a hard time making it to the bathroom. She hangs on me and will hardly let me out of her sight. One day she said to me that she got mad at the baby and made him cry, and that's why he died. I explained to her that it wasn't her fault. The next day I placed her in a preschool, and they have helped her much more than we ever could, since we are so close to the tragedy.

> She [the baby who died] was very special to him [a young adult, age twenty]. When she died, he began having severe problems in school and at home. These diminished somewhat after a year, but reoccurred with his subsequent brother's birth. He ran away from home in the middle of the night, because he was afraid he would cause the new baby to die by staying in the house. Only now, two years later and with the help of a family therapist, are conditions beginning to improve.

> Our son who is mentally retarded was more withdrawn than usual after the funeral. He was also more aggressive. He was not able to express himself in words, so he took it out physically. About six weeks after the funeral he came home from the preschool with rope

burns. He had managed to hang himself in a venetian blind rope. It really scared us as we were not sure . . . still not.

Interviews with the Surviving Children

Seventy-three children were interviewed by their parents about the death of their sibling. The following section includes several case studies of children's feelings about the death of a brother or sister.

A ten-year-old boy said,

> I loved my brother. I loved the way we kissed and hugged, and we would make funny faces and noises at each other. He especially liked it when I gave him candy.
>
> When I think about him I feel sad, because I miss him. He went to live with God and the man on the cross [Jesus]. I am sometimes afraid when I think about the baby, because he is gone, but I know he is in heaven.
>
> When I feel sad about my brother dying, the best thing you can do is to hug me and tell me that you love me.

An eight-year-old boy said,

> The thing I remember about the baby was that he had a stuffed clown, he had a baby swing, and he was born at Christmas time.
>
> It makes me sad that he was buried *in* the ground, under dirt. That also makes me afraid. If I'm feeling sad, it makes me feel better when you show me his book of pictures.

A seventeen-year-old girl remembered these things about her brother who died:

> He didn't seem very happy or healthy, and he was always crying. He was sick and something was wrong, and he wasn't meant to live. I arranged my life so I was away from home when a later child was between three and five months of age, so I wouldn't be around if something happened.

A five-year-old boy described his feelings about his sister who had died:

> I remember that she was pretty, and she was a good sister, a friend. After she died she was cold. Now I miss her because I can't play with her and hug and kiss her. Thoughts that make me happy are

when I remember that she was kind, huggable, snuggable, wiggly, and little.

She died because she didn't have enough power to stay alive. When I'm feeling sad about her, I want you to give me a hug and a kiss.

An eight-year-old girl remembered her sister:

I know that she died of crib death. She was in a deep sleep and forgot to breathe. We didn't have her on a monitor, so she died. Sometimes I'm afraid that I might die. Sometimes I think I might never get to see her again up in heaven.

When I feel sad about her death, I want you to have me sit on your lap. It also helps if you try to make me happy by playing around with me and kidding me.

A fourteen-year-old boy said this:

I wonder what she would be like if she were still alive. Sometimes I get sad when I think about the baby, because I used to tell my mom I wished she hadn't had another baby. I worry that it might be hereditary and might happen to one of my kids or someone close to me.

When I am sad about the baby dying, just let me talk about how I feel.

A six-year-old girl had these thoughts about her brother:

I remember that he wore blue most of the time. He would be two years old now. It makes me sad when I think that he'll never get any more teeth and his hair will never grow. I dream about him.

He died because when he took a nap, he held his breath too long. When I feel sad about his death, just hug me!

One mother asked her two-and-a-half-year-old about the baby who died. He said, "Pretty baby, all gone, huh, Mom?" When asked if they should have another baby, he said, "No more babies."

Clearly, subsequent and/or surviving children have needs, questions, and concerns about the sibling who died. Children have been said to be the lost souls of a family in crisis. Parents are often so numb from the death of a baby that they are immersed in their own thoughts and they spend little time relating to the surviving children. Most specialists in the area of grief counseling would agree, however, that it is important to talk with the surviving children about their feelings.

Here is a list of questions a parent could ask surviving children. These questions could help begin a useful dialogue between parent and child, and help parents become more informed about the feelings of their children regarding the death.

> What do you remember about the baby?
> When you think about the baby, what are you thinking?
> What makes you sad when you think about the baby?
> What makes you laugh or feel happy when you think about the baby?
> Do you know why the baby died? Could you tell me?
> Should we have another baby?
> Are you sometimes afraid when you think about the baby?
> What should I do to make you feel better when you're feeling sad about the baby?

If you as a parent wish to talk with your child, sit down when you are relaxed and the child is also relaxed, maybe after dinner. Let the child know you would enjoy talking about the baby, and hope that he or she would like to talk about the baby with you. Good questions are open-ended and can take the parent and child in many directions.

The parents themselves provide the best advice for families who must go through this experience: Be honest! Even very young children will have questions. They will need very simple answers, answers consistent with their understanding of the world. The children in these families also have a clear message that when they felt sad about the death, they needed "to be hugged," "to be loved," "to look at pictures," or just to talk about the child who died. Children in families where there has been a SIDS death definitely need to be included in the grieving process.

Testimony: The Surviving Children

Almost four years after her son died of Sudden Infant Death Syndrome, this mother shares her story:

"Our son of three and a half months had been attempting to sit up. That night I let him stay up so he could show off for his dad. About nine I put him to bed, and later we went to sleep.

"When we woke up in the morning, we looked at each other and knew that the other had not been up with our baby in the night. My husband took off down the hall to the baby's room. I thought, He's at that age when he will be sleeping all night. Then I heard my husband's scream and knew something was wrong. I said, 'Oh God, no' as I went down the hall. I had to push around my husband standing in the doorway. At first it looked as though the baby had vomited all over his face, but once I got to him I knew he was dead. Still, I unzipped the sleeper to feel his chest for respiration or heartbeat, but in my mind I knew he was gone.

"We called the police, and soon the police and ambulance were sent out. They went past our house, and I had to run out to have them turn around. The EMT was the first one in. He went to the room, looked, and just turned around and said, 'I'm so sorry,' and held me for a second. The other EMT dropped his equipment when he looked into the room and stood there.

"The police officer was standing in the front doorway and wanted to know the situation. My husband was sitting on the couch in shock, crying. The other children were asking questions about what was going on and who were all the people in the house and why wasn't the baby there.

"I let the police officer use the phone to call the coroner, and while on the phone he reached over to help steady my hand as I was spilling cereal and milk. I kept apologizing to him that usually I was not that messy. I wondered if he thought I was a lousy parent. I mean I was not functioning as a good parent when I could not even give the children cold cereal.

"He told me it would be a while until the coroner could get there. The coroner finally arrived, went into the baby's room, and started the examination. When he was finished, I was allowed to go back into the room. I yelled at him [the coroner] that he could have at least cleaned the baby up. I went and got a warm wash-cloth, like the temperature made a difference, and cleaned him up. I asked if I could hold my baby and was told, yes, for a short time. When I picked him up I tried to cuddle him to my breast, but he was so rigid. I remembered the saying that you cannot break a baby, and felt that I would if I moved him anymore. I looked down into his discolored face and said, 'Forgive me.' I just could not bring myself to kiss his face and kissed his hand instead.

"The coroner told me that was enough.

"I said to him, 'I'll know when it's enough. I've got to say good-bye.' I laid him down and went in to ask my husband if he wanted to say goodbye to the baby. He said no. He couldn't even bring himself to go back into the room.

"I told the coroner that he could not use a body bag and to put it away because I did not want him to scare the other children. He asked if he could use a blanket. I gave him the baby's yellow shawl, and he just threw it on our baby.

"I yelled, 'That's not how it goes.' I picked up our baby and laid him on the blanket right. 'The flowers come up over his head,' I explained to the coroner. We put another blanket over him so as not to let the other children see him.

"As they started out the door, our older son, who was six and a half, reached out and grabbed the baby's leg and asked, 'Why is this man taking him?' I just hugged him and said, 'Our baby's dead, and this man is going to take him.'

"The police officer asked if there was anything else he could do for us and then said he was sorry and left. I went over and sat on the couch by my husband, and we just held each other. The other children by this time were crying and wanting to know what was wrong with us. They had never seen their daddy cry.

"The funeral home called and asked if we wanted the funeral the next day. I said, 'No way. Tomorrow is our anniversary and I refuse to bury my son on that day.'

"My dad and stepmom went to the funeral home with us to make arrangements while my mom watched the other children. When we stopped to pick up the children, my mom said she had been in contact with all of her brothers and her sister and had been given permission to have our baby placed in the lower half of my grandmother's plot.

"The funeral home called after we got home and said he was ready for viewing. I went up to the funeral home alone, but I took the camera. I know that this may sound cold, but I wanted to have the pictures to prepare the children for what they would see.

"The next day we went to view our baby. It was very difficult on all of us. So hard to look at our own dead child and have to explain it to the children. Our daughter, who was four, wanted to keep going back to the funeral home to make sure our baby had not left that home too. The funeral director was very nice about that and let me take her back late at night to tell her dead brother good night. Our son, after looking at the baby, did not want to stay around and went to the back of the room and sat. We made arrangements that if the children did not want to go to the funeral, they would not have to and would be dropped off at day care.

"They both went to the services. Our son went in and just wanted to sit down, and we allowed him to do that. Our daughter wanted to reach in and touch the baby all the time.

"At the graveside service I had the pastor read a child's poem that I had picked out. I remember that the ground was soft from the damp, dewy night. My high heels were sinking into my grandfather's side of the plot. I remember thinking how my grandfather had always said never to stand on a grave out of respect for the person buried there. It was difficult for me to continue to stand. I thought, Hey, Grandpa, he [our baby] was named after you and he is with you, so hold him tight for me and give him love.

"The children's first questions were basic, and we answered them as best we could:

"Why is our baby dead?"

"We told them that we did not know why our baby had died, that it's just something that happens to young babies, but that they did not have to worry that it would happen to them.

"Why did they put make-up on him when he was in that box?"

"They put make-up on him to help him look natural. He had lost his color, and we wanted the funeral people to make him look like our baby."

"When will our baby come back?"

"We explained to them that the baby will never come back to live with us, but he can live in our minds. I reminded them of things they had done for or with him, and said those are memories and no one can take them away, ever.

"Why did they put that box in the ground?"

"The casket goes in the ground at the cemetery, and it's called buried and it happens to everyone who dies."

"Is that how babies grow, you plant them?"

"Babies do not need to be planted to grow. They had not been planted and look at how big they were getting. We went through the photo album with them.

"Why doesn't the baby open his eyes? Isn't he going to get hungry and shouldn't we feed him?"

"When someone or something is dead it does not open its eyes, breathe, or need to eat or go to the bathroom."

"Can we go see him, wherever he is?"

"Someday we all hope to go to heaven, but hopefully that will be a long time from now for you."

"Why can't Daddy go get our baby back—he is our baby?"

"Daddy cannot go and get our baby because he is dead."

"Why is everyone crying?"

"Everyone is crying because they miss our baby and they know he is not coming back and we feel bad about that. It's okay to cry when you're hurting, and we are all hurting."

"As time passed, the children had difficulty going to sleep, would wet their beds, have nightmares and cold chills. There were more temper tantrums, or so it seemed, but we were also very upset. After the funeral they began to realize that the baby was not coming back, and they did not want to leave us, even to spend time at their grandparents'.

"Our son was more withdrawn than usual and then at times much more aggressive. I guess not being able to express himself in words, he took it out with physical frustration.

"Our daughter was always wanting to go to the cemetery to make sure he was still there and had not left us again. She would pretend to call him on her telephone and would have long conversations with him.

"They both wanted to know if he was in the big package that our son received for his birthday party a couple of weeks after the funeral.

"Time has passed. . . . Our son is happy that the baby is in heaven and not down in the other place. He remembers the funeral and how everyone sat with their heads bowed and hands folded. Our daughter remembers going to see him and that he had make-up all over his face. She still doesn't know why they had make-up on him. She is unhappy that he had to die.

"We have a routine that we do for fire and tornado drills, and the first thing we grab is the large photo of our dead baby and take it with us. The tornado siren went off once when we were not home, and the discussion was around "Where does God go when it storms?" I told them that he is above the storm and he is okay. 'That means our baby is safe too, doesn't it, Mom?'

"Both of the children, especially our daughter, think we should have had a monitor for the baby and that he would still be alive. Our subsequent baby was on a monitor and she is still alive, so they want to know why Mommy didn't have our other baby on one. I've asked myself the same question. Why was I so ignorant . . . at least when the monitor went off I would have known that I had done everything I could to save him. He would not have died alone . . . I know he still would have died, because a SIDS baby cannot be revived.

"The children also want to know why the two-year-old (subsequent child) was not asked questions (for the survey) about the death of the baby. I told them that she did not know him. They came right back with 'But he knows her, he knows all of us, he still can see us . . . right?' "

12

Can It Happen Again?
Having Subsequent Children and
the Use of Monitors

What is the likelihood of a second SIDS death in the same family? Are parents' fears that this could happen again realistic? In the early 1980s evidence was found to suggest that subsequent siblings of SIDS victims had an increased risk for SIDS.[1] More recently, however, researchers have concluded that the rate of death for a SIDS sibling is only slightly higher than or the same as it is for children who have no history of SIDS in the family.[2] In fact, researchers Donald Peterson, Eugene Sabotta, and Janet Daling conclude,

> Parents can be advised, with considerably more confidence than in the past, that their risk of loss of a child in the future is virtually the same as that among families of like size and mothers' age.[3]

Parents can be assured that it is very unlikely that a second child in the family will die of SIDS. The parents quoted in this chapter discuss the processes parents go through in making the decision to have subsequent children. Further, the chapter will explore the fears parents have when they decide to have a subsequent child, as well as the effect of monitor use on families.

Having Subsequent Children

We asked parents if the death affected their decision to have other children. One mother responded this way:

At first I was going to get my tubes tied, but another parent talked me out of it. Now we have another child and want more. We know it's a risk, but to me it's like a dare. I've had my one in five hundred.

This case is typical of the changing feelings that parents experience about having a subsequent child. Their feelings about having other children usually changed depending upon when the question was asked. Consequently, parents need to be aware that their feelings will probably change, and they should not do anything irreversible about their reproductive capabilities. Here is an example of one parent's changing attitudes toward having additional children:

The evening of her death I announced I wanted *many* children. My husband agreed. Now (sixteen months later) we're back to two children being the ideal number. We'll see. . . .

Typically, parents initially feel they never want another child, for they do not want in any way to try to replace the child who died. As time passes, they feel they cannot bear the pain of going through another SIDS death, but later, after the pain has subsided somewhat, they decide they want additional children.

I'm not sure how I would react to a child for the first six months. There would be fear that the same thing might happen again. I might be overbearing. [a mother whose baby had died ten months earlier]

I want another one but would be too scared at this point. [a mother whose baby had died one year earlier]

I am feeling so drained that I want to wait a while even though I'm feeling age pressure to complete my family. [a mother whose baby had died six months earlier]

I have been afraid to have other children. I'm afraid to have a sleeping baby in the house, and I'm afraid of it happening again. My husband doesn't seem to be in any hurry. [a mother whose baby had died two years earlier]

At first I didn't want any more children, ever! But later I learned about sleep studies and apnea monitors. I knew they weren't 100 percent effective, but it seemed to put the odds more in our favor. Then we decided to have another child, who is now a happy sixteen-month-old and going strong. [a mother whose baby had died four years earlier]

At first I was scared, but as time goes on and I realize that this happened for a reason and may not necessarily happen again, I feel much more comfortable. [a mother whose baby had died three months earlier]

At first I could not think about ever going through a nightmare like this or putting my family through it. Now I trust the Lord. If it is his will, I would gladly be once more part of the creation of a new human being. [a mother whose child had died four months earlier]

My wife says that she could not have another child. I would like to have another, but I don't think I could sleep with another baby in the house. [a father whose child had died five years earlier]

For this mother it took years to decide to have a subsequent child:

I didn't have one for seventeen years. I was afraid I would not be able to live if something happened to another child.

One mother said she had one child ten months after the death, and "I never worried about him." But with a later pregnancy,

I freaked out! The pregnancy ended in a miscarriage, and it was then I decided to have a tubal ligation. I couldn't handle it again, emotionally.

Another woman said she used birth control after the death to avoid becoming pregnant. She did get pregnant, however, and had a very difficult time: "I would never have another after this last child. It is too difficult to cope."

A few parents had vasectomies or tubal ligations after the birth of the child who died but before the death. Then, after the baby died, their feelings about having additional children changed:

We decided to have another child, even though my husband had had a vasectomy. We had the procedure reversed, which was successful.

My husband had a vasectomy when the baby who died was a week old. I was hoping the vasectomy had been unsuccessful. In a way I'm glad the decision is not ours to make.

I am afraid. I had my tubes tied when I had the baby. But sometimes I want a baby so badly I don't know what to do. I'd have to have my tubes untied, and that's not always successful. I just don't know. It's too soon for me yet.

For several parents the death of a child from SIDS eventually led to the birth of at least one additional child. One mother had another child who would be a companion for the remaining child, and also because she did not want to end her childbearing years with the loss of a baby. Other parents had similar feelings:

Originally my husband had an appointment to be "fixed." However, we are going to try again, as we want to raise two children together.

We did not plan on any more. But I did have another baby. Not to replace her, but to have a sibling for our son.

Some parents expressed a need to fill the "hole" left by the child who died:

We were going to have a baby in about three years, but now we decided to have another baby as soon as possible.

I decided I wanted another child as I felt very lost and empty after the death.

It was a big decision to have another baby. But the odds of having it happen again are slim. We felt we needed to fill the "hole" left in our lives.

Clearly, parents struggle with the decision to have a subsequent child; the decisions change, however, as parents move through the grieving process. When struggling with this decision parents should consider the experiences of other parents who have gone through this process, since many of them changed their minds several times about having subsequent children. The bereaved parents should allow the grieving process to unfold slowly. They should avoid making decisions—such as sterilization, which must be considered permanent—quickly. For those parents who decided to have a subsequent child, there was often considerable worry even though they could tell themselves that it probably would not happen again.

Using a Monitor for Subsequent Children

There are no easy answers regarding the use of monitors for subsequent children. Briefly, these devices monitor the cessation of breathing or a slowing of the heart rate of a child. When the respiration and/or heart rate is too fast or too slow, an alarm sounds, and the parent or other caretaker must provide appropriate intervention, such as cardiopulmonary resuscitation (CPR).

The use of the home monitor resulted from development of the theory that SIDS is caused by sleep apnea (abnormalities in breathing control).[4] Although researchers' views differ, some conclude that there is no relationship between SIDS and sleep apnea.[5] Home monitors have been used, therefore, for the past fifteen years to notify parents when a baby stops breathing. Looking back over those years, researchers found no evidence to indicate that the use of monitors has led to a decrease in the number of babies who have died of SIDS.[6] In fact, there are many examples of infants who have died while being monitored.[7] It is important to know that there is no way to identify babies who are at risk for SIDS, and that there are therefore no preventative measures that can be taken for all infants. Home monitoring may be appropriate for certain babies based on their individual histories, but it should be clearly understood that home monitoring should not be widespread and it will not ensure an infant's survival.[8] Home monitoring was used extensively in the early 1980s in an effort to prevent SIDS, but at present it is encouraged for only a small number of cases.

When home monitors are warranted, the parents or other caretaker should be trained in the use of monitors and intervention, and continued support and follow-up should be provided by technical, medical, and social service staff.[9]

For some families a home monitor can be a source of comfort, and it can help family members be less anxious about a subsequent baby's dying. On the negative side, home monitors are also likely to have many false alarms—that is, they sometimes go off when there is no life-threatening change in breathing or heart rate. As a result, parents "die a thousand deaths" every time the monitor goes off, and the baby is awakened unnecessarily. Sometimes reliance on the monitor leads to difficulty and increased anxiety when monitoring is no longer required.[10] The balance between the comfort a monitor may provide and the psychological stress it may create for a family must be weighed by family members and medical personnel in determining whether to use the device.

Families' Experiences with Home Monitors

Several of the families in our study used home monitors. (It is important to remember that these babies were monitored during the mid-1980s when monitors were used extensively for subsequent children.) One parent described using a monitor for a subsequent child. Because this baby lived with the use of a monitor, the older children concluded that the monitor had saved the life of this subsequent child:

> Both of our children think that we should have had a monitor for the baby who died. And if we had used a monitor, he would still be alive. "The last baby was on a monitor and she is still alive, so why didn't Mommy have the other baby on one?" I ask myself the same question. Why was I so ignorant? At least when the monitor went off I would have known that I had done everything I could to save him. He would not have died alone.

Another parent who monitored a subsequent child for nine months describes how others think that monitoring would have saved the child who died:

> People kept saying things about monitoring our subsequent child, as if it were necessary for his well-being. They kept suggesting that the baby would be alive today if we had monitored her. We know better. One friend told me she didn't have to worry about her new niece because she had been "tested" for SIDS.

One couple who monitored a subsequent child for nine months decided as a result that they would not have more children. Their monitor would sometimes go off as many as twenty times per night. Here, a mother describes her struggles with the issue of using a monitor for their subsequent children:

> I experienced extreme depression after the baby died. My doctor was about to put me on antidepressants when we found out I was pregnant again. The fear of the death of another child was overwhelming. I would shake uncontrollably. Finally, my husband and I separated.

The separation was brief, but it gave me time to grieve and welcome my new child, free of the guilt I felt for the baby's death. Then I suffered a brief setback when doctors informed me our new baby had abnormal breathing patterns, and that we should put her on an infant monitor. I was so nervous that I was sleepwalking. On the outside I was quite calm, but it showed up in my sleep.

Testimony: The Seventeen-Year Wait

This Illinois mother was nineteen years old when her five-week-old son died. She reported that she waited seventeen years before having another child because she was terrified that something would happen. She told us her story eighteen years after the first baby died.

"I was breast-feeding, and Sean was colicky. I woke up at about 10:00 on Sunday morning and knew something was wrong because the baby hadn't awakened me to feed him. (To this day I don't remember if I fed him during the night or not. It is a blank.) I went into the baby's room, and he was just lying there limp and blue. He felt cold and had pooped all over himself. I yelled to Johnny that there was something wrong with the baby. He got on the phone.

"I tried to see if there was something in his mouth and put my finger in it, and it came out bloody. I got a little hysterical then. I tried to blow air into him, but I knew nothing about CPR so I'm sure it was wrong. The paramedics got there with my dad. He was a police officer on duty and had heard the call. They took the baby and ran down the stairs. I remember my dad saying, "Oh, shit." I think I said that he would be all right. I felt guilty just from the way my dad acted, like it was my fault. I think I knew he was dead.

"We got to the hospital in our car, and my mom and my husband's mom came running. I don't remember the father's being there. We were all in the emergency room's waiting room. I was rocking back and forth, and they kept trying to stop me from doing that. I don't remember if my husband was next to me or not.

"A doctor came out and wouldn't tell us how the baby was, but kept asking me why I hit the baby. I kept trying to explain about wanting to make him breathe, but I could tell they thought I had hurt him.

"The doctor finally stopped asking me and made me come in a room and lie down. Johnny was standing next to the stretcher holding my hand. I think most of our family were standing around the stretcher, some crying. They must have already known.

"Then the doctor told me my baby was dead, but not really. First he said that Sean would not be going home with us. They kept trying to hold me down. I wanted to see him, and some nurses left and then they came back. They must have tried to clean him up after all the stuff they did to him.

"He was so small lying on the cart. I wanted to pick him up and hold him, but they only let me hold him for a little bit. There was blood on his face by his nose.

"Then my mother and husband walked me down the block to my mom's house. My dad stayed at the hospital. He knew the head doctor and arranged for an autopsy. I remember saying that I wanted one, but they all said I wouldn't want him all cut up. I couldn't fight then.

"My father made the funeral arrangements. My mom gave me a black dress. I remember having to go for pills to stop the breast-feeding process. The only clear day is the day of the funeral.

"I think the funeral was necessary for me to realize Sean was dead. It was hell to go through, but it let me know people cared."

[How did others react at the funeral?] "People were on eggshells around me and would stop talking when I came into a room. Everyone cried a lot. There was less laughing than at an older person's wake. I was real quiet and just sat and listened to their bullshit most of the time. I think I was in shock.

"When they were going to close the casket, I was touching him and trying to kiss him. I remember him being as cold as ice. They must have thought I was trying to take him because they led me away. They shouldn't have.

"I remember going to a restaurant and not being able to stop eating. I just couldn't fill up.

"His being gone was a physical hurt. It hurt in the pit of my stomach. I've never felt such a bad pain in my life.

"I remember the people at my mom's house after the funeral. They started talking about when we were kids, and I started laughing. Then I felt I was the worst person in the world. How could I laugh when my son had just died? Because I am human, I know now. I had to laugh, or die."

[What have you gone through since your baby died?] "I divorced the baby's father one year after his death; married; divorced again; and changed states and professions. I also tried to commit suicide and had major surgery four times. I presently am a single mother of a three-month-old, by choice, following the death of my son and two miscarriages.

"I have felt personal guilt over the death. I thought I must have done something wrong from the look on my dad's face. I wish an autopsy had been performed because then maybe I wouldn't have feelings of guilt. One of the hardest facts to accept about the death is that I don't know why he died and that he is dead. Until they find out the cause, I'll always suffer some guilt. I have also blamed my husband because he had taken LSD as a teenager, and I thought it might have changed his genes. I remember arguing about it.

"I have experienced flashbacks of the death hundreds of times. I see him dead in the crib, on the stretcher, or in the casket. He is cold, white, and unmoving. It's just in my mind, my eyes don't have to be closed. It (the image) rushes in and won't leave. I have to pray or try consciously to think of something else. This thing (questionnaire) has seemed to bring them more frequently. Sometimes I look at my daughter and think she is Sean.

"I wanted to go to sleep and wake up after the pain had gone away. It seemed like it would never end, and I was so empty. My arms hurt. I also tried to kill myself with pills. I took all the pills we had in the cabinet and ran out of the house. I fell asleep behind a church, and the minister took me home. I thought that if I committed suicide then there would be no more pain.

"My marriage was weakened after the death of my son. We were divorced one year following the death. He was macho and kept it all in. He only cried once at the cemetery. He thought I was going crazy. It seemed like the marriage was over since the reason for it was gone. His errors were huge then. I didn't want to have sex with him anymore. It was easier to get away from him since he reminded me of my son whenever I looked at him."

[What things have people done during the time since your baby's death that have been helpful to you?] "Just let matters take their course instead of telling me to get over it. Being there to listen, letting me be vulnerable, and allowing me to talk about my fears."

[What have people done during this time that has made it more difficult for you?] "Saying he was an angel and we must go by God's will. I was pissed at God! Also saying it was better he died before I was attached to him.

"When my son died, in 1969, there was no one to help you. They thought I had hurt the baby in some way and questioned me at the hospital. No one knew what had happened. After a couple of months, people kept expecting me to be over it."

[Which organizations or individuals were in contact with you the first few days after the death? How were they helpful? If they weren't helpful, how so?] "I had lots of contact with my family. There weren't any organizations then, or at least none called. I just remember everyone saying I should have another baby right away. My mother and mother-in-law cleaned out the baby's room. That was wrong, as I wanted to see how it was and if there was something I did. I went to the cemetery a lot.

"Being able to talk to someone who had been through the same thing would have been helpful. Not just that, but someone to talk to about my son and to stop pretending that he never existed. Also, to let me be with him at the hospital and funeral parlor as long as I wanted to, even if it had been for hours. It isn't morbid. You are saying goodbye, and if that means holding him, kissing, and so forth . . . then let the person do it. It helps you realize that life is gone from the body.

"Talking with people from the SIDS support group has been helpful. They listen. They have been there and let me talk about my son. It hurts because it brings it all back, but I never talked it out. Maybe if I can relive it now, I will be able to go on. I can be vulnerable with them and admit how terrible those feelings are."

[What would you like others to know about how to help a person who is grieving over a baby's death?] "It never goes away, but the hurt stops being so bad. There will be days and then weeks when you don't think about him. If you have another baby, whether right away or seventeen years later like me, you are still terrified something will happen. The new baby makes you relive the old, but you love the new baby more. I think you become more compassionate to other kinds of hurts people suffer.

"Before the birth of my daughter, I probably thought of Sean once a week. His birthday and death, Mother's Day and Father's Day, when I see a boy his age, or people who had babies when I did, are specific times when memories of Sean come back to me. Now that I have my daughter, I think of him daily.

"No other crisis in my life has been as traumatic as Sean's death. My dad's death was expected because he was older. Other things end or you adjust to them. This is an irreplaceable loss.

"I waited seventeen years to have another child. I was afraid I would not be able to live if something happened to another child. She is on a monitor. I'm more worried; I hold her more, take more pictures, and don't really trust her with someone else. I'm afraid it [the SIDS death] will happen again to her. I'm always touching her to make sure she's alive.

"Today, it still hurts that I was robbed of him. It hurts now especially because of my daughter. I have a son I can't talk about because he isn't anything good or bad; he is dead. My daughter brought all these feelings out again. That's why I am going to SIDS meetings."

[What good things have you learned about life?] "The human being can survive anything and can also be the most magnificent creature, especially the brain's ability in all its aspects.

"About myself, I have learned that I am capable of caring deeply for my fellow human beings, and as trite as it sounds I want a better world for my daughter. Also, no matter what, you learn from life's errors if you look for the good parts. If I hadn't had my son die, I might not be so concerned about my daughter.

"Hopefully, the future will bring more growth for me, both mentally and spiritually, with more peace in my soul, more compassion and understanding of myself and other people."

13

How Can Families Possibly Survive?

The words *children* and *death* seem contradictory. To associate them seems to violate our sense of what is appropriate. Children symbolize life and growth and future, whereas death marks the end of growth and the end of the future. The death of a young child is shocking and devastating—outside the "natural" order of events.

In our initial study of SIDS families, we found that 50 percent of the parents who had experienced SIDS in the state of Nebraska could not be found for participation in the research. Within six months to two and a half years after the death, half of the parents had moved from their hometowns, leaving no forwarding address. We learned in our subsequent studies that many parents feel that only by leaving their homes and hometowns can they forget or recover from the death.[1] We believe that early participation in a parent support group is helpful for many parents in lessening the sense of isolation they often feel.

Sudden Infant Death Syndrome is estimated to be the cause of 15–20 percent of all infant deaths. With SIDS there is no outcry, no apparent struggle. No one is to blame. It is a disease of exclusion. When the physician rules out every possible cause for the seemingly healthy baby's death, it is called SIDS. The "whys" of a child's death are relentless, and the less one can understand, the more helpless one feels. Death makes us all helpless, but the death of a child deprives people of their feelings of competence as parents, grandparents, and adults. It deprives them of feelings of worthiness. They cannot blame the unknown, so they blame themselves.

What Have You Gone through Since the Death of the Baby?

We asked families to share with us what they had gone through since the death of the baby. Some of their responses follow:

A lot of questioning of the religious beliefs I have been brought up with and believed. Emotionally, it is like riding a roller coaster, but as time goes on the dips are just as deep, but the distance between them lengthens and the length of time spent in the dips shortens. [I need a] real mental push to accomplish anything physical and have the attitude of why do it anyway.

I hardly know where to begin. I've run the whole gauntlet of emotions. Everything, but happiness. I've felt love, hate, bitterness, guilt, and wondering *why* every day since it has happened. Also, somehow I do feel peace for the baby sometimes, but not for myself. Also, I've found I question my relationship with everyone I know. Some people who I've cared for before, I know I'll never care for again. Other people I hardly even knew before will always have a special place in my heart. I also feel tremendous guilt for my sister (she had Patrick when he quit breathing). I know that she will never be the same person again, and I feel responsible. She's so depressed. I've gotten her in touch with a professional counselor, and I hope it will help her. I also feel I've hurt my children and husband somehow. I was responsible for Patrick's total well-being, so I feel the same about his death. I feel I kind of let this happen, and so I've let everyone down and hurt them. They loved him so. I'm more wary of everyone, and I don't seem to like as many people as before. My family and I have been so devastated that I'll never let anyone hurt them. As far as I'm concerned, no one could hurt me now, nothing could touch this pain I feel.

My life has done a complete turnaround. People who have known me say that my personality changed 100 percent. The first years after she died, I could barely live through each day. It was a struggle at first to get out of bed. I was never afraid of anything, and now I can't sleep without a light on. I am scared to death of finding someone else dead.

It has been a sad, life-hurting thing for me.

At first, shock and anger were the biggest emotions. That turned into depression and a feeling of emptiness. Some self-pity followed. Always the question why? Now, I just think about him a lot, miss him terribly, and still wonder, Why?

I feel like I'm not really here. I'm doing things, but I'm not really participating.

First was a mild depressive mood. My business career was somewhat slowed. Socially, I didn't feel comfortable with friends and relatives. The majority of this has been overcome with time.

[I have gone through] depression, anger, guilt, and a lot of doubt.

I feel a loss of innocence, a vulnerability to life's hurts, and a sensitivity to violence and death portrayed in the media. I have begun a new job in a new town and I have grown. Compassionate Friends has been a tremendous source of strength, and I have healed and felt compelled to reach out to others who are grieving as a way of repaying those who were there for me, and because it is a way for me to heal myself as well.

It has been the worst time of my life, and I pray to God I never have to face this situation again.

[I have gone through] extreme depression. I'm learning not to take anything for granted.

For the first eighteen months after the death, I felt a lot of sadness and sometimes rage and guilt. A general "serious" attitude toward life. This let up after one and a half years, and then I started feeling normal again except for feelings of guilt and an aversion to infants. I feel repelled and afraid of tending to infants.

Prior to our SIDS death, we had a stillborn baby about one year earlier. This was the first blow. The SIDS death was the second blow. We both didn't know if we wanted any children. We found our marriage falling apart and sought help from a psychologist. We now have two healthy children. Just a few weeks ago, we had a miscarriage, which was blow number three. Life isn't easy!

Lots of doubts. Whether I could be a better mother. Lots of anger. A better look at life. I've become a more compassionate person.

We have had two more children, each with minor medical problems, but nonetheless scary. Had a major geographical move and two job changes.

[What have I gone through?] I have had my heart broken. I feel that today I'm loosely glued back together. I couldn't sleep at first. I had a pain in my chest and throat that made it feel broken. That is gone. I had no appetite at first, and now I'm eating normally. I couldn't hold a thought or concentrate at first, but now I am feeling competent to talk to people. I was forgetful at first, and now I can remember things. I would get angry at my mother at first, and now I don't fly off the handle with others. I don't talk about Paul's death as much now.

Depression, guilt, self-analysis, professional counseling, marital pressure, and a deep evaluation of the marriage.

At first I felt like I was in a daze. When the shock finally wore off, I felt almost every kind of emotion possible. When I got really down, I'd go to the cemetery and cry for hours. My husband and I started to grow apart. We separated for two or three months. We worked out our differences and are now expecting our second child.

For a while, I just felt numb. I read a lot of books on death, and I slowly accepted it.

Guilt and doubt. I didn't think I could ever have another baby until one day I just decided that I could. My husband and I did have problems resulting from Katie's death, but I think it brought us closer. I started working one week after her death. I literally went nonstop for sixteen hours a day so I didn't have time to think. After six months I quit and slowed down and tried to rebuild our family.

[What have I gone through?] A lot of stress.

Vulnerability as a result of loss through death seems to be most acute when one's child dies. The grief experienced by survivors of the sudden death of a child may be intense because of the type of death, the suddenness of the loss, the resulting guilt feelings, and the shattered expectations of a long and healthy life for the child. When an infant dies, the parents' reliance on the orderliness of the universe is undermined. There is anger at God, doctors, the marital partner, other children, family, friends, and the lost baby.

The loss of a baby seems to cut at the heart of family life. The guilt, the grief, and the lack of knowledge surrounding the loss constitute major emotional stress. The family unit becomes disrupted since no individual family member lives in a vacuum unaffected by other family members. They want to make sense out of nonsense and put the pieces together in a way that will enable them to see a cause and an effect. Most survivors of sudden, unexpected deaths want to reconstruct, in as much detail as possible, the events surrounding the death as a means of coping with the reality of the loss.

Just when a couple may need each other the most, however, they may be most vulnerable and unable to help each other. In her book *Dearly Beloved,* Anne Morrow Lindberg wrote, "Grief can't be shared. Everyone carries it alone, his own burden, his own way."[2] The death of a baby happens to mothers, fathers, grandmothers, and grandfathers; yet their experiences with grief and mourning may be totally different, and their approaches to coping may go in opposite directions. Sharing becomes difficult when a parent or grandparent is in so much pain and surviving each day can become a selfish endeavor. For the individual, it is a matter of rigid concentration: his or her thoughts are narrowed to just getting out of bed, just getting dressed, just getting through one more day. This can take all of an individual's energy, and it is difficult to have any left to share with the spouse.

Angry feelings that spouses have for each other are difficult to deny. Each person will have his or her own ideas about how grief should be displayed, and these will not be the same for any two individuals. Tension may result when the wife feels the husband is having too good a time; he may become resentful when she wants to make love. How could anyone think of sex at a time like this? he may think, revolted.

These feelings can create a separateness at a time when relatives and friends are leaving the family alone to mourn. A person is truly alone, then, when the mate who is counted on cannot understand his or her feelings. Any relationship will experience times of stress, but the loss of an infant represents a time of crisis that is individually devastating and can be totally destructive to a marriage.

Parents and grandparents who have lost a child can find themselves suddenly out of control. A feeling of powerlessness pervades the relationship as they discover that they were unable to protect their child and grandchild; they feel impotent because they must come to terms with the fact that they have no control over whether a child lives or dies.

Shared adversity often builds bonds between people; the sharing of the loss of a child, however, will not necessarily create a stronger bond between a husband and wife. Grief and the process of mourning are a series of small steps that are taken when the individual is ready, and the marriage often takes second place to individual recovery.

What Was the Hardest Fact to Accept about the Death of the Child?

We asked families what the hardest fact to accept about the death of their child was. Some of their responses follow:

[The hardest fact?] The why.

That I could never say to her, "Stacie, I love you." That I could never see her grow up. No Christmas, no first birthday, no learning to walk. She had just begun to giggle.

The helplessness I feel.

Although I believe absolutely in life after death (and resurrection), I am overwhelmed at how permanent the separation feels. It's so unchangeable and final (for now), and I miss the child intensely even six years later.

Not knowing the reason why he died is by far the hardest thing to accept.

I thought I had a perfect family. The hardest thing for me is that I wanted a boy so badly, and I'm thirty-eight years old and feel time pressure to complete my family.

They are gone forever. As I watch this third child grow up, I wonder how similar the others were to him.

[The hardest thing to accept?] That it actually happened to *me*. With odds of one or two out of a thousand, I still find it hard to believe. It's one of those things that's supposed to happen to someone else.

I'll never get to see her grow up or experience the fun of being her mother.

It is so final.

That it was so unexpected and sudden and that there are no reasons or medical facts to explain it.

That he was so young. That I didn't hold him when he fussed the night before as long as I should have.

Families can and do cope, and they are successful at dealing with the crisis of sudden infant death. In researching how strong families cope with crisis, investigators Nick Stinnett, Barbara Knorr, John DeFrain, and George Rowe found that one major factor in coping is the support an individual receives from the family, and that positive growth can occur despite the initial disorganization that comes with crisis.[3]

One mother who participated in our study explained how it was for her:

I have endured the closest thing to hell on earth that could possibly happen. I have found compassion and understanding from perfect strangers, yet cold and heartless emotions from close friends and relatives. All in all it has been a growing process. I found personal strength and power from within which I never knew existed or had ever tapped.

How Do Other Crises in Your Life Compare to the Death of the Baby?

We asked our families if they had gone through any other crises in their lives, and if they had, how they would compare these crises to the death of a baby. A sample of their responses:

I do not think they really can be compared. I have survived many other crises, but most of the time I knew what the cause was or that with help it could be overcome or changed—which this cannot be. If you know your enemy then you can form some type of defense against it or at least a protective device to help you get through the crisis. With no cause or cure it's very difficult to face or accept.

My father died of brain cancer, after a couple of years of illness, when I was nineteen. Losing our son was much harder. We had no warning. And although I missed my father a lot, I didn't feel responsible for his welfare, I didn't experience self-blame, or the depth of loss.

In 1979, I lost my father to a stroke. In 1980, my brother died in a drowning accident. Meagan died in 1984. The deaths of my father and brother were terrible, but nothing like the pain involved with Meagan's death.

[There is] no comparison. The other crises brought about needed changes.

Last year I lost my brother (twenty-nine years old) in a motorcycle accident. His death has been a great loss. We have had subsequent babies, but he was my only brother. The loss of my father suddenly to a heart attack was easier to take than the loss of my baby and my brother.

Having four miscarriages after Danny died was like losing him all over again. I felt that I would never have another baby to hold in my arms ever again. But, now I do.

Nothing can be compared to the death of our child. My husband spent four weeks in the hospital psychiatric ward for depression and a hyperactive thyroid. Both were triggered by Ryan's death. This was extremely stressful.

I had an accident one year ago in which I was electrocuted and revived with CPR. Also, I saw lots of death in Vietnam. *Nothing* compares to the loss of a child, but perhaps having experienced other traumas dulls the loss.

Our first birth was a stillborn baby, but the SIDS death was much harder because we had time to see and enjoy him.

We almost divorced. That's the only other crisis in my life, and it was as a result of our son's death. We never had any other problems or differences that would have caused such serious action as divorce. As far as I'm concerned, there's no other crisis or tragedy in this world that could be as bad as losing one's child.

My father died when I was three. At the time I had no understanding of death. I wanted to know why Daddy left us. This death left a giant scar on me since I was hurt for many years after my father left me. When my baby died, I had grown to have faith enough to feel secure and realize some things like "life is precious" and that with each close death there is a scar that toughens you up to be stronger.

Nothing compares to this. Not my wreck. Not my miscarriages. Not even when we found out my husband had a lung disease. They all hurt and worried me, but nothing like losing Brian.

The loss of my husband's job and the illness of my parents. Nothing can compare to the loss of a baby. What I thought were major losses before are not. I could lose everything tomorrow (material possessions) and I could make it through—it wouldn't matter. Life is precious and short.

My husband was almost killed in a car accident. This was very frightening. The fact that he wasn't killed made me appreciate what we have rather than dwell on what we have lost.

My divorce was difficult. It in no way was as sad or devastating as George's death.

My father committed suicide when I was age eight. Both SIDS and my father's death rendered me a victim. I was not responsible for either of the deaths, and yet I felt helpless by them.

My stillbirth was very difficult for me, but the SIDS death was harder because I had held, fed, and played with him. He was a definite part of my life. My recent miscarriage brought back the heartache from both.

Positive Approaches to Coping

Why is it that one family can find ways to cope with the death of a child, while another may be torn apart? Individually, all members of a family may adjust to and learn to live with the death of an infant, and yet some families do not survive. There is no simple answer, but many factors can improve the family's chances of survival and perhaps move family members in a positive direction after the death of an infant.

Communication, of course, is of the utmost importance to the process of adjustment to the crisis. When an infant dies suddenly, the guilt and anger may cause a wall of silence to be erected within a family. Placing of blame may prevent couples from communicating. A slammed door, a drunken spouse, or a mother so numb with grief that the thought of sex with her husband is repellent—

all can destroy any kind of adequate environment for effective communication.

Effective communication includes sharing, not only between spouses but also with relatives and friends. Finding strength within the family and using it as a resource is important to coping, and when this does not happen the results can affect the individual for a long time:

> Thirty-seven years have passed, and until four years ago I was not allowed to talk about it. Not to my husband or family or friends. It was only with my daughter's neighbor, who had gone through the same experience just recently, that I was finally allowed to talk and receive some comfort. No one knew thirty-seven years ago that SIDS existed, and all I knew was what the doctor said: "Suffocation." Not another word.

The research on strong families reported by Stinnett, Knorr, DeFrain, and Rowe found that many of the families relied on God to help them through crisis experiences.[4] Many individuals suffering a death from SIDS also said that their belief in God was helpful, and that being able to tell themselves that their baby was with God was one of the few comforts they received. Others cautioned, however, that reliance on God was not all they had to help them recover from the crisis. One father from Nebraska expressed it this way:

> Optimism that things will work out for the best, or faith in God's will, is important. But you've got to try actively to help yourself. You can't sit back and wait for God to help. You've got to get out of your rut yourself.

Commitment, togetherness, and the ability to take turns being strong for each other were also seen as positive ways of coping with the loss of a child. Affection and positive communication can also bring strength into a crisis situation.

A final common denominator appears to be a person's simple ability to survive—to get up in the morning and get through the day, to force concentration on tasks that may seem irrelevant to the situation. One woman found herself thinking, How can I scrub this floor? My baby is dead. But she knew she had to keep busy and involved, if even on such a basic level.

For these parents and grandparents, some measure of control

over their lives returns as they realize that they are going to survive the loss, that the pain will diminish, and that they are becoming stronger as a result. In David Mace's words,

> There is always a way out. No problem is insoluble. The resources of the human spirit to meet and triumph over adversity have amazed me again and again. There seems to be almost nothing men and women cannot do when they are wholly resolved upon it.[5]

Many parents and grandparents expressed surprise that they did survive the death of their baby. Once the realization sank in that they would live though their baby did not, they found strength in themselves they never thought they had. Most of them grimly acknowledged the truth of this Illinois mother's words, "Now I can survive anything."

Testimony: Thirty-Eight Years, Bereaved

The Missouri farm mother who tells her story here was twenty-two years old when her seven-month-old baby died. She told us her story thirty-eight years later. She reported that she was very unhappy for more than ten years after the death.

"I certainly felt grief after she died, but mostly guilt because my husband and I were real young (in our twenties) and I thought maybe we had not taken good enough care of her. And my mother also blamed us, saying we must have neglected her.

"We were so poor, and it was in March. We lived on a farm and we got a blizzard and it snowed for days. Our roads were snowed shut, so our old country doctor didn't even come when we called him. So we really weren't even sure it was SIDS that caused her death. When we got our roads cleared and got in to talk to the doctor, I told him that I'd gotten up and nursed the baby at about four o'clock and she seemed okay then, and when we woke in the morning she was gone but her little body was still warm. It still hurts to talk about it, after all these years.

"I found the baby. She was lying face down on her pillow. At first, we thought she had smothered in the pillow. But when we talked to the doctor and told him, he said no. He said that she hadn't smothered. The first day or so, I was just lost without the baby to care for. We spent the time making funeral arrangements and calling relatives and friends. The man from the funeral home couldn't come to pick up the baby until the county sent a snow-plow out to open up the roads.

"My mother, my brother, and my sister came and stayed with us and helped out in any way they could. My sister stayed until after the funeral, and she kept telling 'dumb' stories to get us to laugh and take our minds off the baby. Afterward, I'd think, How could I laugh like this? My baby is dead and I'm laughing! I was horrified!"

[What could have been done to help you that was not done?] "I really don't know. Maybe a lot more understanding and a little more sympathy. I was already pregnant with my third baby at the time, and I had such mixed feelings. I worried that the new baby might not be all right. Someone made the remark to me that when a person dies, it makes room for someone else, and I couldn't accept that because I loved all my babies and I couldn't believe one had to die to make room for another one.

"If we had had a religious background that certainly would have helped. We didn't know anything about the church or the minister, so we felt uncomfortable and I suppose guilty too. The funeral director was kind and helpful, and his wife was exceptionally kind and thoughtful and understanding. I feel she helped us the most.

"[The funeral] was sad. My mother and dad were separated at the time. My mother, brothers, and one sister came. Friends were there. My dad and one sister were not. I don't remember a word the minister said. I think my mother and an older brother grieved as much as we did. My husband's folks were in Oregon and did not come back. They took it rather calmly, I thought!

"I didn't think of suicide after she died. I do not believe in suicide. I feel it is as great a sin as if you killed someone else.

"We lived on the farm, and there were chores and other work to do. And we had our first child (about fifteen months old) to care for. The loss changed the way I cared for my other children. When all of them were babies, I'd jump up every little while, day or night, to check on them. I remember times I'd check on them and I couldn't tell if they were breathing and I'd grab them up and start shaking them. And they'd awaken and cry, and then I'd feel awful for waking them.

"The children would ask, "Just why did she die?" And it was hard to reply because we didn't know ourselves why she died. We could only say, "God will take care of her." The other children are all grown up and gone from home now, but at times when we get together we do talk about our baby that died. And if they ever run across an article in the paper or magazines on SIDS, they always save it for me to read.

"After the baby died, good friends and even strangers came and took me to church with them, and over the years I've become real active in the church and my religious beliefs are very strong. I have great faith in the Lord, and I know that someday we'll all be together again.

"I think of her very often still today. When people ask how many children I have, I always answer, 'I had six girls, but we lost our second baby when she was six months old.' " [Have you gone through any other major crises in your life?] "Yes, divorce. My husband and I divorced twelve years after she died, but it was not related to the death. Divorce is like a death in the family. And the death of my parents. This is sad. But when an older person dies, I feel they have lived their life. When a baby dies, they haven't had a chance to live and grow up and enjoy life.

"It still hurts to think or talk about my baby's death. I try not to think about it. I have learned that life is precious and that we should put our lives in God's hands and he will take care of us. I feel that I have been a good mother to my children. I've learned to take my troubles to the Lord and have faith that he will always be there when I need him." [What will the future bring?] "Only God knows.

"[When people are experiencing hard times] I try to help them any way I can. It makes me feel good to help others whenever I can."

14

Support Groups for Families
Who Have Lost Babies to SIDS

One major difficulty bereaved family members have is finding an appropriate time and place to grieve. People who have not themselves lost a child are often very uncomfortable talking about the death with a parent, and support groups for many bereaved family members satisfy the need to talk about what has happened with others who understand the need not to forget.

Support groups for bereaved families are functioning in countless cities and towns today. A look in the local phone book and a few calls is all it takes to find one. In our most recent study of 127 parents, 83 percent said there was a support group in their vicinity, though some people ended up driving thirty, forty, and fifty miles to the meetings. Some parents who found themselves in a community without a support group got on the phone and created one for themselves and a handful of other bereaved families. Meetings take place in churches or synagogues, living rooms, libraries, hospitals, wherever adequate space is available.

Seventy-six percent of the parents in our most recent study said they had contacted a local support group for information, and 76 percent had attended at least one support group meeting. The mothers in our study who had attended support group meetings had attended an average of ten meetings, ranging from one to one hundred. The fathers in our study who had attended support group meetings had attended an average of three meetings, ranging from one to ten. We asked the parents in our most recent study to describe their personal reactions to the support group meetings they had attended: "What happened? What did you like about the meeting? What did you dislike?

Parents who attended support group meetings regularly were quite positive, in general, about their experiences. Other parents, however, were highly critical of their more limited experiences with support groups. This smaller group of parents had attended a few meetings and decided not to return because of dissatisfaction with the organization. We will begin by reporting the positive responses. These will be followed by remarks from parents who were not particularly happy about their experiences with support groups. We hope that both the positive and the negative remarks will be helpful to those parents and professionals active in establishing and maintaining support groups. Human beings are wonderfully diverse, and it is thus especially challenging to try to provide support services for such a broad range of personalities and approaches to grieving.

Those Who Regularly Attend Support Group Meetings

The best way to outline the benefits of support group attendance is simply to let the parents describe their experiences:

> I found it helpful to talk to others and hoped we could be of help to them.

> We were thrilled. At last we had found somewhere where we could take off our brave faces and grieve. Everyone there had been there and could tell us that we weren't going crazy and that we would survive. They hurt *with us* and *for us,* and the love and concern felt like a warm blanket wrapped around us. We have a terrific social worker in the group who helps us keep the communication going— he is a wonderful person whom we have all grown to love.

> It was comforting because you could sit and talk about your feelings to parents who felt the same way. There were tears and laughter.

> [This mother had already attended forty-eight support group meetings over several years when she told us why the meetings were so important to her.] I like talking to other parents about their experiences. I also started the group as a way to help parents to overcome their grief more easily than I did. I feel it is necessary to talk to someone who truly understands how you are feeling. I was unable

to do that for years. I know I have helped other parents; even though they still have to suffer, they can see someone who has lived through it, and I know that helps.

The first meeting I didn't like because some people did a lot of laughing. Now I can laugh with them and cry with them.

[This mother had a difficult time with her first support group meeting, but she subsequently learned to appreciate deeply the importance of the meetings and became active as a volunteer for the National SIDS Foundation.] The first night I *hated*. It was a Christmas party, and everyone had their babies in tow. It was a group I *did not* want to belong to. I guess it forced the reality of Spencer's death. I ran out crying.

It was very helpful to me to visit with other SIDS parents and see that they had survived.

The SIDS meetings are very informal. Parents have opportunities to share with one another. It helps to know others have similar feelings and reactions. Frequently there are discussions of the "theory of the month." Since SIDS is so vague, many people have differing opinions about their child's death and afterlife. I did not like having their ideas stated as truths to the group.

[This mother called a support group ten years after the death and subsequently attended twenty-five meetings.] My old nightmares came back for a while at the meetings. But then I felt better after I began to talk to others who understood. I kept things bottled up for so long. I had no one who really understood to talk to.

We just talked about the baby and things we do or did to get over the pain. I liked it because it was a place where I could talk about Rob and show his picture if I wanted.

[It was] very helpful. It felt like a release of tension. I could say things about what I was feeling and ask questions without fear. Nobody was uncomfortable or acted like I was crazy. Nobody was ashamed to cry. We occasionally cry and laugh at the same time! I disliked hearing the different circumstances under which others lost children. It made me more fearful for my other children. It's part of the meeting, though. You have to accept it.

Lots of listeners. Most were SIDS parents who have been there for years. They mostly listened. Two other mothers and me were all new

SIDS parents (less than one month). They also showed a film. Then it was a rap session. It was nice. I'm going back.

I attend the Oklahoma City chapter meetings of the SIDS group. I have found the group to be very helpful. It is very reassuring to know that you can make it through this very hard time. I like being there for new parents, also. I am unhappy that recently we have had practically no interest at all in the group. [This mother had attended more than one hundred support group meetings in the twenty-one months since her baby died.]

The meetings were the most helpful thing to us during the first year after our son's death. To talk to other parents who had experienced the same loss. We spoke about everything: the child (alive), the death, the aftermath. Every aspect. [This mother had attended more than thirty meetings in the first year after the baby's death.]

It was very difficult to tell our story, particularly the first few times. But it was the one place where you were actually *supposed* to talk about your child and his death. Having a *place* to go to grieve and sensitive people to share and listen was and is a tremendous source of relief. We found the meetings to be cathartic and catalysts for deep and meaningful conversations with each other afterward. Both of us have cried at meetings, as have others in the group. But everyone there knows that crying is not a sign of weakness but a way of healing yourself by releasing feelings. [This mother and her husband had attended twenty-four support group meetings in the two years following their son's death.]

I needed it. I felt they were the only ones who understood.

Those Less Comfortable with Support Groups

Many other SIDS parents were clearly uncomfortable with support groups, and attended once or twice but did not return. Some were angry about their experiences. Often the dissatisfied parents were those whose babies had died relatively recently. The meetings must have been difficult for them, especially seeing that other parents' pain lasted so long—this perhaps scared them away. It is possible that they will return to the support group later in their journey to healing.

Here are some comments from parents who did not find their support group experience particularly helpful:

It is good for people who need that. I need time for myself and not others, so it's not very helpful for me.

At one meeting, I liked listening to different ways of coping with grief. There was a psychologist speaking. I went to one that was a very painful meeting. We all just talked, and in a way it kind of scared me away.

I felt depressed that there could be so many people whose children died the same way. An M.D. spoke to us and commented on his book. He made me wonder whether anyone would ever find a cause for SIDS, but he was very truthful.

I have mixed feelings about the support group. I only went to two meetings. The commonality of feelings was comforting, but there are so many who have not progressed in their lives since "that night." [This leads us to believe that some parents may feel support groups to be "too much" for them in their early weeks and months of grieving, but that these same people may find it comforting to come back to the group later on when they realize that the pain is a long-term pain.]

I have only been to a couple of meetings. Parts of the meeting are helpful and parts are not. I think (in my opinion) that some of these people are living in the past and can't let go. The loss of a loved one will always be with you and you won't forget him or her. I go to these meetings and find what information I can on SIDS.

A meeting of the group six weeks after Sandy's death was horrible at the time. There was no professional leadership, and we all sat around a table and told what had happened to us. Some of these people had deaths occurring more than five years ago, and all I could think of was that I didn't want to be like them (depressed, and so forth) in five years.

They discussed autopsies, and I came away furious. I just never went back.

The people leading it were grieving over their abortion, and it made me mad!!! Abortion is murder, and those people made me physically sick to my stomach.

We disliked it. The people in the group almost as a whole were bitter, angry, and having marital problems. We were bereaved most recently but felt we had better ways of dealing with it. They discouraged us with their lack of hope.

I think a one-to-one is better than group meetings for me.

I was horrified. "Support" is a misnomer. They were sitting around chatting about trivia and selling notecards when my baby had just died. My marriage is crumbling and I am still devastated by the death, and their meetings resemble a social hour! When I tried to talk about my marriage and grief problems, she responded, "Oh, things will get better." Frankly, I'm surprised they even got this survey to us.

Support groups clearly do not work for all people at all times. Some people are more able to share their feelings with others; some find little comfort in groups. Feelings do change over time, however, and it is good to keep an open mind about the possible benefits one may find in joining a group:

I have mixed feelings. Some comfort in being with others who have suffered the same plight and knowing life does go on. But it is not necessarily always constructive to sit in a room and listen to people talk about the details of their loss. However, that very thing seems to help somehow. Who knows? I'm going to go again.

Suggestions to Support Group Leaders and Members

After studying the parents' comments about support groups, we have some suggestions to make that perhaps will be of use to leaders and other support group members in their efforts to improve services to families:

1. *We believe the best leadership team for a support group unites parents and professionals together.* Professionals who have not personally experienced SIDS are often uncomfortable and afraid in dealing with such a sensitive issue; they need bereaved family members to work with to help them better understand the grieving process. And parents and other bereaved family members often do not have any professional experience in organizing groups, orchestrating meetings, and understanding group dynamics. Professionals can readily provide this expertise, and often are most willing to do so for a small fee or no charge at all.

2. *A clear agenda for meetings is comforting to many people.*

Announcements in advance noting that there will be a speaker or a film followed by open discussion and small-group sharing signifies to the members of the group that there is a course being set and the group will not simply drift. The key is having some set structure with a great deal of flexibility built in to meet individual needs as they arise.

Newcomers, especially, are fearful of being out of control and are looking for some order, something to hang on to. An agenda and a professional on hand are often comforting. Old-timers to support groups know, however, that free-flowing discussion can be enormously beneficial to family members. And, though a professional's presence can be quite helpful, many support group adherents will quickly say that the greatest benefit comes from people in similar circumstances sharing stories of the challenges they face— "I don't feel so alone . . ."

3. *It is important to make a special effort to help integrate newcomers into the group.* They are likely to be fearful of the depth of the pain group members share with each other. And newcomers whose babies have died relatively recently are also likely to think that those who are still grieving after several years ought to "get on with their lives." This sounds like a harsh judgment but perhaps is simply a protective mechanism—for example, "These people are still grieving after years and years. There must be something wrong with them. I know I won't be grieving after so many years. At least, I *pray* I won't be grieving after so many years."

4. *Support groups work wonderfully for many family members, while others are very uncomfortable with them.* We would guess that those who tended to enjoy groups and expressing their feelings to others in a group before their baby died will find support groups heartening. Those who were more solitary, more private before the baby's death will perhaps be less likely to find a support group of comfort. But we would like to encourage everyone to attend at least a few support group meetings. We clearly share one father's enthusiasm: "It's certainly worth a try!"

5. *Support groups are not just for mothers. Fathers, grandparents, and surviving children also experience tremendous grief over the loss of a baby.* Thoughts of suicide and attempted suicide are not confined to mothers, as we have found in our studies. Fathers have tried to kill themselves, a big brother tried to hang himself,

and grandmothers considered suicide because they had not prevented the baby's death.

Many support groups do an excellent job of integrating the whole family into the support group, and they are to be commended for this vital achievement. Fathers and grandparents can be consulted as to how they can best be drawn into support-group activities. And surviving siblings can also be integrated into the group. There can be special activities for the youngsters on some occasions, as well as times when they can be part of the group discussions. A good way to begin would be to have panel discussions: "Fathers Talk about SIDS"; "Grandparents Talk about SIDS"; "Big Brothers and Big Sisters Talk about SIDS." The only thing keeping these evenings from happening is fear.

6. *Support group members often become very close to each other, and that is the wonderful power that a good group has to help members heal. Leaders and members must be somewhat cautious, however, not to get drawn into the trap of believing that "only the support group really understands."* SIDS parents have not captured the market on suffering. To live on this earth is to experience both joy and sorrow. Not everyone can perfectly understand the devastation of a child's death. But everyone can understand a loss of some kind.

Support groups would be most helpful to family members if they could help individuals reach out to many others in their pain, not only other bereaved parents. Pain knows no boundaries; everyone carries sorrow—everyone. That is the burden of being human.

7. *Formal memorial services sponsored by a support group can be a wonderful way of remembering the baby.* Activities can include an interdenominational memorial service at an appropriate nonsectarian site; visits to the graves; services for babies without grave sites; sharing, prayers, tears, and laughter; a potluck picnic, and so forth.

8. *SIDS parents share a common tragedy with parents who have experienced a stillbirth or a miscarriage. An alliance of these parents and other bereaved parents and families would be mutually beneficial.* SIDS parents and concerned professionals have developed an excellent network of support groups in the United States and Canada. We would encourage them to use the strength of their organization in reaching out to other bereaved parents, because

much can be gained by integrating families. Our research clearly indicates that SIDS, stillbirth, and miscarriage are basically the same type of crisis for families: the death of a baby. By uniting SIDS families with the other bereaved families, their organizations could be much stronger. Or perhaps SIDS groups could form stronger bonds with the Compassionate Friends (a group welcoming families who have lost a child of any age) and other support groups. There is indeed strength in numbers.

We realize that some parents have an almost desperate need to talk to others in "the exact same situation." This is the power SIDS support groups have. But a stillbirth is a death, just as a miscarriage is a death. Pain simply cannot be weighed and measured, though bereaved parents sometimes want to cry out that no one on earth hurts as much as they do.

Instead of segregating bereaved family members by the type of death they have experienced, however, we believe there is benefit from being more inclusive. There are eight thousand to ten thousand families affected by SIDS in the United States alone each year. Another thirty-three thousand families are affected by a stillbirth. Perhaps nearly a million miscarriages crush down upon the lives of American families each year. And countless other children die or disappear from their families in a terrible variety of ways. All these families share a common bond: they know what it means to lose a child.

Reaching out to Others in Pain

One of the best ways to deal with our own pain in life is to reach out to others who are also suffering. Seventy-three percent of the 127 parents in our most recent study said they had made efforts to be helpful to others who had lost babies. Here are descriptions of what they have done:

Talked, I guess. I'm not sure it helped.

We visited a couple who lost a baby. Not sure how much help we were, but we let them know they were not alone. Wrote a letter to a couple in another state that lost a baby to SIDS.

Just always being there if they need someone to really talk to.

I contacted a friend who had a stillbirth. I visited with her—mainly just listening.

I have been in touch with several families who have lost babies to SIDS. I have put information packets in local libraries and funeral homes.

I'm current president of the local chapter of the National SIDS Foundation. I design and write a quarterly newsletter. I do four to six public speaking engagements a month. I still occasionally attend parent support meetings. I try to write personal notes to the parents to remember birthdays or anniversaries. I try to make a call when I learn of a subsequent pregnancy. I do telephone parent-contacting whenever needed.

Speak with them about our experience. What helped, what made us feel rotten.

I have written my story, which I have been told is helping others.

I ran in a race to raise funds for SIDS research support groups.

Talked, prayed, listened, cried, hugged.

Two other couples have lost babies to SIDS in Oak Harbor since Melynda died. We've counseled, shared, prayed, talked, cried, laughed, and made new friends.

I told them the pain will be easier, in time.

Testimony: A Single Mother

The single mother who tells her story here was twenty-nine years old at the time her five-month-old baby died. She told us her story nine years later. She reported that her life did a complete turnaround after her baby died. She stated that during the first few years after the death she could barely live through each day.

"I found my daughter dead at 2:00 A.M. She was cold and stiff, and her face was black. I just started screaming and running. My father attempted CPR while I called an ambulance. We went to the hospital; I rode in the ambulance, and the rest of the family followed. We spent about two hours at the hospital and then went home.

"I just lay on the couch curled up until it was time to go to the funeral home. Nobody slept. We called all my family and friends in the morning. I think I smoked two packs of cigarettes that night. The following day was like limbo. We didn't do anything and couldn't go into the funeral home until the next day. I showed her one night at the funeral home and had the funeral the next day. I do not remember much of the funeral. It has always seemed like more of a dream than real.

"Everyone was very subdued at the funeral. They were uncomfortable, more than if an adult had died. I was in shock. I had to be totally supported most of the time. I could hardly walk or talk. I did not want to see my baby in the casket, but once I did, I do remember that she looked peaceful and it made me feel better. She looked better than she had when I found her.

"I would always recommend a funeral. I got to see my baby looking better than she had when I found her dead. My memory of her is much better because of the funeral."

[Which organizations or individuals were you in contact with the first few days after the death? How were they helpful? If they weren't helpful, how so?] "The doctors and nurses at the hospital were very cold. No one told me my baby was dead. They simply came in and asked me to sign papers for an autopsy. My personal physician and my daughter's pediatrician were helpful. They both talked to me to try and explain SIDS to me. The local police were terrible. The priests at my parish were wonderful to me, but since my daughter died on Holy Thursday, we were not allowed to have a funeral mass because of Catholic Church rules. I have since left the church. The National SIDS Foundation sent me a lot of literature and offered their help to me.

"I believe that her premature birth contributed to her death. Several theories relating to prematurity seem reasonable to me. I never had any indication, though, that she had a problem. An autopsy was performed, and everything was normal.

"I did feel personal guilt over my daughter's death because I was not married, and I felt that I had not taken proper care of my baby since I had to work long hours to support us. I have gotten past the initial guilt, but now I think about my prenatal care, which was not the best.

"I have also blamed the doctors I was seeing when my daughter was born. I believe they made several mistakes in my prenatal care which caused a premature delivery.

"My life has done a complete turnaround. People who have known me say my personality changed 100 percent. The first few years after she died I could barely live through each day. It was a struggle just to get out of bed. I was never afraid of anything, and now I can't sleep without a light on. I am scared to death of finding someone else dead.

"Nothing else comes close to the death of my baby. One month after my daughter died, my grandfather died. I was very close to him. My daughter is buried at his feet. My father also had a severe illness that caused him to become disabled. All of this happened within a three-year period. It altogether devastated my family.

"I went back to work one week after she died. I tried to spend as much time away from home as possible. I moved from my home ten months after the death of my baby. The move was related to the death. I couldn't stand the house anymore, so I accepted a job transfer to another city. It was a mistake and turned out very bad.

"I've had flashbacks since the death. For about four years after my daughter died, I was unable to sleep without nightmares. I would imagine everyone in the house was dead, and I at one time ran through the house turning on all the lights and waking everyone up because I was sure they were all dead. I still am afraid of finding someone I love dead. Every now and then I still am unable to sleep because every time I close my eyes I see what my daughter looked like when I found her. Her face was black and her body was cold and stiff.

"I have done many things that I would say are crazy. I would feel like I had to run away from everything, so I would get in my car and just disappear for days, without telling anyone. I was driving my family crazy. I was also addicted to drugs for approximately four years following my daughter's death. I felt it was the only way I could cope with life at the time.

"I thought of suicide because of my baby's death, and I also tried to kill myself. I drove my car down the wrong side of the busiest street in my city the day after she died. I also had very self-destructive behaviors for several years following her death.

"The people knowledgeable about SIDS have helped me get past my guilt feelings. My family stood behind me and gave me the space I needed to get through my grief. They and my close friends were there when I needed them but seemed to know when to leave me alone. The only thing that could have helped more would have been talking to other parents who have had babies die. I did not do that for several years.

"Some people have done things during the time of my daughter's death that made it more difficult for me. There were people who told me I had to forget her and get over her death. There were people who did not understand SIDS and who said things accusing me of not properly caring for my baby. Some well-meaning friends cleared out the house and stored away all my baby's things while I was at the funeral home making arrangements for her funeral. It was a tremendous shock to come home to an empty house.

"Since the death of my daughter, my family has gotten very close. We had never had anything tragic happen to us before my daughter died. We all just went our separate ways. Now we all spend more time together. My parents were very close to my daughter because we lived with them. It was almost as if their own child had died. They also had to deal with me. So, they not only lost their grand-daughter, but their daughter was suffering tremendously, and I know they felt helpless.

"[Several years ago] I started a parent support group in my area. I also worked as a parent contact for four years before I started the group. I like talking to other parents about their experiences. I also started the group as a way to help parents to overcome their grief more easily than I did. I feel it is necessary to talk to someone who truly understands how you are feeling. I was unable to do that for years. I know I have helped other parents, even though they still have to suffer. They can see someone who has lived through it, and I know that helps.

"What still hurts today is the fact that I have been unable to have more children. I have seen several doctors, and I am still trying to get pregnant. I miss having a ten-year-old daughter. I see other children who are ten years old, and it hurts that I'm missing out on the things she would have been doing."

[What good things have you learned about life?] "Life has ups and downs, and even when you feel there is no way you'll ever be up again, it does happen eventually.

"Good things that I have learned about myself are that I am a strong person and that I can be responsible. It is going to take an awful lot to break me down again. I think basically I am a survivor."

[What will the future bring?] "I don't plan for the future; I live for today."

[What would you like others to know about how to help a person who is grieving over a baby's death?] "Don't offer ideas on what caused the baby's death. Offer to help in any way possible and continue to help even a year afterward. Don't ignore the fact that the baby existed, that the parents need to remember the baby. If the parents want to talk about the baby, let them. Don't act uncomfortable every time the baby's name is mentioned. Talk to them about what you remember about the baby. Listen, and don't interrupt."

On Healing and Rebirth

Act out being alive, like a play. And after a while, a long while, it will be true.

—John Steinbeck[1]

The process of healing is long, complex, and fraught with peril. SIDS parents, unanimously, have told us that the death of their baby plunged them into despair. When asked to chart their path of personal happiness, all the SIDS parents we have contacted over the years have drawn a line that crashes dramatically at the time of the death and slowly rises—with erratic, short-term ups and downs—over the months and years that follow.

When we asked SIDS parents to estimate just how long it took to regain the level of personal happiness they perceived they had before the baby's death, they commonly tell us three years or more. So on the average, three years or more pass before one recovers that delicate level of well-being one felt before the death. But three years is not a magic number, because many, many parents are quick to point out that "you really *never* recover from the death."

Soon after the death—even in the first few weeks—most people can "go through the motions of life," almost as if they were on automatic pilot. And, it is clear, the memories become less terribly painful for most as the months and years pass. But recovery, in the sense of going back in life to where one was before the death, is impossible. Life is forever changed.

The wounds caused by the baby's death do heal over, in an

important sense. But the scars will probably always remain, and pain—usually not as devastating—will hide somewhere deep down for many years afterward, only to rise up with the memories.

Though full recovery is probably not possible, then, and healing incomplete, there is still a great deal of hope for bereaved families. This hope lies in a rebirth of good feelings for life and for living: there will be, once again, joy and laughter in the family. If there was joy and laughter before the baby's death, there will be joy and laughter again.

Bereaved families often tell us how thoroughly they have learned that life is precious. Perhaps that should be the whole theme of this book: *Life is precious.* It is finite, it is short, it is often sweet, and life, therefore, is precious. This knowledge, seared into one's consciousness—perhaps branded in one's soul—is important for family members. "I treat my loved ones so much better now," we have been told time and time again. "I tell them how much I care. I fret more when they are away from me, and this makes me so much more kind when they are around."

The knowledge that life is precious gives our lives more meaning. It makes us better people, and this makes our families stronger. Out of the ashes of despair rise hope and caring. Rebirth, in an important sense, is possible; and life can have meaning once again— perhaps even more meaning than it had before the baby died.

Many family members rededicate their lives in honor of their lost baby. This rededication is a kind of symbolic rebirth for people who have suffered greatly.

In this chapter, we will focus on the painful and precious memories parents experience after a death, and on how the nature of the hurt changes with the passage of time: how often people think about the baby; when memories most commonly return to consciousness; whether the memories ever fade with the passage of time; how the death affected relationships in the family; what still hurts as the years go by; the good things people have learned about life and themselves; and what the future will bring.

The Painful and Precious Memories

We asked the parents in our studies how often they thought of their baby. From their responses to this question, it was clear that the memories remain for a long, long time. Some of the memories cause pain to well up inside and tears to fall. Some of the memories bring a smile.

None of the parents told us they ever wanted to forget the baby, but many hoped the memories would not be so painful. With the passage of time, this generally proved to be the case. Memories do remain, and they do not tend to sting as much.

Following are a few representative responses from bereaved parents to the question "How often do you think of your baby?" Before the parent's response is a statement of how much time has passed since the baby died. Some parents think about the baby more than others. Some parents make an effort not to be obsessed by thoughts of the baby, while others let their thoughts flow in hopes that eventually they will not be so burdened by these memories. No one, however, ever forgets:

[Two months after the baby's death.] I don't think of her as much now as I did at first, but still many times a day.

[Two months after the death.] I think of him at least every day.

[Six months later.] When do I think of him? Always.

[Two and a half years later.] Almost every day.

[Three years later.] Almost every day.

[Three years later.] I still think about him a bit almost every day. Mostly the good times we had or about the things he should be doing at this age. Maybe in a store I see something and wonder if he would have liked that toy, would that outfit have fit him, and how good he would have looked in it. Sometimes it's just a fleeting moment.

[Four years later.] At least every day.

[Eight years later.] It's not even once a day anymore that I think of her. Through the holidays we think of her frequently. I am aware of her birthday and the anniversary of her death, but they are not downer days any longer. I probably think of her several times a week.

[Nine years later.] My life has done a complete turnaround. People who have known me say my personality changed 100 percent. The first few years after she died I could barely live through each day. It was a struggle just to get out of bed. I was never afraid of anything, and now I can't sleep without a light on. I am scared to death of finding someone else dead. . . . I think about her quite often. I have lots of pictures of her around me, and it's like she is always with me.

[Eleven years later.] It is still very rare, nearly twelve years later, that I do not think of her every day. Her pictures grace our home. Anyone named Stacie brings her back. I still wish to see her for just a moment on her birthday every year . . . just to see what she would have looked like.

[Seventeen years later.] I thought of the baby before the recent birth of my daughter probably once a week or every two weeks. Now I think of the lost baby daily.

[Thirty-eight years later.] I still think of her very often.

When Do the Memories Return?

We asked the mothers and fathers, "Are there specific times when memories come back?" Their responses are very interesting:

[Two months after the death.] Whenever I see an infant!

[Two months after the death.] After and before work and in the middle of the night. It was at those times I took care of her.

[Six months after the death.] Always. I will never stop remembering him and I don't want to.

[Two and a half years later.] Sometimes shopping. When I see all the pretty little girl clothes. Holidays, when I wonder how Tawnee would be at three years old. She would be so happy. When we are all together as a family, I feel like something is missing. I want to have more children, but it's not having Tawnee there that makes me incomplete.

[Three years later.] The date of his birth, the date of his death. Holidays are also real difficult, as I remember the ones he was there for and the ones he never saw. At the other children's birthdays, I always remember the whole family is not there. I guess that's why some of the holidays are also so hard to get through.

[Four years later.] At night when it's quiet I remember. Or in the day when it gets quiet. At my old job, working with my hands but not talking, it was emotionally exhausting.

[Eight years later.] Birth and death dates, obviously. During subsequent pregnancies, deliveries, infancies. An emergency situation (sirens, hospitals). When "Children of the Heavenly Father" is sung in church (it was sung at the memorial service). When a friend has a baby. When I notice similarities or differences in my living children and wonder what David would look like now, and how he would influence the younger two.

[Nine years later.] On her birthday and the anniversary of her death, I find myself reminiscing. Also when new babies are born in my family I think of her.

[Eleven years later.] On her birthday. On the anniversary of her baptism, death, and funeral. When I hear a Brahms lullaby and a certain song that was popular which they played over and over when I was in the hospital right after her birth.

[Seventeen years later.] I remember on his birthday and death, Mother's and Father's Day, when I see boys his age, or people who had babies when I did. Especially now since I've had another child.

[Thirty-eight years later.] Yes, I remember. When people ask how many children I have I always answer, "I had six girls, but we lost our second baby when she was six months old."

Do the Memories Fade Over Time?

We asked the 127 mothers and fathers in our most recent study, "Have the memories faded over time?" The parents were almost equally divided in response to this question: 49 percent said yes, and 51 percent said no.

"YES, THE MEMORIES HAVE FADED." For almost half of the parents the memories were not as distinct as they were soon after the death. One mother described the almost dreamlike quality of the experience. Perhaps this protects the bereaved from endless, unbearable pain:

[Two months after the death.] At first I talked about him all the time. Now I don't as much, and in a lot of ways, it seems like that year of my life (pregnancy and then having Alexander) was just a dream.

Other mothers and fathers had similar thoughts:

> [Three years after the baby's death.] Everything gets fuzzy—what she looked like and different things that I did get to do with her. It just gets fuzzy.

> [Nine years later.] I have a hard time remembering exactly what she looked like, unless I am looking at a picture of her. If I force myself to think about it, I can remember significant events that took place with her.

"NO, THE MEMORIES REMAIN CLEAR." For the other half of the parents in this study, visions of the baby and the circumstances surrounding the death remained unforgettable. For many of these parents, remembering the baby's life and death in great detail was a way of honoring the baby. Others had difficulty remembering the good things and often were drawn into the painful memories:

> [Two months after the death.] I can see her as if it were today.

> [Six months after the death.] No, the memories have not faded. I won't let them.

> [Three years later.] When I think of him the memories are very clear. I have tried over the years to let myself only really dwell on the happier memories, but that doesn't always work and I will almost have to force myself to think of the happy times to help block out the bad. It's like he will always be close to me, and I want it to stay that way forever. The sad memories are the strongest feelings that I do have, though. But joy is also there a lot too.

> [Four years later.] No, if I start thinking about her, it's not memories of when she was alive. It's that morning. I can't remember a lot about her when she was alive.

> [Eight years later.] I suppose due to [mental] replay, photographs, writing, and speaking, the memories are still vivid. At first, I was afraid I would forget, so I consciously tried to remember everything. Also, the intensity of a first child, first death experience made detail important.

> [Eight years later.] I think I have told myself and her that it's time for the memories to be put away. I won't forget her, but I can't continue to grieve and think of her either.

It is interesting to find the memories come back so vividly at times. I am the co-leader of a local grief group, and there are times when I need to bring back the vivid memories when working with a parent who has had a child die. Sometimes I wish I didn't have to do that, but it seems to help some people so much that I think of it as almost necessary to do at times.

[Thirty-eight years later.] It still hurts to talk about it, even after all these years.

YES AND NO. A few parents talk about reaching a point where some memories are still clear, and others are not:

[Eleven years later.] Some memories are very vivid. Some have faded. It is scary to admit that they have faded, because I do not want to forget her, but it is not as painful now. My memories of her now come through hope, not tears.

How the Death Affected Relationships in the Family

We were very interested in how the baby's death affected family relationships. Fifty-two percent of the parents in our most recent study told us that family relationships had been strengthened as a result of the tragedy. Thirty-nine percent said family relationships had remained the same. Only nine percent said family relationships had been weakened because of the death.

STRENGTHENED. Here is a sample of comments from those who felt the family became stronger:

My son has found he can talk to us about anything now.

I do not take my children for granted . . . We still have our differences at times, but I feel that we are much closer to each other. A couple of my aunts are now also a couple of loving friends. One had lost a son before mine so she was able to help me through some rough times. And now I have been able to do that for another aunt whose daughter I was very close to. My mom and I are much closer.

My family has gotten very close. We had never had anything tragic happen to us before my daughter died. We all just went our separate ways. Now we all spend more time together.

We now know that you have only today to say the things that need to be said. We hold on to each other tighter. We tell each other that we love each other and need each other.

STAYED THE SAME. Here are comments from parents who felt the death had no effect on family relationships:

[Three years after the baby's death.] Nobody else was as close to her as I was. They were there for the big crisis, but not really around for the trying to pull your life back together afterward. I don't rely on anyone else very much.

[Eight years later.] Although my family has lately indicated a respect for me because I "handled Cindi's death so well" (which I resent—they have no idea how I handled it, or handle it today for that matter), our relationships are not good. Her death has had no effect, good or bad, on our family.

WEAKENED FAMILY RELATIONSHIPS. The small percentage of parents who felt family relationships deteriorated in the aftermath of the death tended not to write much. One mother did say seventeen years later that "it seemed like not one of them cared. The grandparents never talked about it."

Families who were doing well before the baby died seemed, in general, to be more able in transcending the crisis, more capable of supporting each other through hard times and of growing in their love. Families who were not functioning cohesively before the death tended to have a more difficult time, for they were not as able to fall back upon each other.

What Still Hurts?

We wanted to learn more about the process of healing and were very interested in seeing whether the nature of the pain changed over time. We asked parents, "Now, today, what still hurts? When does it hurt? Why? What are you doing to alleviate your pain?" Studying their responses carefully, we could not come to any simple conclusions. Perhaps in most cases the pain is less intense as the years go by, but it seems to come in cycles or waves. Each new wave of pain or sadness seems to be triggered by the holidays, anniversaries, birthdays, contact with particular people, sights, or sounds that bring back the memories:

[Two months after the death.] It still hurts to think of the things that might have been. To see children interacting with their parents. I am trying to keep busy, exercise regularly, and take care of myself.

[Two months after the death.] I miss her, all the time. I loved her so much. To help ease the pain, I love God and I love my wife.

[Six months after the death.] Everything hurts, and it hurts always. I deal with the pain by not letting it run my life.

[Three years later.] The thought that he died all alone with no one there to hold him. The empty feeling and the feeling that I failed my son. I should have been able to do something for him. The loss is so great I never will get over it . . . that's my life sentence. It is harder for me at holidays, family reunions, and birthdays when the memories are there to remind me that someone very important to me is missing. When I know the pain is coming, like the holiday season, I try real hard to let the feelings go only when I'm alone. Kind of get it out of my system so that I do not cause problems around others. Get my act together and go on with whatever needs to be done.

[Four years later.] Filling out this questionnaire hurts. Going to the cemetery hurts. I still can't look at her pictures. When it hurts I go play with my other kids, or go sit outside. Sometimes I buy a new tree to plant. It's kind of a symbol or gift to her. Something alive.

[Eight years later.] School just started today, and I think about how she would have been going into the first grade and riding the bus, but it's a passing thought that I know can't be. I just let it go.

[Nine years later.] The fact that I have been unable to have more children hurts constantly. I have seen several doctors, and I am still trying to get pregnant. I miss having a ten-year-old daughter. I see other children that are ten years old, and it hurts that I'm missing out on the things she would have been doing.

[Eleven years later.] The fact that I never got to see her grow up. I still feel cheated at times. I am envious of people who have three or more kids. I cannot tolerate child abuse—hearing or reading about it. I still miss her very much. I wonder what her likes and dislikes would have been. I wonder what life would have been like had she not died.

[Seventeen years later.] It still hurts that I was robbed of him. It hurts now, especially because of my daughter [a newborn baby]. I have a son I can't talk about, because he isn't anything good or bad. He is dead. My daughter brought all these feelings out again. That's why I am going to support group meetings.

[Thirty-eight years later.] It still hurts to think or talk about my baby's death. I try not to think about it.

The Good Things

We asked the parents, "What good things have you learned about life?" and "What good things have you learned about yourself?" We had found in previous studies of how families cope with infant death that in the aftermath of even the most terrible disaster in life, people can see rays of light and goodness shining through. The vast majority of SIDS parents told us of good things that rose from the ashes of despair.

LEARNING ABOUT LIFE IN THE FACE OF DEATH. Many parents told us of the wisdom they gained, in spite of the pain. This mother was especially eloquent:

[Eleven years after the baby's death.] Since she died, I have gone through many years of pain, anger, acceptance, searching, growth, and understanding. The first two years were the most difficult—a pain and a hurt that cannot be adequately described in words. Then years of going through the motions in life. I did get *very* actively involved with the state SIDS Foundation and program about a year after she died, and I just left that capacity after ten years with them. Passive grief was getting me *nowhere*—I had to help. There came an acceptance and understanding about four years ago when I realized the growth that I experienced as a human being. It was then that I knew my daughter taught me more about life by her dying than anyone ever has or will.

"DON'T GIVE UP; IT WILL GET BETTER." This was a theme that many survivors echoed:

[Three years later.] I learned that what my psychology teacher told me at the time can be true: "Fake it till you make it." And I found that I can survive. I get the very much needed strength from somewhere if I try. It also helps to ask Jon [the lost baby] to send some strength from his very special place. Then, yes, I can go on. I may go on just taking very small steps, but as long as I try, that's what counts. *Keep on keeping on.* I can do things that I never dreamed that I would have to do, but if it's important enough to me, I can and do do them.

[Nine years later.] Life has ups and downs. And even when you feel there is no way you'll ever be up again, it does happen. Eventually.

YOU NEED HELP FROM OTHERS TO SURVIVE. Many parents expressed this theme:

[Four years later.] There are people who care about others. I wouldn't have survived it without the SIDS support group, without my husband, without my kids, without the in-laws.

[Eleven years later.] There are *many* loving, caring people out there. We share a strong bond, and we just need to reach out and be there for each other. We are all we have. Make your days count. Learn to risk. To be vulnerable. To love as best and as hard as you can.

I AM A STRONG PERSON. Many people were pleased to find how resilient they were. This knowledge helped them deal successfully with life's subsequent challenges:

[Six months after the death.] I learned you may be able to beat me to the ground, but I won't stay there. I will be back.

[Four years later.] I'm a survivor.

[Eight years later.] Christine's death made me finally gain some self-esteem. I finally realized that I had survived the worst thing possible that could happen to me and I had done it well when everything was considered. Most people I meet haven't had to survive their worst life event possible. I did. I do think it unfortunate that it had to be her dying that made me do that growing, but I am also pleased that I did grow during that period. There are a lot of other things I could have done!!!

[Nine years later.] I am a strong person. I can be responsible. It is going to take an awful lot to break me down again. I think basically I am a survivor.

[Seventeen years later.] The human being can survive anything and can also be the most magnificent creature. I also found I am capable of caring deeply for my fellow human beings, and as trite as it sounds, I want a better world for my daughter.

I AM NOT AFRAID. Six months after his baby died, a law officer spoke about his feelings toward life and death:

I learned that I really don't give a shit if the next bust shoots me. I'm not afraid of death, but I don't go searching for it beyond what my job in law enforcement requires.

ONE CANNOT UNDERSTAND LIFE, BUT THAT IS ALL RIGHT. One mother explained how she learned to accept life, and this brought a measure of comfort:

There is an awful lot I will never understand. No amount of analyzing, reading, studying will give all the answers. And that is all right. Life is worth living anyway. Also, her death was the first real test of my Christian beliefs (maybe second). God is real. God has the answers. When I really need them, he really does give them to me.

GOD LOVES ME. Two months after her baby died, one mother noted that one good thing the tragedy had brought was "I have learned that God loves me."

LIFE IS PRECIOUS. One of the most common and enduring themes survivors talk about is the fragility and value of life. This knowledge leads them to treat themselves and others with greater care and concern:

[Two months after the death.] I have learned that life is *very* short, and that you better enjoy it to its fullest while you have it.

[Thirty-eight years later.] I learned that life is precious. That we should put our lives in God's hands, and he will take care of us.

What Will the Future Bring?

The final question we asked the 127 parents in our most recent study was "What will the future bring?" Everyone hoped for good times to come, but all had been severely traumatized. No one seemed ready to hazard much of a prediction, though many had fervent hopes and prayers.

[Two months after the death.] I don't know what the future will bring . . . maybe another child, maybe sinking deeply into my career. Working on my M.B.A. and seeking career advancement.

[Two months after the baby's death.] More children, I pray.

[Six months after the death.] I don't know, and I don't want to know. Life is full of uncertainties you just have to take. Fight back when possible, and move forward. Never stop fighting.

[Three years later.] No one knows what the future will bring. Just have to try to take it a day at a time, and never give up on your hopes and dreams. Make plans. It's okay. But be ready to change or adapt if things do not go the way you wished. Expect the unexpected.

[Four years later.] Hopefully, more kids.

[Eight years later.] ???? I know that I can't plan the future. I can live for today and maybe try and plan for tomorrow, but not much further than that. I will make today what I can.

[Eight years later.] My thoughts about the future are generally positive. But [she asks the researchers] how about *you* telling *us?* How do parents feel fifteen years, twenty years, forty years later? By four years after his death I felt I was in an uncharted territory of grief. Books only deal with the first two years or so.

[Nine years later.] I don't plan for the future. I live for today.

[Eleven years later.] I hope the future will bring a cure or prevention for SIDS in my lifetime. I worry I will have to be afraid for my grandchildren when they are babies. I do not want my children or anyone else to have to go through this.

[Seventeen years later.] Hopefully, more growth for myself, both mentally and spiritually, with more peace in my soul, more compassion and understanding for myself and other people.

[Thirty-eight years later.] Only God knows what the future will bring.

So be it.

Testimony: The Dream

The Idaho mother who tells her story here was in her early twenties when her baby died at the age of three and a half months. She told us her story three years later.

"The funeral was beautiful. My husband, Bill, and I felt that we would never again be able to do anything for Annie, so we wanted to do as much of the funeral ourselves as possible.

"My husband dug the grave by himself, by hand. We have a tractor we could have used, but he did it all by hand. The ground was frozen and his hands bled. I wanted to dress her, but they wouldn't let me. But I arranged her in the coffin with her blankets. And we gave her a picture of the whole family together.

"My husband and I carried her casket from the car to the grave, and we chose special songs to be played. We had a graveside service in which she was spoken of the whole time, and we prayed. Then my husband and Shelley [the older daughter] and I placed one red rose on her coffin and lowered her into the grave and each put a handful of dirt in the grave. Then Bill covered her up. But he was overcome with grief, and his brother and brother-in-law finished. To me it helped make it real to see her covered up . . . We laid her to rest and made sure it was done right. Since then we have made our own headstone and we take care of her grave. It all helps.

"I think that I have dealt with the loss of our baby fairly well, considering. My husband and I had a hard time with our marriage. That would have to be the hardest thing. My husband had a harder time dealing with it. At first, maybe three months afterward, I asked him to move out. He became almost unbearable to live with. We've gone through some extremely low lows . . . Since that time things have gotten much better, but at the time we almost got a divorce. I wanted another baby right away and my husband didn't. We did get pregnant six months after she died. We now have a healthy one-year-old son. But when he was born my husband would not hold him or even touch him hardly. I felt that he didn't want to get close to him. But my husband became hard to live with again. In the meantime I became very attached to our new son, almost obsessed. I've had a hard time dealing with our older daughter. My relationship with her has suffered very much. It is something that is getting better as our son gets older. I think that now I do treat them more the same, and my husband has since developed a very close relationship with our son. So it has gotten better.

"The day she died I was at my job working in the sheriff's office from 4:00 P.M. till midnight. I had a high school girl come to the house and stay with the kids until Bill got home from work. Well, that night at work I had an upset stomach, for no reason. I still feel it was a premonition. Well, I decided to go home early. It was the first time I had ever missed work, but I went home early about 7:00 P.M. My husband never got home until around 9:30 that night. I had spent a nice evening with the kids. I wasn't used to being with them in the evening, and I really enjoyed it. I had fed Annie and Shelley supper and gotten them all washed up and [had put] clean pajamas on Annie.

"Anyway, when my husband got home, he had been at the bar and had had a few beers. I was mad that he hadn't called. He smarted off to me and then fell asleep on the floor. I was really mad and decided to take a drive. (I had never left before. This was the first time, and that has always seemed so strange to me.) I put the kids to bed. They were both asleep, and I left to take a drive to cool off. I stopped downtown and made a phone call to wake my husband up to let him know that I was gone and to listen for the baby. She usually would wake up crying two or three times a night. He answered the phone but hung up when it was me.

"I drove to a friend's house a few miles away and visited with her. I decided to go home early in the morning because it got late. Around 5:00 in the morning the phone rang. It was the deputy sheriff at work. He is a good friend. He told my friend to bring me straight home, that Annie was sick, and they had taken her to the hospital. I thought that maybe she got the flu or something, but I didn't know because she had been fine when I left, so I called the hospital and the nurse told me, 'Oh! *That* baby died.'

"I remember screaming and then a total calm came over me. I guess I didn't really believe it could be true. When I got home my husband was walking around crying, and he ran out of the house and grabbed me and was hugging me and he was shaking and crying. I kept saying, 'Would you knock it off and tell me what's going on. It's not a funny joke.' The sheriff was there, and he took me in the house. We are good friends with all the deputies and the sheriff, and one of their wives was there looking after Shelley. So there were a lot of people around.

"They were taking pictures of Annie's room and crib. They wouldn't let me in the room. I sat down with Bill and asked him what had happened. I had heard of SIDS, but the thought never crossed my mind. Bill told me that he had gotten up and checked on the kids about 2:00 A.M. because he couldn't sleep and they were both okay. Then around 4:30 he woke up and checked them again and he couldn't hear her breathing. He picked her up, and she was cold and had foam around her mouth. I wanted to see her then, so the sheriff (Al) said he would take me to her.

"Before leaving I called my mom, who lives in another town forty-five miles away. I remember being so calm and just saying, 'Annie's dead; would you please come over?' She started crying and becoming hysterical but said she would be right over. She was in a real state of shock. Al then took me to the funeral home so I could see her.

"She looked so empty. Like something was gone from inside her. I cried, but not really. I called my pastor and asked them to come pray for her, and he came right over. It was like such a nightmare. I guess we stayed there for quite a while . . .

"They said that an autopsy had to be performed on her. I didn't want one. It was such a terrible thought, but Al told me it was the law—if someone died at home, and maybe it might help them find out the cause to help other babies. That was when I was told that they thought it was SIDS. I didn't have any idea up till then. After leaving there they took me home, and my mom had come. Then I just remember a lot of people coming over and a lot of phone calls.

"My husband was like a zombie. I had to do everything for him. He just cried and shook and walked around in a daze. Up until now Shelley had not been told anything. I sat her down and explained that her sister had gone to live in heaven and wouldn't be living with us anymore. That God had taken her to be with him. She cried some, but didn't really understand what was happening. I made all the phone calls to the relatives and stayed so calm.

"It wasn't until in the late morning—around 10:00 or 11:00 A.M.—that it hit me. I remember starting to shake and realize the full force of what had happened. I wanted to hold her, I wanted that so much I lost control and started vomiting uncontrollably.

That lasted maybe an hour, and it was back to being sort of numb. The rest of the time seems to be a dream and all really hazy.

"The sheriff's office and the funeral home were very helpful after she died. The director of the funeral home was supergood. He helped us make all the decisions. At that point, I remember not being able to decide which way to go when we backed out of the driveway, all decisions were so hard. He helped us with them all, but still helped us feel like we made them ourselves. He guided us through the hardest decisions of our life. The sheriff's office was great friendshipwise. One of the deputies there had lost a son to SIDS seven or eight years before and came right over. He didn't say much but his just being there helped. Also, they were really good and explained all the legal things like the autopsy having to be done since she had died at home.

"I have had a good friend who lost a teenage daughter. She helped me most by just being there to talk and mostly to listen to me. Just being there to listen to me at any time or whenever I needed someone. Or sometimes to listen to me even when what I might have had to say wasn't or didn't seem all that important. To understand that grief sometimes can be anger or guilt or sometimes feelings that might not be so nice.

"It hurts a lot when everybody seems to have forgotten about my daughter. She is a part of me, as much now as when she was alive. I wish it didn't upset people so much to talk about her. I still feel like she's my daughter and still like to talk about her, and sometimes dream about what she would have been like now at three years old. To talk about her is my way of keeping her alive as time fades my memory.

"After two or three months the novelty of what had happened was in the past for everybody but my husband and me and our other daughter. We were expected to carry on, stop hurting, act normal, and go on with our lives like nothing had happened. I think that if I had been allowed to grieve longer or had not been expected to be so strong for everybody else's sake it would have been better. I got so tired of hearing how strong I was . . . or how well I was taking it. I felt that I wasn't allowed to have bad days, or at least nobody understood if I did. I think from being told how strong I was I felt that I had to live up to everybody's expectations of me and tended to bury my feelings instead of dealing with them.

"My friend, as I said earlier, mostly listened. I could really be myself. She wasn't shocked by my feelings. Since she had been through the loss of a child before, she understood even if she had never experienced that certain feeling. She understood and realized that I was okay, that I wasn't really a bad person for some of my thoughts. She also allowed me to cry and be down even as much as one year or longer after our baby died. We still stay very close, although I don't call or talk to her as often anymore, at least about the death of our baby. I can now talk of other things that are important in my life.

"Listen to a grieving person. Listen to them. Let them say *whatever* they feel and don't condemn them or judge them. Just be there and care for them. Don't say that you know how they feel if you have never experienced it. That tends to put down their feelings. Unless you have been through it, don't tell them what to do or how they should feel. Make suggestions to help, but keep them light. Some people don't need advice as much as they need someone to turn to whenever they get down. Even if it's not a convenient time.

"Grief sometimes hits at the happiest times. Even if bereaved parents seem okay and 'back to normal' on the outside, don't expect that they never hit lows again. They always will. Let them grieve if they feel like it. Don't set your time limit on people who have lost their own blood and their future for when you think they should be over it.

"I explained earlier that when I called the hospital to see how the baby was (I had only been informed that she was sick and had been taken to the hospital), the nurse very coolly informed me, 'Oh! *That* baby died.' No sympathy at all. The physician never talked to me about anything or helped explain what might have happened. The pastor I called to say a prayer for our daughter was wonderful. He helped us tremendously. Counseling and otherwise. Our funeral director was very helpful with all the decisions we had to make.

"I had heard of SIDS before but never thought about it. I just thought it had to be some terrible joke. I do have a personal theory. Sometimes when I have a cold and I sleep at night, I can't breathe through my nose, and I will forget to breathe and wake up with a start and my lungs hurt. Annie (our daughter) used to wake up crying a lot with a start when she had cold. I think that night she forgot to wake up or not in time.

"I wasn't satisfied with the results of the autopsies. The first autopsy said she died of choking. When it was gone over by the head pathologist, he said that it was SIDS. That when the ambulance crew tried to start her breathing, they blew the bolus into her windpipe. I don't know which is true . . . Whether the other pathologist changed it because of the effect that 'choking' had on us, mostly my husband, of guilt. In his letter he said something about how our peace of mind might be better with SIDS on the death certificate, but really now we just wonder what is right.

"I have felt guilty, because I was not there that night, and maybe she did cry and nobody heard her and I wasn't there to take care of her so maybe she did choke. I knew that my husband was a heavy sleeper and did not hear the kids if they woke up or cried at night. When I first heard she was dead, I wondered if my husband had done something to her, but thank God I had enough sense never to say anything like that because my husband would kill himself before he would ever hurt his kids. It makes me feel bad now to even say that I had thought something like that.

"I am very interested in any theory that comes out in the papers or on TV. I read all I can. I have sent for studies on SIDS. It helps me deal with it. Maybe the fact that I feel someone is trying to save our babies helps. But I don't think they really know what the cause is, and I feel that the cause is different in different cases of SIDS.

"I spent most of the night before the funeral with Annie and said my goodbyes then. I didn't cry at the funeral. Neither did my husband. I felt more or less detached. The services were beautiful. Even on the most nasty, gray day. We made the funeral as special and as much like her as we could. The funeral helped to make it real. Having her grave is important to Bill and me. We plant grass and flowers and shrubs. We can't take care of her anymore but we can her place of rest. She might not know it, but it is comforting to us.

"The hardest fact to accept is that we will never hold her or kiss her or tell her we love her again. I won't see her grow and change. I will never hear her call me 'Mama.' She won't experience any of the wonders of life. I won't know what she would have looked like all grown up. I'll never see her walk or hear her talk. But mostly, I can never hold her again.

"I think of her almost every day.

"I had been in a terrible car accident only six weeks before Annie died where one person had been killed in the other car. It was totally devastating, but it has no comparison to losing a child. I felt that I had lost my future. A very big part of me had just been taken away. I not only lost my child, I lost out on all the memories I would have had if she'd have been on earth longer.

"For about the first six months after she died all my husband and I did on the weekends was drink. We went out all the time. It seemed like we could not stay home. But now that things have gotten better, we don't go out hardly at all. We have other interests and reasons for living again.

"I remember before the funeral, the night before, I wanted to go down to the funeral home to be with her. I was telling my husband to come with me. I can't remember what happened, but my husband grabbed my face and shoved me up against the wall, and in the same minute we were both crying and holding each other. He did get violent very easily after Annie's death. But like everything else, time does heal.

"My husband would sometimes hold Annie's picture and rock her in the rocking chair like he did when she was alive and talk to her while patting her picture on the back, and he'd be crying. One night I came home from work and found him hysterical, holding a gun at his head. Right after she died. Within two weeks when it gets the hardest.

"The pain is so intense right after. It's more than a person can bear. Sometimes I just wanted to go to sleep. It would just be easier not to have to deal with the loss of a baby you've only known for such a short time but was as much a part of your life as your right arm.

"Suicide does not solve anything. If you would think of the pain you're going through from the loss of one you loved, think about the loss and the pain you would be bringing to your own family that loves you and cares for you. Would you want to inflict that very same pain that you feel on someone else? It is just the most selfish act one could think of to do.

"The pain was so intense for both of us that we couldn't even deal with our own pain, let alone deal with each other's. It seemed like we just didn't have anything to give anymore, and when you're not giving in a marriage at all times, that marriage can quickly fall apart. Time does heal, and with time we did deal with our grief and then learned how to give again and deal with each other.

"I tend to talk about it. To everybody or anybody who is interested or cares. Not that I really show my true emotions. My husband has a hard time talking. It was hard for him to talk at first, but now he is slowly getting much better. As the pain eases for both of us.

"It was me who stayed strong for everybody else to lean on and to make sure that everyday life got taken care of. I kept things going, ignored my own feelings. I think I just built a wall so I wouldn't remember or think about it. My husband just came unglued.

"We separated for a time after the baby died. I needed time for a while to help deal with my grief without Bill around to make things worse. I had also gotten pregnant because of the feeling of being so empty, and my husband didn't acknowledge it, and for me it was the hope I clung to to keep going.

"I have had a hard time dealing with our older daughter, who is now six years old. It has gotten better with time, but at first I just didn't have any tolerance for her at all. I pulled myself away from her at first.

"Shelley wanted to know why Annie died. She wanted to know if it was because she didn't like living with us: 'Is that why she went to heaven?' She wanted to know what had happened to make her die and wondered if she would die too. Or if Mommy or Daddy would die. We told her Annie loved us and we loved her, but God wanted her to come live with him and she would be very happy with God too. She died because sometimes little babies forget to breathe, and it would not happen to her [Shelley] because she was too old. Everybody had to die sometime, and we would too, but not for a long time.

"Shelley got harder to discipline and acted up more for attention. I think this was my fault because I was so wrapped up in myself that I didn't give her the attention she had been used to. But time heals, and with time we have learned things all over again. We just have a different relationship.

"[My religious beliefs were helpful.] I believe that if it is someone's time to die, then they will die, and circumstances have nothing to do with God's will. I had to believe this or the guilt of not being home and being there for my baby would have destroyed me. God will take his children to be with him when it is his time and only he sets the time for anyone. He felt she had served her time, and maybe if she hadn't died she would have had a life of severe pain or heartache. And thank God he took her in such a peaceful way.

"The general idea of support groups is good. But the one I went to, it seemed that for some people who had been going to it for five to ten years, they had never really dealt with their grief, and it was a way for them to grieve over and over about something that should have lessened by now. I think people should learn to go on with their life and to find happiness. Not to dwell on things to a point where it controls their life. But I do believe that people helping other people deal with things that they might have experienced in their own lives is good.

"I have had several people referred to me when they lost a child to crib death. I mainly just try and listen and answer questions they might have about what we have gone through, which is about everything. I want to be able to help other people, because without my special friend I would never had made it. I would like to do that for other bereaved parents. I have thought about trying to start a support group in our own community, but there are not enough people.

"It gives me a sense that my experience of having my daughter die does not have to be in vain if, because of my experience, I can help someone else who may be less fortunate or who has experienced the loss of more than one child.

"There are good things in this world and in life. We have two beautiful, healthy children. We made it through an almost unbearable time and we survived. They say God will never give to you more than you can handle. I believe that. And I believe that in time you will know the meaning in everything that happens to you. Good or bad.

"I am a good person and I am strong. I am proud of the person I am and think I have done and been through a lot for my twenty-five years. I have learned that I can help other people through my experiences. I think I have a bright future. We have plans to raise our children to be happy, self-sufficient adults, and to be happy ourselves. I know that there is no such life as one without problems, but they can be dealt with. A person can make it through some pretty tough times and come out a better person from it all.

"I would do anything to help someone else through the pain.

"I remember a dream. It was right after she died, and I had cried so hard just to be able to hold her one more time. That night, she came to me in my dreams.

"I held her, but she was different. I can't explain. She said she was okay, and happy, and she loved me and knew I loved her.

"I never had a dream like that about her after that. It sounds so strange, but I really do believe that she came to me that night and I got my wish to hold her one more time."

Coping: A Self-Study Guide

As the reader has seen, the process of coping with SIDS is a long and complicated one. For this concluding chapter, we have developed a series of study questions that a parent can answer about how well she or he is doing in adapting to the crisis. (Grandparents will also find most of the questions useful to think about.) The questions can be answered in writing, on audio or videotape, or in the mind. We believe it would be most useful to reply to the questions in a format that can be saved and studied months or years later. A person can then clearly see the progress that he or she has made in transcending the crisis.

Coping with a crisis is like a child growing: unless you have a photograph or an aunt who does not visit very often to tell you how fast your child is growing, you just do not see the changes. Your recorded answers to these questions can be that photograph or that aunt. You can look back in the months and years ahead and see how far you have come in your journey.

Couples might find it helpful to answer the questions individually and then discuss how their responses are similar or how they differ. A discussion of these issues can go a long way toward easing the tensions and preventing misunderstandings. Remember, as Rabbi Earl Grollman says, "Anything mentionable is manageable." If a couple simply cannot discuss these matters together, however, we suggest they try it with the aid of a family therapist or other type of counselor. A professional working with SIDS parents would play the role of mediator and referee—making sure that each person understands the other, and that communication between people proceeds in a positive manner. (Counselors could have parents answer these questions before counseling sessions begin, and follow up at the end of treatment by having them answer the questions again.) Support group leaders will also find these questions useful in leading group discussions. At each session the group leaders could focus on a different area of concern. The process of grieving moves along better, we believe, if it is a shared experience with loved ones and friends.

If you wish to answer these questions, simply get several sheets of paper, something to write with, and a handkerchief or some tissues. You will find that answering these questions takes a long time—several hours, perhaps over several days or weeks. And you will find that tears come easily and quickly while you are thinking about what has happened. That is good; that is part of the healing.

The questions here are very similar to those we have asked parents over the years in our studies.

Coping with Sudden Infant Death: A Self-Study Guide

1. Please write down what you have gone through since your baby died.
2. What things have people done during this time that have been helpful to you?
3. What things have people done during this time that have made it harder for you? Have you told them so, in a kind but straightforward manner?
4. What would you like people to know about how to treat a person who is grieving over a baby who has died? What do you feel the general public doesn't understand?
5. Could you describe at length (and we know this is terribly difficult) what happened at the time of your baby's death? (Who was caring for the child? Who found the child? What did they see? What happened after the child was found? Please tell the story of the first day or so after the death.)
6. When you first realized the baby was gone, what went through your mind as a probable cause of death?
7. Which organizations or individuals were you in contact

with the first few days after the death? How were they of help? If they weren't helpful, how so?

8. Did you ever feel personal guilt over the death? If so, why?

9. Did hardship during pregnancy, delivery, and so forth, make the death of your baby even harder to accept?

10. What was the hardest fact or facts to accept about the death of your child?

11. Do you consider your baby a part of your family?

12. How often do you think of your baby? Are there specific times when memories come back? (For example, birthdays.) Have memories faded over time?

13. Do you ever worry that you won't be able to remember details? (For example, what your child looked like.)

14. Was an autopsy performed?

15. If so, did knowing the results and their explanation help?

16. Were you satisfied with the results of the autopsy?

17. Did you have a funeral for your baby?

18. Comment on the funeral. (For example, how did others react to the funeral? Was there an open casket? Were pictures made?)

19. Do you feel that having a funeral and going through a formal ceremony helped you and others accept your baby as a part of your family and as a worthwhile individual in her or his own right?

20. Rate the quality of professional care provided by the following professionals involved in the crisis: physicians; nurses; religious personnel; funeral directors; family therapists; social workers/counselors. Explain the rationale behind each of your ratings.

21. How does the loss of your baby compare to other crises you have experienced in your life? List each major crisis and note similarities and differences.

22. (If you were or are part of a couple) Who resumed normal activities first after the death, you or your partner? Why?

23. (If you were or are part of a couple) Presumably, you and your partner have different ways of coping with the death. What are they, and why are they different?

24. If you feel you need to talk with someone, whom do you turn to most often?

25. Irrational thoughts are common in a crisis. Have you had any? What were they?

26. Did you move from your home and/or your community? Why? Was the move related to the death?

27. Did you have so-called flashbacks of the death—that is, pictures in your mind of the dead baby or some related nightmare—that would intrude into your thinking at odd or inopportune times? If so, estimate how many flashbacks you have had since the death.

28. Could you describe the flashbacks?

29. Has drinking or other drug use increased in your family because of the death? If yes, please explain.

30. Did any family violence occur as a result of the death? What happened?

31. It has been said that when a baby dies it is "almost normal to go crazy." Could you describe anything you have done that made you wonder sometimes if you were going crazy?

32. (If you were or are married) Could you describe anything your partner has done that made you wonder sometimes if she or he was going crazy?

33. What about other people?

34. Did you ever just want to go to sleep and wake up after the pain has gone away?

35. Have you ever thought of suicide because of the death?

36. Did you try to kill yourself because of the death?

37. What are your arguments for suicide?

38. Why shouldn't you kill yourself?

39. (If you were or are part of a couple) Has or was your marriage affected by the death?

40. If yes, how? Strengthened? Weakened?

41. (If you were or are part of a couple) Did or does your way of coping with the death differ from that of your spouse? If so, how?

42. Did your sexual relationship with your partner change after the death? If so, explain.

43. Did you ever consider a divorce in the aftermath of the death?

44. Did you and your partner separate in the aftermath of the death?
45. Did you actually divorce in the aftermath of the death?
46. If you divorced, was the baby's death one of the causes?
47. How has the death affected your relationships with other members of your family? Strengthened? Weakened? Stayed about the same?
48. How were the baby's grandparents affected by the death?
49. If you have other children, have there been changes in the way you care for them as a result of the death?
50. Did the children ask questions about the death? If so, what questions? And how did you reply?
51. Was there any difference in the children's behavior after the death? If yes, what differences?
52. Has the death affected your decision to have other children? If so, how?
53. If there was a funeral, did the other children attend? If so, how did they react?
54. (If you have surviving children) Children have been said to be the lost souls of a family in crisis. Parents are often so numb from the death of a baby that they are lost in their own thoughts and spend little time relating to the surviving children. Most specialists in the area of grief counseling would agree, however, that it is important to talk with the surviving children about their feelings. Would you sit down with your other youngsters and ask them a few questions? The discussion might prove very beneficial to your family, though it will certainly be both a sad and a happy time.

    The discussion should be very open and free-flowing. Rather than give you any specific formula, here are a few suggestions: Sit down when you're relaxed and the child or children are also relaxed—Maybe after dinner sometime, or after school or on Sunday afternoon. Anyway, let the children know you'd enjoy talking about the baby, and hope they would like to talk about the baby with you also. Good questions seem to be open ended. The list of questions could go on and on. Write down some of the things your children say about the baby; they will be very important to have later on.

Some good questions for children:

What do you remember about the baby?
When you think about the baby, what are you thinking?
What makes you sad when you think about the baby?
What makes you laugh or feel happy when you think about the baby?
Do you know why the baby died? Could you tell me?
Should we have another baby?
Are you sometimes afraid when you think about the baby?
What should I do to make you feel better when you're feeling sad about the baby?
Want a hug?

55. Has your baby's death had an influence on any religious beliefs you may have? Strengthened? Weakened? Changed? Or perhaps you didn't think of the death in religious terms at all?

56. Were your religious beliefs helpful to you in this crisis? If so, how? If not, why?

57. Was your church or synagogue itself helpful to you in this time of crisis?

58. Could you describe your religious beliefs as they relate to the death?

59. Does your community have a support group for grieving parents?

60. Have you called the support group for information?

61. Have you attended a support group meeting?

62. Could you describe your personal reaction to the meeting? What happened? What did you like about the meeting? What did you dislike?

63. How many meetings have you attended now?

64. Have you done anything to help other people who have lost babies? If so, what have you done?

65. In order to get an idea of how the baby's death affected you personally, circle the appropriate number to describe your feelings for each period of time.

	Very Unhappy	Somewhat Unhappy	Average	Somewhat Happy	Very Happy
1 year before the death, I was	1	2	3	4	5
9 months before the death	1	2	3	4	5
6 months before the death	1	2	3	4	5
3 months before the death	1	2	3	4	5
At the time of the death of the baby	1	2	3	4	5
3 months after the death	1	2	3	4	5
6 months after the death	1	2	3	4	5
9 months after the death	1	2	3	4	5
1 year after the death	1	2	3	4	5
1 year 3 months after the death	1	2	3	4	5
1 year 6 months after the death	1	2	3	4	5
1 year 9 months after the death	1	2	3	4	5
2 years after the death	1	2	3	4	5
2 years 3 months after the death	1	2	3	4	5
2 years 6 months after the death	1	2	3	4	5
2 years 9 months after the death	1	2	3	4	5
3 years after the death	1	2	3	4	5
4 years after the death	1	2	3	4	5
5 years after the death	1	2	3	4	5

	Very Unhappy	Somewhat Unhappy	Average	Somewhat Happy	Very Happy
6 years after the death	1	2	3	4	5
7 years after the death	1	2	3	4	5
8 years after the death	1	2	3	4	5

66. Now consider your family organization or integration in relation to the various time periods surrounding your child's death. (In other words, consider how smoothly the family was functioning as a whole.)

	Disorganized	Somewhat Disorganized	Average Level of Organization	Somewhat Well Organized	Very Well Organized
1 year before the death, I was	1	2	3	4	5
9 months before the death	1	2	3	4	5
6 months before the death	1	2	3	4	5
3 months before the death	1	2	3	4	5
At the time of the death of the baby	1	2	3	4	5
3 months after the death	1	2	3	4	5
6 months after the death	1	2	3	4	5
9 months after the death	1	2	3	4	5
1 year after the death	1	2	3	4	5
1 year 3 months after the death	1	2	3	4	5
1 year 6 months after the death	1	2	3	4	5

	Disorga-nized	Somewhat Disorga-nized	Average Level of Organi-zation	Somewhat Well Orga-nized	Very Well Orga-nized
1 year 9 months after the death	1	2	3	4	5
2 years after the death	1	2	3	4	5
2 years 3 months after the death	1	2	3	4	5
2 years 6 months after the death	1	2	3	4	5
2 years 9 months after the death	1	2	3	4	5
3 years after the death	1	2	3	4	5
4 years after the death	1	2	3	4	5
5 years after the death	1	2	3	4	5
6 years after the death	1	2	3	4	5
7 years after the death	1	2	3	4	5
8 years after the death	1	2	3	4	5

67. Now, today, what still hurts? When does it hurt? Why? What are you doing to alleviate your pain?
68. What good things have you learned about life?
69. What good things have you learned about yourself?
70. What good things have you learned about your family?
71. What strengths of your family have helped you pull through this crisis?
72. What will the future bring?
73. What are you going to do to help other people who have been to the edge?

We are sure that answering these probing questions about the crisis you are experiencing in your life has been a difficult process. We hope that answering these questions has helped you sort things through in your mind. We hope you keep your answers, if they are written or taped; and perhaps it would be useful to share what you have written with loved ones and friends so that they may better understand what you are going through. Again, anything mentionable is usually manageable.

Best wishes to you in your journey of healing.

Appendix A
Eighteen Ways to Help People Who Have Been to the Edge

Our final question to the parents and grandparents in our most recent study was "What are you going to do to help other people who have been to the edge?" Following are eighteen representative responses in people's own words which contain the collective wisdom of the group. No single human being could possibly do all of these wonderful things, but anyone could choose one or two or three to offer for the good of humankind:

1. I will do whatever I am strong enough to do.
2. I will listen if they want to talk, and tell my story if they want to hear it.
3. I will lend a shoulder to cry on.
4. I'll lend a helping hand, whether it's doing small chores, helping with their children, fixing a meal, anything.
5. I will be patient and kind and encouraging. I will be there.
6. I will tell them it's all right to be angry, as long as you don't get stuck there.
7. I will tell them that in every day of darkness there is a ray of light and a glimmer of hope.
8. I will tell them it is normal to grieve and to feel depressed. I will tell them the first year is hell, but that after that your life begins to reconstruct and time helps heal the horrible pain. I will assure them that it will get better and that they will be happy again.
9. I will talk . . . pray . . . hope . . . talk some more . . . and pray some more.
10. I will love them.
11. I will seek them out. A stranger is only a stranger until

you've knocked on their door and said, "I'm sorry, my baby died too."

12. I will pray to live to see the day that Sudden Infant Death Syndrome is cured or a preventive medicine is found that will save the lives of other babies and my children's babies.

13. I will teach my surviving children that to live is to laugh, to risk, and to cry.

14. I would like someday to be a counselor to parents who have lost a child. But I must first get a little farther away from the edge myself.

15. I will get involved with others, because life is truly precious. I will stay active in my support group and help people see that they are not alone. It makes me feel good to help others whenever I can.

16. I will volunteer my time and talents to SIDS organizations. I will help raise the needed funds for research so that others may not have to experience this loss.

17. Eventually, I will help them remember their little one with smiles, not tears, and that is the moment when healing really begins.

18. I will be there to listen and show that one can and does survive what I consider life's greatest tragedy.

Appendix B
Selected Readings

Readings for Adults (Parents, Grandparents, Professionals)

Borg, Susan, and Judith Lasker. *When Pregnancy Fails: Families Coping with Miscarriage, Stillbirth, and Infant Death*. Boston: Beacon Press, 1981.

A very competent guide based upon the authors' extensive reading, interviews, and personal experiences as mothers who have felt the pain of the death of a baby.

The Compassionate Friends. *Grieving, Healing, Growing*. Oak Brook, Ill.: The Compassionate Friends, 1982.

The Compassionate Friends is a nationwide organization with local chapters in most major cities. They offer emotional support and friendship, educational and social activities for bereaved families. Activities are even included for surviving children.

This book is a compilation of writings by professional people and bereaved parents taken from Compassionate Friends newsletters. The mailing address of the Compassionate Friends is P.O. Box 1347, Oak Brook, IL 60521.

Culbertson, Jan L., Henry F. Krous, and R. Debra Bendell, eds. *Sudden Infant Death Syndrome*. Baltimore: Johns Hopkins University Press, 1988.

This book is made up of twelve articles on the medical aspects of SIDS and infantile apnea; acute loss and grief reactions; the family and SIDS; family reactions to home monitoring; the apneic infant; and the story of the National SIDS Foundation.

DeFrain, John, Leona Martens, Jan Stork, and Warren Stork. *Stillborn: The Invisible Death*. Lexington, Mass.: Lexington Books, 1986.

More than 350 parents from across the United States share how they managed to survive the stillbirth of an infant. There are chapters on the marriage relationship, God, surviving siblings, and ways to cope.

"One of the most outstanding books of the decade dealing with death and dying. It is definitive . . . it is helpful . . . it is *so* human. It should be required reading for social scientists and bereaved people alike."

—Rabbi Earl A. Grollman, D.D.

Grollman, Earl A. *Talking about Death: A Dialogue between Parent and Child.* Boston: Beacon Press, 1976.

A book parents can read and study, and then read to their children. Awarded a UNESCO citation as "one of those books in the world which has changed public opinion."

Grollman, Earl A., ed. *Explaining Death to Children.* Boston: Beacon Press, 1979.

A book of readings for parents and other adults to help them guide children, "the lost souls of a family in crisis," through their grief.

Guntheroth, Warren G. *Crib Death: Sudden Infant Death Syndrome.* Mount Kisco, N.Y.: Futura, 1982.

A professor of pediatrics at the University of Washington discusses the pathology of SIDS; epidemiology of SIDS; near-miss SIDS; theories of cardiovascular causes of SIDS; possible respiratory causes of SIDS; miscellaneous theories about the cause of SIDS; maternal factors in SIDS; and management and prevention of SIDS. Especially strong on the medical aspects.

Harper, Ronald M., and Howard J. Hoffman, eds. *Sudden Infant Death Syndrome: Risk Factors and Basic Mechanisms.* New York: PMA Publishing Group, 1988.

More than forty articles from a meeting of international investigators gathered in Santa Monica, California, to discuss information on the risk factors and underlying mechanisms of SIDS. The book describes the history of SIDS research over the last twenty years, and new research findings reported by epidemiologists, pathologists, and physiologists. An excellent sourcebook for those interested in the medical aspects of SIDS.

Kastenbaum, Robert, and Beatrice Kastenbaum, eds. *Encyclopedia of Death.* Phoenix: Oryx Press, 1989.

Offers a broad range of information on death written by recognized authorities in their particular areas. Sections relevant to SIDS families include adolescence and death; autopsy; awareness of dying; children and death; Compassionate Friends; death anxiety; death education; funerals; grief; grief counseling; humor and fear of death; life after death?; religious beliefs; SIDS; and suicide.

Kushner, Harold S. *When Bad Things Happen to Good People.* New York: Avon, 1981.

Why do the good die young? How can we retain a sense of hope and goodness in an insane world? Rabbi Kushner, who lost a son, addresses these questions in a most meaningful way. A nationwide best-seller.

Ring, Kenneth. *Heading toward Omega: In Search of the Meaning of the Near-Death Experience.* New York: Morrow, 1984.

A discussion of the possibility of "life after life" by a noted psychologist. Ring concludes that science cannot verify one way or the other whether there is some kind of existence after death, but his research has indicated that millions of people's lives each year are transformed by near-death experiences.

Schiff, Harriet Sarnoff. *The Bereaved Parent.* New York: Penguin Books, 1977.

"A beautiful book. It speaks to all those who have lived through the experience of the death of a child. It does not make death beautiful, it does not console in an unrealistic way—but it tells the truth—and is very reassuring and helpful because of it. I will give it to many parents who will pass it on to others—and thus will know that they are not alone and that they will be able to live again."

—Elisabeth Kübler-Ross, M.D.

Schwartz, Peter J., David P. Southall, and Marie Valdes-Dapena, eds. *The Sudden Infant Death Syndrome: Cardiac and Respiratory Mechanisms and Interventions.* New York: New York Academy of Sciences, 1988.

Includes nearly sixty articles written for presentation at an international scientific meeting held in Italy in 1983 to discuss the search for the causes of SIDS, which is "a puzzling scientific problem and one of the greatest challenges for contemporary medicine." A highly technical book, especially of interest to those seeking an in-depth understanding of medical research and its efforts to prevent SIDS.

Westberg, Grainger. *Good Grief.* Philadelphia: Fortress Press, 1971.

What happens to us when we lose someone or something important? The author gives important insights into our overwhelming grief experiences. This short book has comforted millions of people.

Books about Death for Children

Bernstein, Joanne E. *Loss: And How to Cope with It.* New York: Clarion, 1981.

Writing for children age ten and older, the author argues that life is a series of losses and that in celebrating our humanness we must face loss directly. Topics include what happens when someone dies; children's notions of death;

living with survivors; feelings; the death of particular individuals (parents, grandparents, siblings, friends, pets, and so forth); and unusually traumatic deaths (suicide, murder, war).

Bernstein, Joanne E., and Stephen V. Gallo. *When People Die*. New York: Dutton, 1977.

The authors explore life, death, and loss by looking at the death of an older woman: the process of aging; efforts to stay healthy; the good life; what is medical death; methods of checking for signs of life. Various religious and cross-cultural beliefs about burial, funerals, and the nature of the soul are also discussed. The authors define the soul as "everything about a person except the body. The soul is the thoughts, wishes, and feelings of the person. It is all those qualities which make one person different from all others."

Buscaglia, Leo. *The Fall of Freddie the Leaf: A Story of Life for All Ages*. Thorofare, N.J.: Slack, 1982.

"Dedicated to all children who have ever suffered a permanent loss, and to the grownups who could not find a way to explain it." Written by an internationally acclaimed and beloved professor of education at the University of Southern California.

Chin-Yee, Fiona, and Bill Johnson. *Sam's Story*. Toronto: Canadian Foundation for the Study of Infant Death, 1988.

Infant death seen through a child's eyes. A storybook, lovingly written, beautifully illustrated, and meticulously validated through research. For parents, children, and grandparents. Available through the C.F.S.I.D. National Office, 586 Eglington E, Suite 308, Toronto, Ontario M4P 1P2 (416-488-3260).

Grollman, Earl A. *Talking about Death*. Polson, Mont.: Creative Children (P.O. Box 1212), 1985.

A workbook for children and parents. The parent can read the booklet to the child and write down the child's responses to questions about her or his feelings. The child can also color the pictures in the booklet. An excellent tool for beginning a discussion on death with one's youngster.

Klein, Norma. *Confessions of an Only Child*. New York: Dell, 1975.

The story of nine-year-old Antonia, whose prematurely born baby brother dies. Written for children eight to twelve years old, the book is appropriate for those whose families have had a SIDS death.

Levin, Erin Linn. *Children Are Not Paper Dolls: A Visit with Bereaved Siblings*. Greeley, Colo.: Counseling Consultants, 1982.

Direct quotes from six children in a bereaved-siblings discussion group. Appropriate for children eight and older. The brothers and sisters died in a number of ways, including accidental hanging and shooting, and death shortly after birth. Discussions of funerals, family life, friends, school, feelings, and holidays.

Richter, Elizabeth. *Losing Someone You Love: When a Brother or Sister Dies.* New York: Putnam, 1986.

"It takes courage and sensitivity to be able to examine a traumatic event in one's life, and these young people have offered to share their grief experiences in order to be of help to others. One can only admire their candor and honesty."

—Eda LeShan

Rofes, Eric E. *The Kid's Book about Death and Dying.* Boston: Little, Brown, 1985.

Fourteen children offer facts and advice to young readers in an effort to increase understanding of death.

Notes

Chapter 1

1. Janet Michel Nakushian, "Restoring Parents' Equilibrium After Sudden Infant Death," *American Journal of Nursing* 76 (1976): 1600–1604.
2. J. Bruce Beckwith, *The Sudden Infant Death Syndrome*, DHEW publication no. HSA 75-5137 (Washington, D.C.: U.S. Government Printing Office, 1978).

Chapter 2

1. John DeFrain and Linda Ernst, "The Psychological Effects of Sudden Infant Death Syndrome on Surviving Family Members," *Journal of Family Practice* 6 (1978): 985–89.
2. John DeFrain, Leona Martens, Jan Stork, and Warren Stork, *Stillborn: The Invisible Death* (Lexington, Mass.: Lexington Books, 1986). See also John DeFrain, Leona Martens, Jan Stork, and Warren Stork, "The Psychological Effects of a Stillbirth on Surviving Family Members," *Omega: Journal of Death and Dying* (Fall 1990).

Chapter 4

1. A.B. Bergman, J. Bruce Beckwith, and C.G. Ray, "Sudden Infant Death Syndrome," in *Proceedings of the Second International Conference on Causes of Sudden Infant Deaths*, ed. A.B. Bergman, J.B. Beckwith, and C.G. Ray (Seattle: University of Washington Press, 1970).
2. Carl E. Hunt and Robert T. Brouillette, "Sudden Infant Death Syndrome: 1987 Perspective," *Journal of Pediatrics* 110 (1987): 669–78; Marie Valdes-Dapena, "Sudden Infant Death Syndrome: A Review of the Medical Literature, 1974–1979," *Pediatrics* 66 (1980): 597–613.
3. Marian Willinger, "SIDS: A Challenge," *Journal of NIH Research* 1 (1989): 73–80; Eileen G. Hasselmeyer, "A Perspective on Sudden Infant Death Syndrome Research Development," in *Sudden Infant Death Syndrome*, ed. R.M.

Harper and H.J. Hoffman (New York: PMA Publishing, 1988), 3–19; Marie Valdes-Dapena, *Sudden Unexplained Infant Death, 1970 through 1975: An Evolution in Understanding,* DHEW publication no. HSA 78-5255 (Washington, D.C.: U.S. Government Printing Office, 1978).

4. Willinger, "SIDS: A Challenge."
5. Ibid.
6. Hasselmeyer, "A Perspective on Sudden Infant Death Syndrome," 18.
7. Willinger, "SIDS: A Challenge."
8. Ibid.
9. Ibid.
10. Donald R. Peterson, "The Epidemiology of Sudden Infant Death Syndrome," in *Sudden Infant Death Syndrome: Medical Aspects and Psychological Management,* ed. J.L. Culbertson, H.F. Krous, and R.D. Bendell (Baltimore: Johns Hopkins University Press, 1988), 3–17.

Chapter 5

1. Robert Browning, *The Pied Piper of Hamlin* (New York: Rand McNally, 1910).
2. Therese A. Rando, *Parental Loss of a Child* (Champaign, Ill.: Research Press, 1986).
3. Charles Dickens, *A Tale of Two Cities* (New York: Peebles Press International).

Chapter 7

1. Anne Tyler, *The Accidental Tourist* (New York: Berkley Books, 1986).

Chapter 9

1. Harper Lee, To Kill a Mockingbird (New York: International Collectors Library, 1960).

Chapter 12

1. D.C. Shannon and D.H. Kelly, "SIDS and Near-SIDS," *New England Journal of Medicine* 306 (1982): 959–65.
2. Donald Peterson, Eugene Sabotta, and Janet Daling, "Infant Mortality among Subsequent Siblings of Infants Who Died of Sudden Infant Death Syndrome,"

Journal of Pediatrics 108 (1986): 911–14; S.M. Beal and H.K. Blundell, "Recurrence Incidence of Sudden Infant Death Syndrome," *Archives of Disease in Childhood* 63 (1988): 924–30.
3. Peterson, Sabotta, and Daling, "Infant Mortality."
4. Richard Naeye, "Sudden Infant Death Syndrome: Is the Confusion Ending?" *Modern Pathology* 1 (1988): 169–74.
5. Eugene Robin, "Risk-Benefit Analysis in Chest Medicine," *Chest* 91 (1987): 765–68.
6. Robert Beckerman, "Unexpected Death in Infants Monitored at Home," *American Journal of Diseases of Children* 142 (1988): 1033–34; Anne Gilmore, "Apnea Monitors of Little Use in Preventing SIDS," *Canadian Medical Association Journal* 140 (1989): 1072–76; National Institutes of Health, "Infantile Apnea and Home Monitoring," *Conference Statement* 6 (1986): 1–10; Robin, "Risk-Benefit Analysis."
7. National Institutes of Health, "Infantile Apnea"; D.P. Southall, "Commentary: The Prevention of Sudden Infant Death Syndrome: Is There a Role for Home Monitoring?" *Journal of Medical Engineering & Technology* 9 (1985): 259–60.
8. National Institutes of Health, "Infantile Apnea."
9. Ibid; J. Michael Coleman, "Sudden Infant Death Syndrome," *Minnesota Pediatrician* (1989): 15.
10. Gilmore, "Apnea Monitors"; Southall, "Commentary."

Chapter 13

1. John DeFrain and Linda Ernst, "The Psychological Effects of Sudden Infant Death Syndrome on Surviving Family Members," *Journal of Family Practice* 6 (1978): 985–89.
2. Anne Morrow Lindbergh, *Dearly Beloved* (New York: Harcourt, Brace and World, 1962).
3. Nick Stinnett, Barbara Knorr, John DeFrain, and George Rowe, "How Strong Families Cope with Crisis," *Family Perspective* (Fall 1981).
4. Ibid.
5. David R. Mace, *Success in Marriage* (Nashville: Abingdon, 1958).

Chapter 15

1. John Steinbeck, *East of Eden* (New York: Penguin Books, 1952).

Index

About the Authors

John DeFrain, Ph.D., is a professor of family science in the Department of Human Development and the Family, University of Nebraska, Lincoln, where he has been on the faculty for the past fifteen years. In 1975 he received his doctorate from the University of Wisconsin, Madison, studying parent education, family therapy, and child development. From 1976 to 1984 he codirected a joint postgraduate training program in marriage and family therapy at UNL. He was a cofounder of the National Symposium on Building Family Strengths, which for ten years examined nationwide efforts to enhance family relationships. In addition to his teaching and research responsibilities today, he consults with the Cedars Home for Children, focusing on the needs of children and families in crisis, and writes about families for the Cooperative Extension Service. Besides this book, Dr. DeFrain has coauthored *Secrets of Strong Families* (with Nick Stinnett, 1985, Little, Brown); *Stillborn: The Invisible Death* (with Leona Martens, Jan Stork, and Warren Stork, 1986, Lexington Books); *On Our Own: A Single Parent's Survival Guide* (with Judy Fricke and Julie Elmen, 1987, Lexington Books); and *Parents in Contemporary America* (with E.E. LeMasters, 1989, Wadsworth). His research on healthy families and families in crisis has been published in two dozen professional articles and reported in many newspapers and magazines, including *Parents Magazine, Redbook, Ladies' Home Journal, Psychology Today, Good Housekeeping, McCall's Working Mother, Reader's Digest, USA Today, the New York Times,* and the *Washington Post*. He has appeared on NBC's Today Show with Jane Pauley in New York, and has testified on the development of family strengths before a congressional committee on Capitol Hill in Washington. DeFrain and his wife, Nikki, watch the growth and development of their three daughters, Amie, Alyssa, and Erica, with great amazement.

Linda Ernst, Ph.D., is an assistant professor in family resources at St. Olaf College in Northfield, Minnesota and also teaches home economics education part-time at the University of Minnesota, St. Paul. She has a background in social work, family social sciences, and education. Her graduate work was completed at the University of Nebraska, Brigham Young University, and the University of Minnesota. Teaching responsibilities have focused on adult education, AIDS education, and family studies courses. Her most recent research interest has been in the area of values in parent education and is concerned with making parent education relevant for families from diverse cultural and socioeconomic backgrounds. She has provided staff development for parent education programs throughout Minnesota. Future research interests include developing educational models for family-life education programming for families from diverse cultures. Dr. Ernst has spent the last several years doing research and publishing in vocational education and has focused on such issues as equity in vocational education and purposes of vocational education in public schools. Along with her professional interests, she has volunteered in religious organizations, 4-H, and social action groups. Dr. Ernst is married to Rev. Roger Ernst and they have three teenage children, Sara, Jennifer, and Aaron. Things which are important to Dr. Ernst are: her relationship to God, her family (both nuclear and extended), and her personal and professional relationships. An ongoing goal in her life is to be an advocate for families, whatever form they may take, since the family is the best place for so many human needs to be met.

Deanne Jakub, M.S., is an adoption and unplanned pregnancy counselor for the Lutheran Family Services in Omaha. She received her master's degree in human development and family studies from the University of Nebraska, Lincoln, writing her thesis on the effects of SIDS on grandparents. She has also served as a home-based family therapist for the United Catholic Social Services of Omaha.

Jacque Taylor, M.S., is director of the Office on Family Violence and Sexual Assault in Riverton, Wyoming. She chairs the Wyoming Crime Victim Compensation Program and is active nationally in victims' rights issues. She speaks regularly about domestic violence around the country to professional and lay groups, and made a recent appearance on the Oprah Winfrey Show in Chicago. Jacque received her bachelor's and master's degrees in human development and family studies from the University of Nebraska, Lincoln. Her interest in SIDS began in 1980 when she wrote her master's thesis on how the syndrome affects families. Jacque lives with her husband, Parnell, and their three children, Darren, Nathan, and Brennan, in Wyoming.